AF556084

THE IDEA OF NEW INDIA
Essays in Defence of Critical Thought

Pramod Kumar

The Idea of New India: Essays in Defence of Critical Thought
Pramod Kumar

First Published 2021

ISBN 978-93-5002-691-5

Published by
AAKAR BOOKS
28 E Pocket IV, Mayur Vihar Phase I
Delhi 110 091 India
www.aakarbooks.com

In Association with
INSTITUTE OF DEVELOPMENT AND COMMUNICATION
Sector 38 A, Chandigarh 160014
www.idcindia.org

Laser Typeset at
Arpit Printographers, Delhi

Cover Design: Manjot Kaur

Printed at
Sapra Brothers, Noida

Dedicated to my parents
who lived for others

Contents

List of Tables

List of Figures, Boxes and Maps

Figures

Boxes

Maps

Abbreviations

A & N	Andaman and Nicobar Island
D & N	Dadra and Nagar Haveli
J & K	Jammu and Kashmir
AAP	Aam Aadmi Party
ACP	Assistant Commissioner of Police
ADGP	Additional Director General of Police
AICC	All India Congress Committee
AIDMK	All India Dravida Munnetra Kazhagam
AIIC (T)	All India Indira Congress (Tiwari)
AIMPLB	All India Muslim Personal Law Board
AITC	All India Trinamool Congress
ANM	Auxiliary Nurse Midwifery
ASHA	Accredited Social Health Activist
ASI	Assistant Sub Inspector
BDO	Block Development Officer
BJP	Bharatiya Janata Party
BJS	Bharatiya Jan Sangh
BLD	Bharatiya Lok Dal
BPI	Bolshevik Party of India
BPRD	Bureau of Police Research & Development
BSP	Bahujan Samaj Party
CAA	Citizenship (Amendment) Act
CAD	Community Affairs Division
CEC	Chief Election Commissioner
CFC	Citizen Facilitation Centres
CMO	Chief Medical Officer
Covid-19	Corona Virus Disease 2019
CP	Commissioner of Police
CPC	Community Police Centre
CPI	Communist Party of India

CPM/CPI (M)	Communist Party of India (Marxist)
CPMU	Community Policing Monitoring Unit
CPRC	Community Policing Resource Centre
CPSC	Community Policing Suvidha Centre
CRPF	Central Reserve Police Force
D.S.P.	Deputy Superintendent of Police
DCPO	District Community Policing Officer
DDR	Daily Diary Report
DFID	Department for International Development
DIG	Deputy Inspector General of Police
DMK	Dravida Munnetra Kazhagam
DSK	District SAANJH Kendra
ECI	Election Commission of India
EPF	Employees Provident Fund
EPW	Economic and Political Weekly
ESI	Employees' State Insurance
FBL (MG)	Forward Bloc (Marxist)
FBL (RG)	Forward Bloc (Ruikar Group)
FC	Financial Commissioner
FCI	Food Corporation of India
FDI	Foreign Direct Investment
FGD	Focused Group Discussion
FIR	First Information Report
GAIL	Gas Authority of India Limited
GDP	Gross Domestic Product
GER	Gross Enrolment Ratio
GMP	Good Manufacturing Practices
GRU	Grievance Redressal Unit
HIV/AIDS	Human Immuno Deficiency Virus/Acquired Immuno Deficiency Syndrome
HMS	Hindu Mahasabha
HRD	Human Resource Development
I.T.	Information Technology
ICS (SCS)	Indian Congress (Socialist-Sarat Chandra Sinha)
ICS	Indian Congress Socialist
ID	Identity
IDC	Institute for Development and Communication
IGP	Inspector General of Police

IIPO	Indian Institute of Public Opinion
IIT	Indian Institute of Technology
IMF	International Monetary Fund
INC (I)	Indian National Congress (I)
INC (U)	Indian National Congress (U)
INC	Indian National Congress
IPC	Indian Penal Code
I-T	Income Tax
JD	Janata Dal
JD (S)	Janata Dal (Samajwadi)
JD (U)	Janata Dal (United)
JDS	Janata Dal Secular
JNP	Janta Party
JNP (JP)	Janta Party (JP)
JNP (S)	Janta Party (Secular)
JS	Jan Sangh
KLP	Krishikar Lok Party
KMPP	Kisan Mazdoor Praja Party
LKD	Lok Dal
LKD (B)	Lok Dal (Bahuguna)
MACT	Motor Accidents Claims Tribunal
MC	Municipal Committee
MGNREGA	Mahatma Gandhi National Rural Employment Guarantee Act
MLA	Member of Legislative Assembly
MRG	Matter Related to Governments
NCO	Indian National Congress (Organisation)
NCP	National Congress Party
NCT	National Capital Territory
NDA	National Democratic Alliance
NFHS	National Family Health Survey
NGO	Non-Government Organisations
NHRC	National Human Rights Commission
NOC	No Objection Certificate
NRC	National Register of Citizens
NRI	Non-Resident Indian
NSSO	National Sample Survey Office
NYKS	Nehru Yuva Kendra Sangathan

OBC	Other Backward Class
PEPSU	Patiala & East Punjab States Union
PGRC	Punjab Governance Reforms Commission
PHC	Primary Health Care
PIL	Public Interest Litigation
PM	Prime Minister
PNDT	Pre-Natal Diagnostic Techniques
PPP	Public-Private Partnership
PRI	Panchayati Raj Institution
PRP	People's Republican Party
PSOC	Police Station Outreach Centre
PSP	Praja Socialist Party
PSSK	Police Station SAANJH Kendra
PUNSUP	Punjab State Civil Supplies Corporation Limited
PWD	Public Works Department
RCPI	Revolutionary Communist Party of India
RCT	Randomised Control Trials
RJD	Rashtriya Janata Dal
RRP	Ramrajya Parishad
RSP	Revolutionary Socialist Party
RSS	Rashtriya Syamsewak Sangh
RTI	Right to Information
S.P.	Superintendent of Police
S.S.P.	Senior Superintendent of Police
SAD	Shiromani Akali Dal
SAP	Samata Party
SC	Scheduled Caste
ST	Scheduled Tribe
SCF	Scheduled Caste Federation
SDM	Sub-Divisional Magistrate
SDSK	Sub-Division SAANJH Kendra
SEZ	Special Economic Zone
SHO	Station House Officer
SHS	Shiv Sena
SLCRC	State Level Coordination and Review Committee
SMS	Short Messaging Service
SOC	Socialist
SP	Samajwadi Party

SSP	Samyukta Socialist Party
SWA	Swatantra Party
TA/DA	Travelling Allowance/Daily Allowance
TADA	Terrorist and Disruptive Activities (Prevention) Act
TDP	Telugu Desam Party
TMC 'M'	Tamil Maanila Congress
UPA	United Progressive Alliance
VHP	Vishwa Hindu Parishad
VIP	Very Important Person
YSRCP	Yuvjana Sramika Rythu Congress Party

Acknowledgements

The thought of writing a book on *The Idea of New India: Essays in Defence of Critical Thought* has come from the receding tradition of dialogue through peaceful means. It has also coincided with the purging of adventurism involved in the exploration of new knowledge. After more than seventy years of Independence, the evolution of the relation between the trinity, i.e. State, civil society, and the market intermeshed with nationalism, secularism, and socialism, also offered an opportunity to capture its various manifest forms.

I am especially grateful to my colleagues for not only encouraging me to venture into this area but, they also enriched my understanding of the social and political theory and theme-based knowledge of the subjects covered in this book. The comments and critical observations from my esteemed colleague Rainuka Dagar have benefited the book, particularly in an essay on the Dalit Identity Architecture, a part of this has been co-authored with her earlier.

Interactions with Atul Sood have helped me immensely to build linkages of the economic process with the phenomena of the divergent sort. The essay on 'Governance for the Margins: Tensions and Faultlines' was an outcome of the work done by the Punjab Governance Reforms Commission (PGRC) and contributions made by R.N. Gupta and J.R. Kundal, former civil servants and members of the PGRC, are highly appreciated. Further the case study on Meeting Trust Deficit: Rationalization of Affidavits were written together with R.N. Gupta and J.R. Kundal. I acknowledge the assistance of Amit Kumar for providing valuable support in organising and locating the original materials relating to the election speeches and bibliographical references.

In the final stages of preparation, the book has benefited from the comments of Dipankar Gupta and H.S. Shergill. The final outcome was expedited by Akshat, my son, as he cautioned me, not to be trapped by the researcher's curse. The improvement in the flow of thought and grammar brought clarity to the manuscript by J.R. Kundal. I am thankful to him. The support and contribution of the following are thankfully acknowledged: for data support, Harsh Chopra; designing, Sunil Arora and typing, Ashwani Kumar and Sanjeev Kumar.

Preface

There is always an urge and need to explore knowledge to seek answers to make the living more humane. At the same time, attempts are made to build a consensus on the values which do not question the path of development that argues that 'the efforts to realise other utopias are counterproductive.' The main thrust of their argument is that a particular path of development is the only source of growth, and a particular type of nationalism as the core value.

History has witnessed that the better way to love one's country and have pride in its greatness is to appreciate and tolerate critical ideas and strive for justice. I remember having been interviewed once by a self-appointed custodian of Indian nationalism, a television anchor, on the hanging of Kasab (accused in Bombay 26/11 terrorist attack). He reprimanded me for not supporting his idea that Kasab should be hanged expeditiously rather than getting bogged down to the time-consuming legal processes. He asserted that not hanging him will make India look weak in the comity of nations. In other words, the idea that the countries emerge stronger by becoming justice-oriented was branded as anti-national by this anchor. And, if these ideas are institutionalised, the logical outcome will be to exclude certain activities and viewpoints outside the scope of factual enquiry. And, institutionalisation is the most effective way to acquire legitimacy as it penetrates the people's belief system even at the expense of undermining the facts, leading to the perpetuation of the status quo. The natural outcome of this is to purge the scope of academic adventurism and innovative experimentation from the places of learning.

If the centres of learning have to become places of creativity, innovation, and excellence, they have to transcend the boundaries demarcated by 'status-quoism' for marching towards achieving a more humane social existence. Of course, creativity must be grounded in the content rather than shine only in the banners.

The status quo has become unsustainable as it negates the notion of nationalism based on cultural pluralism and growth with equity. There is, however, a very thin line between secular nationalism (based on cultural pluralism) and cultural nationalism (based on majoritarian religion). The idea of 'New India' is the most debated, feared, and a popular construct in the twenty-first century after 70 years of India's independence. It has become a central issue. The trinity of cultural nationalism, market fundamentalism, and interest-based global alignments are being pursued with intensity. However, it must be underscored that all these tendencies were pervasive earlier also, but the kind of legitimacy and dignity that has been attributed recently to these has been distinct and disturbing to the discerning minds. As a consequence, the country has willingly become a hostage to the market fundamentalism that is considered a panacea. Not that the Nehruvian project was without its follies. Instead of building a welfare state, it constructed 'state led capitalism with socialist pretension.'

In this context, the most relevant question is: can the 'Idea of New India' become acceptable without reinventing the State? The idea of cultural nationalism is not merely an illusion or the conglomeration of myths, but it does represent the reality selectively though, a world view and, the same can coexist with the critical wide range of the competing representation of the world views. The dominant politics has adopted the content, language, and symbols drawn from the way of life of the majority of the population. It has transformed the three core principles of politics, i.e. mixed economy, secularism, and non-alignment movement. These have been replaced by the market economy, cultural nationalism, and interest-based alliances in the global sphere for building a self-reliant nation.

These issues have been debated through three essays. The first essay 'Unfolding Challenges of Democracy in India' is an elaborated version of a lecture delivered in Asian and African Area Studies (ASAFAS), Kyoto University, Japan in 2019. This essay captures the changing spectrum of interactive relationships between the economy, politics and society in three phases.

During the first phase from 1952-77, along with building state capitalism, secularism was presented as a supra-religion, which in turn led to pauperisation of a large section of the society, accompanied by disintegrative social process reflected in communalism, regionalism and casteism in the post-mid 1960's. The deepening of these tendencies led to invoking of the nationalistic fervor.

In the second phase from 1977 to 2014, the mismatch between electoral promises and the economic policies led to the trust deficit in the leadership. And, at the ideological level in the political practice, the religious, caste and ethnic cleavages were converted into electoral capital. It also provided continuity to authoritarian trends, of the emergency era, to curb various forms of dissent. The answers to these crises were found in globalisation, liberalisation and privatisation of the economy in 1990's.

And, the third phase from 2014 provided continuity to the neoliberal reforms and manufactured new electoral architecture not merely for power politics, but also for social dominance.

These trends have been conceptualised in terms of the faultlines, i.e., the convergence of the market fundamentalism with the religious fundamentalism, centralisation of power and bargaining federalism, and locating (Cultural) civilisational symbolism under the umbrella of secularism. The crisis emanating from the path of development, and the emerging faultlines shifted the focus of politics from the norms of dissent and consent to 'forced consensus.'

These faultlines are moderated by making minimal concessions to the popular resistance through a reductionist interventionist strategy. In this, the citizens experience exclusion in their interaction with the State, and that has been made central to the political discourse and not the exclusion of the marginalised sections from the market and the dominant politics. Having blurred the structural inequalities, commonalities of the experience of the (deficient) citizen interaction with the State are captured for providing access to the so-called good governance, discussed in detail in an essay on 'Governance for the Margins: Tensions and Faultlines.' This is an exhaustive version of a lecture delivered on the occasion of celebration of the Civil Service Day in Vigyan Bhawan, Delhi on April, 2013.

The third essay has analysed the Dalit identity architecture as it is getting nurtured and evolved within the given cultural specific variations at the regional level. This is based on a paper presented in International Institute for Asian Studies, Leiden University, The Netherlands in December, 2012. In each context, the dynamic interactions with the social processes and the value-laden public policy interactions are leading to the distinct formation of the institutions, behavioural codes of conduct and social capital.

The policy of administrative fragmentation of the population based on caste and religion, within 'restrictive citizenship,' has multiplied social cleavages and led to the denial of full citizenship. In this background, the use of caste as a political capital leading to distorted policies has been examined whereby choices are exercised to redistribute the resources from the whole to the caste collectively and to the individuals belonging to the group.

It has nothing to do with equal or a little less than equal access to justice. As a consequence, the nature of growth remains exclusivist; it acts as a toxin to the various social faultlines leading to conflicts.

To consider the assumption of the nature of development and governance beyond question is not only lethargic but also dangerous; the difference lies in the details notwithstanding the consensus on the assumptions. The present book, in general, deals with the issues, such as, whether 'cultural nationalism' would be compatible with the multiplicity of cultures and religions and, cherish the values of democratic rights, tolerance and freedom of expression. And, an attempt has also been made to critically examine the relationship between the market economy and the institutions of the State, political parties and the civil society for ensuring equity to mitigate fear, insecurity and conflict and enhance justice, safety and equality.

The inclusive growth cannot be reached without the productive engagement of the large marginalised population. It has been argued that the policies of inclusion have to be based on creating conditions for the historically disadvantaged groups to participate in the growth process and can have access to the assets, livelihoods, jobs and investments.

Importantly, it would be worthwhile to describe as to how is the present nature of social, political and economic development self-limiting and also provides not only legitimacy but the justification to the marginalisation of the people without means and besides ensuring multiplication of wealth for the few.

The whole texture of social life through nurtured subjectivity for the evolution of new political identity has to be restructured. The tinkering with the existing institutional structure, public policy and socio-economic and political practices may not be sufficient. There has to be much more than that. It is equally important to indicate that there does exist the possibility of alternate politics with a change in the specific institutions to transform the society for the better.

There is a need to rethink a new development path which includes key elements, socially—a just growth, redistributive and sustainable development, and productive engagement of the citizens. The alternate path of development has to move beyond the conventional growth and poverty debates.

Chandigarh **Pramod Kumar**

Introduction

The idea of 'new India' has acquired currency with the fading away of the left and marginalisation of the left of the centre politics. With the adoption of neo-liberal market reforms initiated in the 1990s and the subsequent emergence of a broad consensus amongst competing political parties provided the structural base to the new path of development. At the super-structural level, historically, it continued to persist along with the dominant tendency of secular-nationalism. However, it became more pronounced with right-wing politics having captured the political power. The global eco-system, the neoliberal path of development, and the absence of competitive alternate political and economic model, and the empirical level provided much-needed justification for this thought. This neoliberal path of development is being presented as the only source of growth, and a particular type of nationalism alone is presented as real. (see Camus 1943)[1] There is a concerted effort to build an eco-system rendering the members of the civil society virtually incapacitated to think of any alternatives. And, any departure from the status quo is considered as a rank deviation. For combating corruption, individual honesty is marketed as a supreme value. No doubt, continuation of the dialogue has to be based on honesty; otherwise, no exchange or dialogue shall have a future. The basic question remains: honest exchange for whom and for what purpose? Well, individual honesty can be an instrument of retrogression or progression. The claim to individual honesty per se does not have any finality, and it not only blurs the real issues but also saps the humans' revolutionary urges and might go to legitimise the unequal status quo.

A narration of a situation in a novel titled *Raag Darbari* by Shukl (1968: 35-37, 216) uncovers the dimensions of the relationship between the political leadership, civil society and the citizens. It has shown the complexity of these interactions and also how it saps the human urges to transform the existing terms of exchange.

The novel vividly captures the citizen's (villager) interaction with the district administration to procure a copy of the land records. He goes to the tehsil office for this where he is asked to pay a bribe of Rs. 5, whereas, the going rate of the bribe was Rs. 2. The citizen resented the enhanced rate of the bribe. The argument between the citizen and the office clerk became loud. The citizen was willing to pay, but not the increased rate. The legal practitioners tried to convince both to accommodate each other. They even offered to pay the enhanced amount to resolve the conflict. But, both of them remained adamant. The selected excerpts are being reproduced.

Third Person: What is the citizen fighting for?

Principal (of a college): He needs a copy of the land-record (*Fard*) from the office of the Tehsil. He has taken an oath that he will not give a bribe and receive a copy of the record as per the rules. On the other hand, the officer has also taken the oath that he will not accept a bribe and give the document as per the rules. And, the fight is all about this.

Third Person (a member of the civil society): His (citizen) wife has died, has an issue with the children and so, lives separately, the life of a saint. Earlier, he used to sing devotional songs, and now it seems he is tired of that too. So, with nothing left to do, he filed a case in the court, and for that purpose, he needs a copy of the land record. His application got rejected twice for some error in the application filing process. And, when he went to sort out the matter, the copyist asked for Rs. 5, but the argument ensued over the increased rate of bribe from Rs. 2 to 5.

Advocates (to Copyist): Let's settle this matter for the time being and agree to a lesser amount that he (citizen) can afford. Instead of being bribed, he will be praising the act of your mercy.

Copyist: No, I can't. Now, it's an issue of my word, and a real man, once committed, cannot take his words back.

Advocates (to Citizen): We know that the usual price rate (of the bribe) has increased, but you (citizen) must also understand that the copyist also has other priorities (he is also a family man, has unmarried daughters) to look after. So, why don't you agree to this new rate (of the bribe)?

Citizen: This is not the way to deal with such matters. The copyist must have set his priorities accordingly. He spends his earnings thoughtlessly and expects others to cover his extra dues.

Copyist: If he (citizen) thinks I am not efficient about my duties, if this is the way he wants, then I don't even need anything (no bribe at all). Now, whatever I need to do, I will do as per the rules and regulations.

Citizen: All right, then. If you (copyist) want to settle things as per rules, so be it. You will not get anything from me. I have applied again. Though it might take a long time, sooner or later I will get it...

Citizen: It's been 15 months since that day. The error in the application form has been corrected. The case file has got back to the Tehsil from the **Sadar** (District). The copyist has taken the matter in hand now and is working on the same. I am sure that I will get a copy of the land record within three-four days.

Advocate (to Citizen): What is this unreasonable

struggle for? It's been days. If you had come to us or any other advocate, we would have arranged the record within three days.

Citizen (to Advocate): There was no need for any advocate. The fight was about righteousness. If I had given Rs. 5 to the copyist, I could have taken the copy of the record in three hours. But, both of us (copyist and citizen) were not interested in that kind of modus operandi. As I said, the fight was about honesty and truthfulness. But, you are an advocate. You will not understand...

Leader (to Citizen): You are fighting for Dharma (ethics). What help can I render in that fight?

Citizen: You are right, sir. In this fight, you cannot do anything. When I need 'Sifarish-vifarish' (any recommendation or approach), I shall beg for the same.

The rather long narrative clearly shows that the resolve to have an honest exchange between the official and the citizen has been characterised as a conflict disturbing the existing consensus. This is seen as an exception to the disadvantage of both the government officials and the citizens. The trigger of conflict is located in the arbitrary increase in the rate of bribe, but the same is conceded as a prerogative of the power, and it is also justified as the official has a large family to support and a 'liability' of a daughter. The concerned citizen, on the other hand, is seen by the civil society as a societal dropout without a family to support who took a rigid stance in the negation of the efforts made by the civil society to pool an additional amount to settle the dispute. The inference is that no rational citizen will disturb the existing status quo. The civil society lamented that the younger generation government officials do not uphold the legitimate terms of exchange and keep enhancing these in violation of the consensus. The political class and the officials of the court, i.e. the lawyers are seen as irrelevant to this conflict and for the maintenance of the status quo. The representatives of the civil society, political class, officers of the court and the opinion-making section took this existing code of conduct, values and the overall system as given and beyond intervention: "Taking the existing order of the facts for granted and the existing 'values' as somehow beyond rational enquiry."[2] (Singh 2008: 94).

The ecosystem that has been nurtured has the potential to dilute the critical impulse, unnerve the exercise of the human mind to explore the truth and reflect on other possibilities. The ecosystem that is located in an ideology that represents a particular way of life, using the language of power rather than justice, majoritarian hegemonic policies and mass mobilisations, diversionary discourse on the issues and/or politics of personal vendetta—all that is bound to deter the expression of alternate politics; in short that is the politics of fear. It may remain within the confines of law and constraints of a democratic system, but it violates the spirit of free expression and critical enquiry.

We are told that the existing structure is beyond scientific enquiry and that there are no alternatives also, that any exploration to discover and realise other utopias is not worthwhile.

These are difficult times, no doubt, and the idea of globalisation, technological revolution and holistic knowledge are marketed as the new dawn for emancipation and universal progress. In this, the sovereignty of the State has been surrendered to the market. It is the market which shall govern and not the State. And, the market is invariably secular. It is not meant to hear the voices of any caste, class, religion or creed. And, it excludes those people who neither have assets nor the capabilities. For the people without assets, the opportunities are, of course, assured, but no provisions are made to empower them to avail those opportunities. The public policy statements promise to make the people productive through education. The education policy document makes it quite clear that it is the market which will create jobs; the government can only build capacities. Since it is not possible to predict the skill set needed in the market, the thrust would be to create the capacities that are flexible enough to acquire multiple skills for the jobs over time. To quote:

> It should be emphasised that higher education must build expertise that society will need over the next 25 years and beyond. Simply tailoring people into jobs that exist today, but that is likely to change or disappear after some years, is suboptimal and even counterproductive... Single skill and single discipline jobs are likely to become automated over time. Therefore, there will be a great need to focus on multidisciplinary and 21st century competencies for future work roles–these are indeed the capabilities that will separate humans from robots... By focusing on such broad-based, flexible, individualised, innovative, and multidisciplinary learning, higher education must aim to prepare its students not just for their first jobs–but also for their second, third, and all future jobs over their lifetimes. In particular, the higher education system must aim to form the hub for the next industrial revolution (Government of India 2019: 202-203).

As is evident, the goal is not to develop a particular skill, but to build capacities supposedly necessary for the future. The relevant question arises: a capacity for what and for whom? This has been left to the market.

> But a project for society or civilisation cannot be built based solely on the market. A project for civilisation is born out of a collective will, a collective effort over the long term. It is not the fruit of the instantaneous confrontation of supply and demand... Markets and statistics are being made to say things that they are incapable of saying (Sen, Fioussi and Stiglitz 2011: XV).

It is not that the State does not have the policy options within a particular path of development. The policy options available range from becoming subservient to the market, to moderation through welfare policies, to the integration of domestic markets and local diversities with the global capital. And, the option that the State opts for is largely dependent on the ideological and political predisposition of the ruling establishment.

> In the last half-century, the State, in all the rich countries in the Western world, has become a democratic "Welfare State", with fairly explicit commitments to the broad goals of economic development, full employment, equality of opportunity for the young, social security, and protected minimum standards as regards not only income but nutrition, housing, health and education, for people of all regions and social groups (Myrdal 1960: 45).[3]

But, the State in the Third World countries like, India, has to reinvent itself. On the contrary, the State is working overtime to create a crisis for capitalism. 'It is not only the State that has to constantly act or intervene apparently against capitalism but really on its behalf, to alleviate the anarchy of the market to prevent major depressions, to save capitalism from its own self-destructive consequences' (Mohanty 2017: 235). The reality of globalisation has nurtured a new terrain for the trinity, i.e. the State, the market, and the civil society either to surrender or reinvent. It is not that the world was not globalised earlier. But now, the notion of globalisation has given a new orthodoxy. To quote: 'Geography without distance, history without time, value without weight, transactions without cash' (Singh 2006: 685). The nature, scale, scope and speed of the circulation of capital and commodities is unprecedented. This includes the speed of instant cash transfers, the speed of investments, the stock market, of general data collection (Crosthwaite 2011). The speed kills the deliberative, reflective and dialogical time required for critical analysis. The interpretive possibilities and well-thought countermeasures have been replaced by a reactive exchange. Every human practice, social relationships, social institutions and cultural spaces, including, the natural environment, have been subjected to the requirements of the morality of the market. The role of the ideology is to influence the behaviour and enforce the acceptance of ideas embodied in the instruments of the market. The most important institutions are those that are in the business of generation and dissemination of knowledge. The dominant trend in contemporary politics is to shape the political discourse by appealing to the lowest mental capacity of the people living on the margins.

> Knowledge is reduced to slick, pre-digested, easy to understand capsules, inducing people to want simple answers to the difficult problem... at the ideological level brainwashing of the people, diverting them from any advanced social ideas and implanting in their minds bland, illusory and often downright false and reactionary views of social and political realities (Singh 2007: xlii).

That knowledge is generated and disseminated, which reinforced the ideas of the ruling class to acquire legitimacy without questioning the structural base. And, technology is presented and used as a panacea. Technology is a great facilitator. This has been amply demonstrated in dealing with the unprecedented crisis caused by the COVID-19 pandemic. For instance, it facilitated the maintenance of social distance through 'work from home' by using technological innovations, having positive implications for sustainable environment-friendly development. But it also reinforced that it is no replacement of human compassion and basic needs of human existence as it is not possible to download food, medicines and other essentials from the internet directly without the delivery persons. And, capital on its own cannot produce essential commodities without workers. Further, the patients cannot be treated through telemedicine alone without hospitalisation. The cities and villages could not be sanitised or put under lockdown without human labour. And, the households cannot be run with technology-driven gadgets as one needs the people to take care of the elderly or do babysitting etc.

Legitimisation Through Institutionalisation of Ideas

To achieve societal conformity of the ideas so generated, the process of legitimisation involves institutionalisation, usages of the symbols, categories of social analysis, practices and activities to seek uniform responses to the common problems. It involves influencing behaviour. To acquire legitimacy, the foremost step is the institutionalisation of these ideas.

In other words, the ideological processes are not merely the articulation of ideas, but these also involve institutionalisation through constitutional amendments, redefinition of the role of institutions, both 'Ideological State Apparatus and Repressive State Apparatus' (Althusser 2006: 127-186).[4] This is, perhaps, the most effective mode to enforce and obtain acceptance of the ideas. The ideas which support the ideology propagated or adopted by the ruling establishment, and the powers that be and the social institutions in favour of the status quo acquire normative and constitutional dignity. For example, the Nehruvian nation-building project in India relied excessively on the conception of secular nationalism through the Constitution by including the word, secular in the Preamble to the Indian Constitution. And, through the ideological State apparatus like, the judiciary, executive, legislature, educational system, social groups, mass media– the idea of secularism was legitimised. Notwithstanding the fact that these were not in conformity with the political and social space governed by the religion-centric discourse at the societal level intermeshed with the electoral realities of the contemporary Indian politics. The main thrust of the Nehruvian secular nationalism has been to ensure that in the secular domain, the majority religious community would not dominate the religious minorities.

In the Nehruvian vision, it was assumed that developmental nationalism would provide the basis for the emergence of secularism. In this paradigm, secularism was seen as the opposite of communalism. To quote Nehru:

> I am afraid, I cannot get excited over this communal issue, important as it is temporarily. It is after all a side issue, and it can have no real importance in the large scheme of things. Those who think of it as a major issue think in terms of British imperialism continuing permanently in this country. Without that basis of thought, they would not attach so much importance to one of its inevitable offshoots. I have no such fear and so my vision of a future India contains neither imperialism nor communalism (Gopal 1975: 190).

The perspective was that with the initiation of the process of development of science, technology, industry and with the steady spread of literacy, communalism and other such retrogressive tendencies would automatically get subsumed and would lead ultimately to the emergence of new kinds of social and economic groupings and identities undercutting the base upon which the communal (i.e. caste, religion, tribal, racial) social relations and politics rest. It was believed that "religious particularism" would be submerged by the universalistic character of the market forces. And, this was termed as 'development nationalism'.

> But, once the initial economic boom was over, and the conditions of the masses started worsening and the faith in the government started declining, this ideology lost all its meaning. Since the 1960s, there is no such common ideology though an attempt was made through slogans like *Garibi Hatao*, etc. This lack of ideology has led to a hiatus between the ruling class and the masses threatening the ruling classes with a complete loss of legitimacy. Communalism is one such ideology which can be a nationwide ideology binding the majority of the people, diverting their attention from the real issues and securing the interests of the ruling classes. This is

> the reason why even the ruling party is coming out more and more openly with its communal bias (Desai 1985: 42).

It was indicative that the left of the centre political parties for historical, electoral and socio-cultural reasons surrendered their ideological and political position, which in turn provided the much-needed legitimacy to the emerging right-wing political discourse. The competing ideas exist alongside having a basis in society. These ideas, when provided institutional dignity, acquire currency in the political discourse. The transition of politics from the left of the centre to the right centric politics initiated movement from developmental nationalism to cultural nationalism through the process of institutionalisation. To illustrate, the legitimisation of the right-wing politics was constitutionally initiated with the constitutional amendments to reverse the judgment of the Supreme Court on the Shah Bano case.

> There are at least three crucial events in this chronology; the Shah Bano-Muslim Women's Act affair of 1985-86, the BJP's defection in 1990 from the United Front government of V.P. Singh, and the ongoing Mandir-Masjid saga. By overturning the Shah Bano decision in the widely publicized case, available and explicable to a nationwide audience, the Rajiv Gandhi Government gave apparent credence to the widespread and long-held charge against the Congress that the substance of its secularism was "pseudo-secularism," communally divisive "vote bank politics," and "pampering" Muslims in order to get their votes (Stern 2003: 185-86).

The Ram Janmabhoomi movement (See Annexure 1.1) and, to counter this, a caste-based political co-option strategy spelt out in the Mandal Commission Report also led to the redefinition of the secular space. This was provided continuity with the constitutional amendments relating to the status of Jammu Kashmir through the amendment in Article 370, and banning the practice of Triple Talaq amongst the Muslim community and to provide a life term for sacrilege by codifying the Blasphemy law adopted by the Punjab Assembly through the insertion of Section 295 AA into IPC. This was a movement towards reinforcement of the concept of cultural nationalism.

Legitimisation Through Symbols, Labels, and Social Categories

The complex architecture for influencing the human behaviour involved invoking the ideas with attributed values incorporated in and disseminated through the institutional framework, usage of the societal customs, rituals and symbols through the labels (civilisational or otherwise) for power enhancement.

Usages of Symbols: For Legitimisation

Along with institutionalisation, the symbols and religious categories were simultaneously invoked to legitimise the acquired normative institutional dignity. For instance, the 'Hindu' civilisational symbols have been invoked to build a 'narrative' to fertilise an identity to hegemonise the political discourse, redefine the cultural and social spaces, rights and claims of the populations labelled as 'majority and minority'. For example, the use of the notion of Ramrajya by Gandhiji was against colonial domination and for the democratic righteous rule.[5] (see Gandhi 1919: 305) The use of Ramrajya was also a reference to the country's civilisation, and it transcended the boundaries of caste and religion. It was not to reinforce religious monoliths. In no way did it propagate and project Ramrajya as synonymous with the Hindu identity. On the contrary, the recent use of the notion of Ramrajya has been antithetical to its Gandhian use. The meaning of the term 'Indian civilisation' is restricted to mean "Hindu" civilisation. Ramrajya is used to mean the Rule of the Just rooted in a particular world view. The central thrust of this politics is to bring to the foreground the need for establishing a monolithic 'Hindu identity.' Once this identity gets recognised and established as propagated, it will make a crucial difference in determining the personal, social and institutional relationships to the benefit of the so-called *Hindu Samaj*. This cultural stream has been ingrained into the dominant culture of politics. The contention is not with the civilisational values and ethics that are propagated like the Rule of the Just (Ramrajya), but with the prefix of 'Hindu'. The appropriation of the dominant cultural practice as an ideology has transformed the conception of the 'idea of India.'

The social categories like the Hindu or the Muslim, for instance, signify some traits and characteristics, but these may not be shared beyond the demarcated boundary. There are characteristics and values which the people share as a member of a social group irrespective of their religion. However, the categories of social analysis based on religion are a powerful tool for political mobilisations. Even the secular space has been defined by taking religion-based categories for exhorting the majority religion to be generous, accommodating and tolerant towards the minorities.

The religion-based 'majority and minority' categories are presented as compatible with the secular nationalism. For instance, the dominant right-wing discourse in India projects the Hindu majority as liberal, tolerant and values the freedom of expression. The liberals also use these categories to exhort the 'Hindus' to be magnanimous and generous towards the Muslim minority. 'He (Nehru) always like, Gandhi, took the line that it was for the Hindus, as a majority community, to make concessions while the communal problem lasted'. This, in itself, despite the call to magnanimity, assumes a communal approach, however, subconscious: The argument is based on the belief that the majority community is a privileged one and the minority community has a reason to be communal (Gopal 1976: 183).

> The very tools of analyses have been contaminated by it (communalism) as a result of the ideological conditioning of the last 100 years, when the middle classes and the intelligentsia were perceptually surrounded by a communal outlook in politics, in the press, in literature and, particularly often, been viewed in the social sciences, as and in real life, through conscious or unconscious communal assumptions. For example, if one's analysis starts by accepting the communal leaders as leaders and representatives of their 'communities'—and if one refers to the Hindu, Muslim or Sikh communalists as Hindu leaders, Muslim leaders, or Sikh leaders—or if one accepts communal political activity of their 'communities', one is already accepting the basic communal framework of thought and analysis. On the other hand, if no communal, economic, political and social interests exist, the communalists cannot be representing such interests and are not, therefore, representative of their 'communities' (Chandra 1984: 101).

It implies that the religious groups are homogeneous in nature and their members have common social economic and political interests which bind them together.

In this sense, the religious categories of the majority-minority have a thin line with secular nationalism. But, at the same time, it is contextual. For instance, non-secular countries based on the religion of the majority may not have the same connotations for the minorities as in a secular country, for instance, in Punjab, in Jammu & Kashmir, the Hindus are in the minority.

The religious-based majority-minority categories are inadequate, partial, and distortion for making cross religious-cultural comparisons. These categories carry political meaning. To brand politics, individual or above all, ideologies as majoritarian, otherwise assume that the religious beliefs are at the core of their socio-economic and political existence. It is precisely the reason when decisions relating to the citizenship rights are made based on the 'majority-minority' categories; it is bound to promote exclusivity. Interestingly, the political ideology emanating from the partition of India on religious lines provides a moral basis to this kind of politics. Not only the partition of India, but the historical evolution of the nation-states in the South-Asian region witnessed religio-cultural identities intermeshed with the conception of nation, nationality and the nation-state.

Politics in the post-colonial South Asia was guided more by the territorial concept of sovereignty and nurtured through the appropriation of religio-cultural capital leading to the reinforcement of ultra-nationalism. Within the complex processes of territoriality, in this volatile region, the unbound cultural, religious, social and political existence plays a dominant role both in 'solidifying and challenging' the diverse domain of the multi-dimensional boundary formation. The dichotomy between territorial nationalism and religio-cultural needs of the minorities having cultural similarities transcending territorial boundaries lead to overactive violent reactions.

The historic correction applied at the time of independence, preceded by a partition based on religion, shaped the political developments in India. In political discourse, the emphasis was to lessen the role of religion in politics and economic development and, on the other hand, attempts were made to treat all the religions as equal by giving certain concessions.

The focus of the Nehruvian nation-building project has been on monocultural and hegemonic nationality. In other words, secular nationalism was nurtured as a supra religion with its doctrine, code of conduct for politics and the State apparatus and civil society, and with demarcated national boundaries. It claimed to be catering to the needs of the collectivities, justifiability, irrespective of the religion, and moral and ethical governance.

The interaction of the monocultural secular nationalism with a multicultural social reality produced divisive faultlines. Given the common cultural and religious history in South Asia, the assertion of the faultlines transcended the territorial boundaries. For instance, the assertion of the Punjabi identity transcends the territorial boundaries of India and Pakistan, the Tamil identity—India and Sri Lanka, Bengali identity—India and Bangladesh, Gorkha identity—India and Nepal, Sindhi identity—India and Pakistan.

To protect the territorial nationalism, expedient politics used the religion-based categories to weaken the process of identity formation, transcending territorial boundaries. This leads to nationalist myth-making. The hypersensitive response to the territorial sovereignty in the context of cross border linkages with the population having similar cultural and ethnic basis resulted in excessive State enforcement to check illegal immigration and reinforcement of the cultural bondage.

This was mainly the result of the institutionalisation of the Western notion of the inalienable rights of the individual in the secular nation-building project, whereas politics and social discourse relied on ascriptive categories for the mobilisation and maintenance of their support base. 'The Western notion of the inalienable rights was incompatible with the interests of the colonial powers, which were slow to promote the notion among the colonialised' (Peterson 1990). On the contrary, the focus of the British colonialism was to sharpen the distinctions by institutionalising the practices on the basis of religious and caste group identities. There was a conscious policy of misappropriating perceived notions about the ethnic superiority and inferiority of the groups and providing access to economic and political or social opportunities based on these notions. The underlying assumption of these policies was the incompatibility of economic and political interests of the groups and, therefore, the need for separate politics in South Asia. This kind of political activity emphasised the particularistic aspects of social existence specific to the nature of socio-cultural or economic and political development in each country of South Asia. For instance, the Citizen Amendment Act of 2019 in India advanced the argument that the religious minorities in the countries of Bangladesh, Pakistan, and Afghanistan with Islam as the State religion are persecuted and, therefore, shall be granted citizenship in India. For this purpose, the 'minorities' who have been identified are the Hindus, the Sikhs, the Buddhists, the Christians, etc. The Muslims have been excluded as they are in the majority in these countries.

The categories used are 'religious majority and minority' by right-wing politics to frame this law. And the argument advanced is that the religious minorities in Pakistan, Bangladesh, and Afghanistan are non-Muslims who are persecuted by the Muslim majority in the countries having Islam as their State religion. It is argued that the Muslim 'majority' is intolerant in these countries, while the Hindu 'majority' is tolerant in India. Hence, the Citizen Amendment Act 2019 to provide citizenship to the persecuted religious minorities in Pakistan, Bangladesh and Afghanistan.[6] (see "How Pak's Hindu" 2020) To hinge arguments by comparing data from the non-secular States of Pakistan and Bangladesh with the secular and democratic State of India, using religious categories in secular spheres is a misnomer. No doubt, religious differences may be real and taking these to be the main inner contradiction in secular spheres, like citizenship or right to citizens, is to blur the real social existence. The attribution of values, i.e. persecution of the religious minorities in Pakistan, Bangladesh and Afghanistan attached to nationalism leads to the mystification of the real issues and blur the real placement of the individuals or collectivities or both affected by it.

Further, it also implies that the religious groups, i.e. the majority or minority as separate categories, are homogeneous in the secular domain, but these categories are dissimilar and divergent from each other. The use of these categories for policy prescription is to take the symptoms as the causes.

The quest of the post-colonial States to emerge as nations by melting the diverse interests into a monolithic entity has led to the subversion of, for instance, the rights of cultural and linguistic identities. The process of homogenisation by undermining multicultural realities and disparate aspirations and identities has led to the negation of the rights of many collectivities. These collectivities started redefining their boundaries. Consequently, implicitly cross border linkages with the population having similar cultural and ethnic basis were subjected to the State controls. The inability to control the cross border migration was seen as evidence of a soft State. As mentioned earlier, mobility of the capital, goods and services are accepted facts and, therefore, transcend the conventional definition of sovereignty. But, the mobility of human beings continues to be seen as a transgression of the territorial nationalism.

Usages of Categories of Social Analysis: For Politicisation

In this context, the Citizen Amendment Act 2019 is an assertion of a strong nation backdrop of the capacity of the States to control immigration. Even the secular parties used these categories to protect religious minorities and were accused of being 'pseudo-secular'. This was widely believed to be correct by the members of the 'majority community'. These parties were also accused of revivalism by serialising the great Hindu epics, the Ramayana and the Mahabharata (1987-89). The rise of the Sikh militancy was also attributed to the Hinduisation of Indian politics and in popular political discourse, articulated by the Sikh militants, branded the Indian State as 'Hindu Bania', its leadership discriminatory to the minorities. The then Prime Minister of India, Indira Gandhi was referred to as Bahamini (the feminine version of Brahmin, a derogatory casteist label). It was alleged that the Congress Party is appropriating Hindu religious icons and symbols.

The apologetic politics of the dominant political parties towards the minority communities justified the Bharatiya Janata Party's idea of India, a derivative of the concept of Hindutva advanced by Savarkar. That only means that everyone who has ancestral roots in India is a Hindu, and all such people collectively constitute a nation (Savarkar 1969: 104).

A process of shifting the focus from one variety of ideological monotheism to another, i.e. from the upper caste to the lower caste, from the majority religious group to the minority religious group or vice-versa has become a dominant political practice. This process negated the forces of ideological pluralism.

In this context, politics has produced a major shift from the minority religious group to the majority religious group, from the nationalisation of Hindutva to the regionalisation of Hindutva. The nurturing of the regional sentiments and aspirations around Hindutva is a unique experiment which has serious implications for the nation-building project. It has not only reversed the secular nation-building project launched at the time of independence but has also distorted the RSS concept of the nationalisation of Hindutva. For example, the whole tenor of electoral mobilisation in Gujarat was a clever blend of Gaurav of Gujarat and Hindutva identity. Earlier, a similar blend between regionalism and Islam had been witnessed in Kashmir. This process has a built-in potential of leading to disintegration of the country. For instance, if the movements like Punjab for Punjabis

(Sikhs), Kashmir for Kashmiris (Muslims), Maharashtra for Marathas (Hindus), Assam for Assamese (Hindus), Gujarat for Gujaratis (Hindus), gain momentum, it will result in not only disintegration but can also cause religious and ethnic cleansing.

The massive response to the future of the Hindutva ideology and regional leadership can be understood in the backdrop of globalisation. The process of globalisation has undermined the concept of a nation. Having compromised on economic sovereignty, countries like, India and Pakistan, have surrendered their political sovereignty, as maintenance of domestic peace has been pushed into the realm of global political decision-making and diktats. It is in this context that President Pervez Musharraf raised the question of the Gujarat riots at the United Nations and the 'Mian Musharraf' symbolism gained currency in the Gujarat elections. The process of globalisation has provided an impetus to the son-of-the-soil movement.

Legitimisation Through Blurring Structures

Given the consensus amongst the political parties, be it the Congress or the BJP, on the process of globalisation of the neoliberal path of development,[7] (see manifestos; Bharatiya Janata Party 2004 and Indian National Congress 2004) electoral discourse conveniently located crony capitalism, unemployment, poverty and inequalities in policy paralysis. In other words, during the Congress regime, it was attributed to policy paralysis and now to the incapacity of the incumbent leadership to address the causes. The consensus is on the path of development, to provide continuity through the legitimisation of laws of the market, surrender of the State to the moralities of the market, and intervention of the State at the superstructural level. For instance, the excessive emphasis on reforming the citizens' interactions with the State, irrespective of structural inequalities, provides much-needed legitimacy. It is claimed that the interests of the citizens are universal, common and rational. In a particular context, the illusion of all interests of all the members to the common remains blurred but with the broadening and deepening of governance reforms reveal the fallacy of this claim. To illustrate, in the 2014 parliament elections eradication of corruption was articulated as a common interest and not building its linkages with the redistribution of income which is a structural issue. It excludes the structures from analysis as these are seen as non-problematical. A body of knowledge is institutionalised, which identifies the problem areas and strategy for problem-solving without questioning the structure. It also prescribes value about what is right or what is wrong within the boundaries so demarcated. For example, the initiation of competitive politics since the mid-1960s brought to the fore a peculiar feature of Indian politics, i.e. a threat and a need paradox of democracy. The ruling elite felt threatened by the same institutions, groups and individuals which provide legitimacy to its rule. The institutions comprising, to use Althusser (2006: 127-186) categories, the ideological and the repressive state apparatuses were used to strengthen the power base of a political leader. In the process, the leader became all-powerful, and with the passage of time, it became obvious that the leader, in fact, had become powerless to effect any radical change in society. As a result, participatory institutions were either made ineffective or defunct. The dissent was either muffled or projected as a threat to national unity. The process has been one of gradual de-democratisation, whittling down of the basic rights of the people, the abdication of the basic obligation of the system, and downgrading of the most precious facet of democracy: Legitimacy.

The institutional decline, which was caused by the threat perception of these leaders, was selectively reversed. Having curtailed the democratic functioning of various institutions, these leaders frequently misused the paramilitary forces to overcome the crises. The 1980s saw the revival of the law-enforcing agencies with overactive police; as a result, the heroes of the 1980s were the super cops. The 1990s produced an 'overactive judiciary' which took upon itself all the functions of the State, including the moral and ethical role of the non-state institutions. The Chief Election Commissioner shared the glory of performing the role of reforming the system single-handedly. The armed forces also could not resist the temptation of showing to the political executive that the latter was not capable of taking the right kind of decisions. Each institution has been trying to emerge as the sole saviour of the system by taking upon itself the task of reconstructing the system. Now, in a changed context, both domestic and global, the onus of building up a just, honest and humane society has been attributed to the 'Jan Lokpal'. But, somebody has to take out heavy insurance against the future failure of Lokpal—there comes a talk of the second republic to start the process all over again. The whole process can be described as the Hindu Cyclical Movement—in that the ruling class feels threatened by the same institutions, which build up a cycle of which they need to remain in power. Paradoxically, therefore, the undermining and revival of the institutions appear to be taking place simultaneously.

The contemporary crises are either characterised, as a crisis of secular values located in the empirical reality of the incidences of targeting the minority religious groups and caste groups or crisis of inequality as a decline in the income and rise in the prices of the essential commodities in criminalisation of the politics. All these factors are considered without building causal connections leading to the non-identification of the 'cause of the causes.' The very crisis lies in the nature of politics.

The dominant trend is to isolate the institutions, glorify or condemn them and insulate the system. The system must not be questioned. In the process, the people either question an institution and / or an individual. This approach reinforces the status quo and doubles up as a cover-up mechanism for the inadequacies of the system.

Further, having built the consensus on a path of development, the political parties have uprooted themselves from their past ideological persuasion to build alliances. The nature of coalitions transformed in the post-liberalisation phase; it has provided justification to the political parties to build bridges with ideologically divergent groups. 'Bridge-Politics' tends to blur the ideological differences. The competing political parties, rather than responding to each other, tend to co-opt ideologically divergent fringe groups to provide a 'stable government' thereby claiming to have saved the people from frequent elections. These politically opportunistic acts are justified in the name of saving people from instability; therefore, the demand that once elected, a five-year term be fixed for the Members of Parliament. The legitimate question is: Can any government be stable without adhering to the norms of democratic, secular and just politics? Further, can a government be stable without restoring the autonomy of the institutions, the legitimacy of all the organs of the State? In the name of stability of government, alliances are made with corrupt, communal, fundamentalist and casteist political parties.

The quest for capturing power, in the negation of the norms of political behaviour, moral veneer, which go to justify political acts, actually made ideologies look redundant. For instance, in the initial years, the coalition for the electoral purpose was formed amongst the political parties which were on the same side of the ideological spectrum. In Punjab, the Congress Party and the Communist parties stood for electoral coalitions representing the left of centre and the Bharatiya Janata Party and the Shiromani Akali Dal on the right-wing political space. And, in post-1990s after the neoliberal reforms, the ideological difference between the political parties vanished. For instance, in 2019, a post-election alliance between the Shiv Sena (an extreme right-wing party), the Indian National Congress and the National Congress Party (centrist parties) in Maharashtra symbolised the recognition of the majoritarianism and hegemony of the right-wing pro-majority agenda.[8] This has the potential to redefine the terms of political discourse in the country. To illustrate, the political parties, like the Indian National Congress, have been caught at the crossroads. The option to launch a long drawn struggle around its basic philosophy of secularism, liberalism and equity has been allowed to go by default. However, the mixed model for contesting elections of endorsement of some of the right-wing policies, like abrogation of 370, supporting Balakot-kind of anti-Pak operations and going low-key on personalised anti-Prime Minister Modi rant and, along with this, aggressively articulate regional and local agenda as has been done by Bhupendra Singh Hooda (Leader of the Congress Party in Haryana) has acquired currency with some of the leaders within the Congress. For entering into post-election alliances, the anti-BJP has emerged as a sole criterion. It was in this backdrop that the Congress Party entered into an alliance with the extreme right-wing Shiv Sena in which both gave tacit consent to put their principled positions on the back-burner for the time being. It is a different matter that the Shiv Sena Chief Minister of Maharashtra has asserted that there was no question of abandoning the agenda of Hindutva. These coalition governments may appear to be merely power-sharing arrangements but have legitimised the right-wing political discourse.

Not only this, as mentioned, the legitimisation

function has been institutionalised through constitutional amendments, power dynamics, political mobilisations and protest movements in exclusion to the examination of the structural basis.

Legitimisation Through Practices and Activities

Further, the practices and activities emanating from the neoliberal path of development, leading to unemployment, inequalities, capital accumulation and social deprivation, etc., were legitimised through the ideology of mystification of the social reality for the marginalised population. For instance, the abrogation of Article 370 of the Indian Constitution (See Annexure 1.2), Citizen Amendment Act 2019, declaring the practice of triple talaq as unconstitutional, etc.—all these shifted the term of discourse in the domain of identity politics. This kind of politics aimed at freezing the status quo not through change, but by shifting the equilibrium in favour of a theoretical counterpart rather than building an alternate discourse. For instance, the dominant philosophical understanding of the present right-wing political dispensation is that our future lies in the past knowledge base, yet to be fully discovered, be it science, ethics, social living, human values, etc. The revivalist movement has been used as the myth of a glorious past. The efforts are being made to present mythology as science to nurture a narrative of India's glorious past. The Minister of State for Human Resource Development, Government of India, said that "students in premier engineering institutes like IITs must be taught about ancient Indian discoveries, such as, Pushpak Viman, which is mentioned in the Ramayana" ("Mythology, Science and BJP" 2018). For instance, a professor in IIT started teaching the technology of spirituality. He observed that "our ancestors called Geography 'Bhu-Gol' means the earth is round... our ancestors were also aware of the knowledge of the properties of metals and their production and purification and so on. Now the question arises, how did our ancestors have such knowledge, was it that "all our scientists were saints. All of them did Yoga, all of them did Pranayama, and all of them did Meditation..." The very basis of science is spirituality ("Technology of Spirituality" 2015). The general result is to make it quite plain that the myth is out of sync with the facts, that it assumes absurdities or implies them, and that it either paralyses action towards a better world or stimulates action towards a worse one. In other words, 'myths make the believer an escapist or a Stormtrooper' (Barrows 2007: 25). Undoubtedly, it is essential to know one's past to shape the future. But, to accept the past without question is to generate myths and dogmas, which in turn, strengthen the forces of revivalism. It is understandable that when hopes are belied, the present is full of disappointments, and the future is uncertain, then nostalgia produces revivalism. This kind of discourse has blurred the distinction between revivalism and 'renewalism.' 'The event, incident and activity, etc., are investigated in isolation as if they have no structural roots. It excludes specific areas of social activity, which on the surface, appear to be unproblematical and therefore, need not be subjected to critical enquiry and attributed causality' (Allen 1975: 24). For instance, this is like an experiment conducted by the 'Godman' called Mahesh Yogi. This Yogi has been credited with having trained his disciples in the art of flying without wings. They were pushed into the air from a height. They all fell to the ground and broke their limbs. When the Yogi was asked to explain this bizarre experiment, he accused his disciples of lack of concentration. The Yogi ought to have known that in the case of physical objects, the power of earth's gravitational pull is stronger than the power of meditation. He claimed to have imparted knowledge relating to multiple factors, like the technique of flying, body discipline, surroundings, and meditation. However, the cause of all the causes that gravitation pull was taken as given, assuming that this can be neutralised by the super-structural factors. The activity was based on holistic knowledge, but could not build interconnections between the various factors and attribute primacy to a factor without which a phenomenon cannot surface.

The process of legitimisation was carried out through practices and various activities in the mainstream of electoral politics and political ideology, like revivalism and glorification of the past through Hindu civilisational symbolic categories. Similar is the case of the cow politics, promoting yoga, promoting territorial nationalism (through websites like 'Bharat Ke Veer'), etc. The notion is to join the activity, supported and justified by random statements, followed by conducting some studies and further legitimised through practices. For instance, to establish a commoners' understanding of yoga and infrastructure, Mr. Modi placed yoga above everything. He said, "We should make efforts to take yoga from cities to villages, tribal areas. Yoga is above the region, above faith, above everything." Along with it, he further stressed the infrastructural needs that Yoga requires to work efficiently ("Yoga Integral Part" 2019). On other aspects of cow politics, political leaders gave bizarre statements, such as linking cow with love jihad ("Mashable News Staff" 2019), cows exhaling oxygen or producers of oxygen, claims of cow dung being capable of curing cancer, assertions like cow's hump, has gold in it, etc. ("Samayam Malayalam" 2020). A study conducted by the researchers at Junagadh Agricultural University claimed that the cow urine contained gold (Lee 2016).

'The holistic knowledge believes in a plurality of causes, but does not build a hierarchy of causes and, therefore, does not specify the cause of all causes' (Carr 1961: 90). To interpret a phenomenon, it is always desirable to identify multiple causes and, thereby establish a hierarchy of causes. It also necessitates building a causal connection between the causes to identify the final trigger for the event to acquire a manifest form.

The main focus ought to be to address those causes which are rooted in the structure and address those that may bring limited changes in reality. For instance, if the dropout rate amongst the school children is on the rise, the reason is attributed to the children's sickness or student-teacher ratio, i.e. within the education system rather than in the system per se. A phenomenon is broken into the various parts, and the solution is offered in the micro context without locating it in the 'cause of all the causes'. It depends on which facts are selected to hinge the arguments. The selection of facts for prioritising is a political decision. It involves a value judgment.

Similarly, the use of measures is also inseparable from our politics. To consider the measures to be beyond question is not only lethargic but dangerous.

> Our measuring systems make us reason on the basis of averages. But, if we go on reasoning in averages, we will forge our beliefs and build our decisions on data that are increasingly divorced from real life. The average individual does not exist, and heightening inequality is detaching this average even more from the real experience of life, for talking about the average is a way to avoid talking about inequality (Sen, Fioussi and Stiglitz 2011: XIV).

If we stop asking questions, then what would we be measuring and to achieve what outcomes; simply put, it will be disastrous for sustainability. For instance, the green revolution strategy for food production was marketed as a powerful engine of growth in Punjab, India. It contributed to a higher GDP. However, two decades later, it came as a 'discovery' that it has led to a depletion of the water table, environment damage and soil degradation, besides, the decline in the farmers' income. The consequence of a single-digit measurement obsession like the GDP led to the endangering of the future of farming, farmers and the entire generation of the people.

It has to be recognised that the system is facing a challenge due to the complexity emanating from the interaction between the paradigm shift in the path of development, the evolution of corresponding institutions, and shaping of the diverse expectations in a multicultural society. It has been evident that the development per se may not lead to equity in the allocation of resources and also bring about the collapse of the retrogressive ideological structures. There is, thus, a need to debate as to how to reframe the policies to build the capacity of the people on the margins and create conditions to enable them to get integrated into the productive processes and secular democratic institutions. And, as an outcome, they are likely to gain access to the assets, livelihood, jobs, and investment and a tolerant diversity, sensitive politics and society.

These issues have been critically examined in three inter-related essays. The first essay deals with unfolding of the challenges of democracy; and the limits and reinvention of the State in response to the challenges of the market. The essay on Governance for the Margins: Processes, Tensions and Faultlines also empirically identifies the limits of the political intervention to bring about pro-people reforms; and the third essay deals with the need to understand the social faultlines in a regional context titled 'Dalit Identity Architecture: Selective Adaptation of Cultural Symbols to Nurturing Extensive Sites.'

NOTES

1. Albert Camus: 'And I should like to be able to love my country and still love justice. I don't want any greatness for it, particularly a greatness born of blood and falsehood. I want to keep it alive by keeping justice alive' (Camus, 1943: 90).

2. 'A theory with a static basis deals with problems in such a way as to exclude specific areas of social activity as being non-problematical. In other words, it precludes structures from analysis and in this way specifies that they do not present problems and need in no way to be altered' (Allen 1975: 20).
3. The reason for the historical development of the welfare state are contextual. These have been listed by Richard Titmuss. 'Fear of social revolution, the need for law-abiding labour force, the struggle for power between political parties and pressure groups, a demand to remove some of the social costs of change—industrial accidents—from the backs of the workers, and the social conscience of the rich are played a part' (Titmuss, 1964: 34).
4. Althusser argued that the power is exercised by the public and private institutions, and all these provide legitimacy and dominance to the ruling class. And these constitute an ideological state apparatus. It functions primarily on ideology and secondarily on repression. The repressive state apparatus functions primarily on repression while functioning secondarily on ideology (Althusser, 2006: 127-186).
5. 'By Ramrajya I do not mean Hindu Raj. I mean Ramrajya, Divine Raj, the Kingdom of God. For me Rama and Rahim are one and the same deity. I acknowledge no other God but the one God of truth and righteousness' (Gandhi, 1919: 305).
6. In parliament while presenting the Citizenship Amendment Bill it was mentioned that in Pakistan, the Hindus were 23 per cent in 1947 and have been reduced to 3.7 per cent at present. But the given census data shows that the population of Hindus in West Pakistan was 1.3 per cent in 1951 which increased to 1.6 per cent in 1998 ("How Pak's Hindu" 2020).
7. The Bharatiya Janata Party election manifesto for the 2004 parliament elections highlighted its commitment to 'further broadening and deepening the economic reforms based on a self-reliant approach, sustained double-digit GDP growth rate to achieve complete eradication of poverty and unemployment, end of regional and social disparities and bridging the urban-rural divide' (Bharatiya Janata Party, 2004). The Congress manifesto asserts that, 'it would broaden and deepen economic reforms. The overriding objectives would be to attain and sustain year after year a 8-10 per cent rate of economic growth and to spread this growth over all sectors, particularly agriculture and industry... aimed at local level economic and social transformation

that directly benefit the poor in rural and urban India, bringing prosperity to the 6 lakh-odd villages of India and improving the living conditions of the urban poor' (Indian National Congress, 2004).

8. Interestingly, the Bharatiya Janata Party (BJP) and the Shiv Sena fought the 2019 Maharashtra assembly elections as a pre-election coalition partner and won the elections with the thumping majority. In the house of 288, the BJP and the Shiv Sena together won 163 seats. Notwithstanding, their ideological similarities, they could not reach an agreement on power sharing. And ideologically, divergent parties, i.e. the Shiv Sena, the National Congress Party (NCP) and the Indian National Congress formed the government.

1
Unfolding Challenges of Democracy in India: 2019 Electoral Verdict

Introduction

The main function of democracy is to multiply choices and ensure people's participation in decision-making and not merely their presence. Elections are meant to offer choices. And, also filter the claims, shape entitlements and rights and mould opinions, of course, maybe with manufactured facts. In each election, filters ranging from nationalism, caste, religions to survival needs, etc., are applied in varied proportions to woo the voters. The electoral system, for that matter, any other system, is directed by the individuals or/and the groups to pursue their concerns, interests and power ambitions.

Historically, Indian politics has undergone a shift from a command economy to the neoliberal market economy, and the movement of the pendulum from the Congress-led one-party dominance[1] to a coalition of political parties to the BJP-led one-party dominance;[2] from institutionalised developmental nationalism to cultural nationalism. This shift has shaped certain paradoxes providing content to the idea of new India radically transformed from the one envisioned by the makers of the Indian Constitution.

These paradoxes are the Nehruvian mixed economy to market economy (see "Selected Works" 2006: 618),[3] mono-cultural institutional secularism (see Secular Nationalism, cited in Chandra et al 1999: 48)[4] to a unified conception of indigenous (Hindu) nationhood, and the threat and need of the democratic institutions and from the non-aligned (see Huntington 1996: 21)[5] to the interest-based global alignments.

As a result, it may not be methodologically appropriate to label the political leadership and parties as a pro or anti-neoliberal economic reforms, secular, pseudo-secular or non-secular, casteist or non-casteist. The political spectrum, by and large, endorsed the market reforms and allowed redefinition of the secular space and, for electoral purposes, made opportunist alliances, notwithstanding the noises made in opposition to the market reforms and communal politics. Briefly, these paradoxes can be located in three distinct phases, i.e. 1952 to 1977, 1977 to 2014 and, 2014 onwards. To provide a historical background to the post-2014 phase, the salient features of the first two phases are being listed.

First Phase 1952 to 1977

In the first phase, the electoral promises were ideologically in convergence with the path of development and institutional secularism. The hallmark of the Nehruvian phase was the promise of equitable distribution of the resources as expressed through the various policies like land to the tiller, industrialisation with the increased government ownership and creating employment in the public sector. In the 1971 parliamentary elections, the slogan of 'Garibi Hatao' (poverty eradication) provided continuity by Indira Gandhi to social justice for all as envisioned by India's first Prime Minister, Jawaharlal Nehru. Along with this, it was envisaged that with the initiation of a process of development of science, technology, the spread of modern education and build-up of the modern industrial complex—all would lead to a collapse of the retrogressive identities based on caste, religion, tribal and social, and reinforce the secular social groupings and institutions. These institutions were nurtured, and their autonomy was protected.

There was another reality reflected in the politics that could curb the authoritarian tendencies irrespective of the fact that it was one party dominant rule without much competition.

The effective numbers of the parties in this phase ranged between 1.80 in 1951 to 2.12 in 1971. This was a single party dominant phase. In this, the Congress Party launched a nation-building project which promised a model of mixed economy government-supported capitalism with Five Year Plans. In a brief building, a welfare state based on the socialistic pattern of society.

Table 1.1 Effective Numbers of Parties in Lower House Elections

S. No.	*Year*	*Effective Numbers of Parties (Votes)*	*Effective Numbers of Parties (Seats)*
1	1952	4.53	1.80
2	1957	3.98	1.76
3	1962	4.40	1.85
4	1967	5.19	3.16
5	1971	4.63	2.12
6	1977	3.40	2.63
7	1980	4.25	2.28
8	1984	3.99	1.69
9	1989	4.80	4.35
10	1991	5.10	3.70
11	1996	7.11	5.83
12	1998	6.91	5.28
13	1999	6.74	5.87
14	2004	7.60	6.50
15	2009	7.98	5.01
16	2014	6.92	3.45
17	2019	5.27	3.03

Source: Journal of the Indian School of Political Economy, XV / 1-2 (January-June 2003), Statistical Supplement, Tables 1.1-1.13: 293-307. For 2004, the index was calculated by the Centre for the Study of

Developing Societies, New Delhi; In: E. Sridharan (2014), editor, *Coalition Politics in India: Selected Issues at the Centre and the States*, p. 52, Academic Foundation: New Delhi. For 2014 and 2019 the index is calculated by the author.

In a mixed economy model of Nehru, the State was to play a leading role in creating a structural base by investing in the strategic industries like iron, steel, etc., science and technology research, and producing technical human resource. And, the private sector was expected to produce essential consumer or wage goods, but as an integrated whole.

The emphasis was to produce essential consumer goods and ensure their distribution amongst the people living on the margins. The instrument of Five Years Plans was envisaged to seek a basic transformation to curb individual greed and to ensure equitable distribution of political and economic power (see "Selected Works" 2005: From the Editorial Note).[6] To quote Nehru:

> It is true that a socialistic economy must provide for a welfare state but it does necessarily follow that a welfare state must also be based on a socialistic pattern of society. Therefore, the two, although they overlap, are yet somewhat different, and we say that we want both (*Jawaharlal Nehru's Speeches* 1958: 17).

The outcome was measured in terms of the rapid economic growth, arts, culture and science and technology development, nurturing of technical human resource and scientific temper. Along with, the idea of secular nationalism was institutionalised meaning thereby freedom of religion and conscience, including freedom for those who may not have any religion. And secularism was presented as a supra-religion. It was attributed as a superior value to maintain order, brotherhood, tolerance, peaceful coexistence and explore truth without the shackles of dogmas and ritualism. To Nehru, 'religion, though it has undoubtedly brought comfort to innumerable human beings and stabilised society but its values, have checked the tendency to change and progress inherent in human society' (Nehru 1946: 511). He further advocated the need for a scientific approach and temper to overcome the religious dogmas and explore the truth. 'The scientific approach and temper are, or should be, a way of life, a process of thinking, a method, of acting and associating with our fellowmen' (Nehru 1946: 512). The emphasis was to put secularism alongside 'scientificism' and hoped that it brings down the collapse of ideological structures which, on their own, proved to be historically fallacious. The structural logic of this kind of development led to pauperisation of the large section of the society accompanied by disintegrative social process mirrored in religiosity, revivalism, fundamentalism, communalism and communal riots in the post-mid-1960s. As a consequence, the disintegrative tendencies became a dominant and persistent feature of socio-economic development.

The interaction of the State-led nation-building project with the path of development threw up challenges for political leadership. The leadership started feeling threatened by the same institutions which had empowered them. A process of the centralisation of power in the leadership led to deinstitutionalisation of governance amid mass movements. From 1971 till 1975, the Congress Party led by Mrs. Gandhi centralised power through the weakening of the regional Congress leadership and replaced them with those leaders who owed their allegiance to her, In spite of this, the state leadership continued to remain faction-ridden. Having made the institutions non-functional, leaders who were all-powerful, increasingly become powerless. The need was felt to bring about the necessary changes and provide stability to the system. The economic recession leading to food shortages, price rise and the collapse of the democratic party system produced a popular mass movement. The movement in the States like Bihar and Gujarat even turned violent amidst discontentment amongst some of the Congressmen known as the Young Turks, led by Chandra Shekhar, Mohan Dharia and Krishan Kant. In March 1974, a Sarvodaya leader, Jayaprakash Narayan (JP) took the leadership of the movement and made it a national movement and directly challenged Mrs. Gandhi's authority by labelling her regime as corrupt and authoritarian. During this time, Mrs. Gandhi's 1971 election was set aside on the grounds of corrupt practices by the Allahabad High Court on June 12, 1975. These movements and political challenges led to the imposition of internal emergency. In the words of Myron Weiner (1989: 269):

> In Smt. Gandhi's view, Congress organisations with local leaders independent of the centre, hostile opposition, a critical press and an independent judiciary had impeded a movement towards a modern socialist, equalitarian social and economic order. The gradual democratisation violative of the basic rights of the people initiated the reversal of the idea of India as envisaged by the leadership at the time of independence.

To provide for constitutional dignity, the 42nd amendment in 1976 brought about certain changes by including in the preamble, 'Secular and Socialist' and unity of the nation to 'unity and integrity of the nation'. It curtailed democratic rights in the country and gave the parliament unrestrained power to amend any parts of the Constitution without judicial review.

During the constituent assembly debates in 1946, K.T. Shah proposed an amendment seeking to declare India as a Secular, Federal, Socialist nation. B.R. Ambedkar stated:

> My objections, stated briefly are two: in the first place the constitution... is merely a mechanism for the purpose of regulating the work of the various organs of the state. It is not a mechanism whereby particular members or particular parties are installed in office. It can't be laid down in the

> constitution itself, because that is destroying democracy altogether. He further added that the amendment was 'purely superfluous' and unnecessary, as "socialist principles are already embodied in our constitution, through fundamental rights and the Directive Principles of state policy" (*Constituent Assembly Debate* 1948: 401-402).

The economic crisis of the mid-1960s and the fading away of the aura of national freedom and its leadership, and demystification of the 'national' prefix attached to 'economy', 'integration', 'mainstream'—all that produced intractable problems. This led to the delegitimisation of their politics as they obscured the most basic faultlines in our society of castes, religions, regions, ethnicity, classes, etc. The deepening of the crisis led to the invoking of nationalism to blur the social reality for the people. This could succeed because of the failure to develop alternate politics. The poverty eradication policies could not pay much attention to the role of the institutions like caste, religion, family, kinship, which have many potentials to perpetuate inequalities as also to promote equity.

Second Phase 1977 to 2014

The second phase from 1977 to 2014 saw the slogan 'justice for all' being replaced by 'justice for Backward Castes, Dalits and Minorities'. It provided hope to the people living on the margins; in other words, opportunities were promised without creating the conducive conditions for enabling the same.

In the 1990s, the Indian economy was passing through turbulent times. The rising inflation, multiplying unemployment, a steady decline in the public saving rate, drop in the foreign exchange reserves, and the external debt had ballooned.

Even during the Nehruvian phase, the economy passed through such a balance of payment disasters in 1957, 1961-

62, 1965-66, 1974 and 1979-80. At the centre of this was the shortage of the food-grains but the policy response was to strengthen the trade regulations, whereas, the crisis of the 1990s had been shaped by a demand-led economy rather than the 'supply-side shortages'.

> Coupled with the drop in foreign exchange reserves; the Gulf War leading to trembling of oil prices, violent agitation triggered by the Mandal Commission, and an increase in interest rates on international borrowings. The political response was to initiate policy decisions for liberalisation and to integrate the economy with the global economy rather than building a conducive environment to build alternatives (Ramesh 2015).[7]

The argument advanced against the State-led mixed economy is that the promotion of the common good by the State is nothing but common good as interpreted by the self-seeking politicians and civil servants, and the argument in favour of the market-led reforms is that 'the self-seeking actions' of a multitude of individuals would be amalgamated into the common good.

The neoliberal reforms and integration with the global economy necessitated major changes in the institutional framework, and reportedly even the appointment of the Finance Minister was dictated by the Global Finance Institutions. 'Given the grave financial situation, we knew that the first priority would be the appointment of the Finance Minister...one who commanded the trust of the IMF and the World Bank' (Ramesh 2015).

The market fundamentalism package unleashed a process leading to the integration of the developing countries into the new economic global order without having any autonomy to dissent. It is in this context that the *Human Development Report* (2000) recorded:

> Small and poor countries generally participate little in global economic rule-making for a host of reasons, starting with

> the costs of participation and policy research. Just as the nation requires an inclusive democracy to guarantee respect for human rights, so the system of global governance needs to be transparent and fair, giving voice to small and poor countries and releasing them from their marginalisation from the benefits of the global economy and technology.

This mismatch between the electoral promises and the economic policies adopted led to widespread discontentment amongst the people and reinforced the trust deficit in the leadership. The term anti-incumbency acquired currency to explain the people's mistrust. The political parties in power supported the economic reforms and, at the time of elections, made promises contrary to these reforms. And, the answer to this was found in coalition politics—non-ideological marriages of convenience and justified to provide a stable government to the electorate. To put it simply, power-sharing through cabinet berths and portfolios and to share the spoils of power. These are justified as a necessary evil to remain afloat in the business of politics to serve their support base.

The anti-incumbency, therefore, provided an honourable exit to one party to be replaced by another party with a similar track record. When in power, they implement economic reforms through rationalisation of employment in government, public sector disinvestment, privatisation of the public services, elimination of subsidies etc. And then conclude that the electorates are against the incumbent political party. Are the people so irrational to be against the incumbents? It is because the government takes initiatives to reduce employment in the public sector and promotes jobless growth for ensuring the fiscal fix. And exhort the people to participate in the self-help groups and launch small businesses of their own in the face of intense global competition relying on quality, cost-cutting and efficiency. Nor can they tell the people to mind their health while the government provides subsidies to build private hospitals. And to build their stakes, they are motivated to pay for the life-saving services even if they do not have the opportunities to earn a livelihood.

The emphasis was to shift the role of the State as the provider of services to being merely a facilitator. At the election time, political parties oppose neoliberal economic reforms and promise doles.

> Both Dr. Manmohan Singh and Dr. Montek Ahluwalia were better known for their commitment to neoliberal reforms rather than to concerns of the disadvantaged people. It was only Sonia Gandhi who tried to temper hard market fundamentalism with compassion and equity, and this I believe was her most valuable and least acknowledged contribution to Indian life (Saxena 2019: 192).

The politics of populism became a predominant mode to outcompete each other. And, simultaneously, the policy formulation for poverty eradication and mitigation of inequalities through the instrument of reservations based on caste, i.e. from the Scheduled Castes to the Backward Castes has been given priority.

The Mandal Commission acknowledged this contradiction. To quote:

> When a backward class candidate becomes Collector or a Superintendent of Police, the material benefits accruing from his position are limited to the members of his family only. But, the psychological spin-off of this phenomenon is tremendous; the entire community of that backward class candidate feels socially elevated. (Mandal 1980: 57)

At the ideological level, it was used as a strategy to co-opt different castes by multiplying the caste cleavages and also to counter mobilisation of the Hindu majority by using the Mandir-Masjid conflict. For instance, BJP's electoral tally increased from two seats in 1984 to 182 in the 1999 elections.

This also coincided with the Shah Bano matrimonial

Table 1.2 Seats Won and Percentage of Votes Polled in Parliament Elections, 1984-2009

Year	*Seats Contested*	*Seats Won*	*% of Votes Polled*	*% of Seats Won Out of Contested Seats*
1984	224	2	7.74	1
1989	225	85	11.36	38
1991	468	120	20.11	26
1996	471	161	20.29	35
1998	388	182	25.59	47
1999	339	182	23.75	58
2004	364	138	22.16	38
2009	433	116	18.8	27

Source: *Statistical Reports of General Election to Lok Sabha (1984-2009).* Election Commission of India.

dispute leading to the amendment in the Indian Constitution to overcome the Supreme Court judgement. The Operation Blue Star led to the demolition of the Sikh Shrine Golden Temple, followed by the assassination of Indira Gandhi, leading to the Sikh carnage in 1984. Also, these developments reinforced the right-wing political discourse. This was a departure from the first phase to which the dominant thrust of politics was to articulate institutionalised secularism into the public sphere that was not governed by the caste and religious-based cultural reservoir. Subsequently, political practice compromised institutional secularism to convert the religious, caste and ethnic reservoir into electoral capital.

This was also reflected in the formation of the governments, which were largely a coalition of various political parties. These coalitions of the political parties consisted mainly of the conglomeration of religious, caste, tribal groups, etc., at the regional level. In seven general elections from 1989, 1991, 1996, 1998, 1999, 2004 and 2009, no single-party could get the majority, and the elections system became highly competitive and more diversity sensitive; the effective number of parties by seats increased from 4.80 in 1989 to 7.90 in 2009. (See Table 1.1). As mentioned, in these elections, the vote share of the Bharatiya Janata Party (BJP) multiplied from 11 per cent (1989) to 22 per cent (2004) and that of the Congress Party, declined continuously. These coalitions were largely for power-sharing and to keep some party out of power. However, the common-minimum programmes evolved by both the centre-right or centre-left were woven around the issues of social and economic equity. And, these coalitions marked a shift from the catch-all approach to caste and community-based policy programmes.

The gap between the electoral promises and the government performance in the first and second phase was there, but the reasons were different. In the first phase, electoral promises were in conversation with the ideological predispositions, whereas in the second phase, the electoral promises were ideologically divergent. The reasons for this ranged from structural causes to choices exercised by the leaders. In the first phase, the leadership was committed to implementing their promises, but could not do it due to structural constraints—This led to a crisis of discontentment. In the second phase, the electoral promises made were divergent from the path of development, leading to a crisis of trust in the leadership.

With the decline in one-party dominance, the national parties started to build bridges with the ideologically divergent regional parties based on caste, language, tribal and religious considerations. It blurred ideological boundaries. For example, the Congress Party, responsible for the atrocities against the Sikhs in 1984, aligned with the secularists, while the BJP, explicit in their commitment to

Hindutva was in alliance with the former socialists and liberal democrats.

This phase also symbolised excessive corruption. Faced with popular discontent and disorder in the civil society, the ruling Congress Party's response was rather indifferent. The popular discontent gave rise to a massive protest movement led by Anna Hazare, a civil rights activist. Interestingly, the political discourse shaped by the civil rights activists was institutional, i.e. for the creation of oversight of the Jan Lokpal to check corruption. Whereas, the State response was procedural, legalistic and threatening. It was procedural when the government abdicated its responsibility to deal with a political protest against corruption and gave all the authority to the Delhi Police. Though it was not a recent development. Earlier too, the State had abdicated its responsibility in favour of the market for providing access to education, health, livelihood and distributive justice to the people.

It was legalistic, as was asserted that the civil society activists misappropriated the function of the Parliament to enact laws. Not recognising the fact that the laws are enacted by the Parliament, but are evolved as per the needs of the times, protest movements as nurtured by the rights-based consciousness, globalisation and marketisation. For instance, the introduction of the Women's Reservation Bill was a consequence of a long protracted struggle of the women's movement in the country. These are testimonies of a vibrant democracy where the right to dissent and consent are protected as a cardinal principle.

The State's response was quite intimidating as it started witch-hunting of those who were leaders of the protest movements. First, it targeted Baba Ram Dev, a Yoga Guru and a business person, and followed by Anna's team. They were accused of corrupt practices. The signal was loud that if you support an anti-corruption campaign of Anna

Hazare, be ready to be targeted for your past mistakes. The anger was so deep that all these tactics could not deter the people from coming out in large numbers in support of the anti-corruption movement.

The language of the anti-corruption crusaders was liberating for the people with the means or resources from the shackles of corruption and harassment. It is also in celebration of the creation of the super icons like the Jan Lokpal. The 1980s have seen the birth of super cops in the fight against terrorism. This role was passed on to the judiciary in the 1990s. Now, we have an overactive judiciary with super-judges trying to perform all other functions except their own. The backlog of the cases is daunting. People have to wait for more than 10-15 years to get justice. Earlier, the country witnessed the rebirth of the Election Commission with Super Regulator T.N. Seshan. All these encompassing overactive institutions like the overactive police in the 1980s, the overactive judiciary in the 1990s and an overactive Election Commission did perform some exemplary role in their respective fields. But, the damage they caused to the system cannot be overlooked. It took quite some time to make the Election Commission function without violating the space of other organs. It required a tremendous effort to send the police back to the barracks and redefine its boundaries. The stress and strains caused by the judiciary by their constant day-to-day interference in the functioning of the legislature and the executive have now come under the lens. There are lessons to be learnt from these developments.

Now, in a changed context, both domestic and global, the onus of building up a just, honest and humane society has been attributed to the 'Jan Lokpal'.

Undoubtedly, the issues raised by the anti-corruption protests were relevant as they stressed the need to have an autonomous and transparent institutional mechanism for reducing corruption. But these protests were without any vision for the redistribution of income and to provide justice to the people living on the margins.

Politicians and aspirants use this moral space to pull different strings. And, what is bad and good is situational and contingent. Corruption is bad, and honesty is good. Personal honesty has a higher value because it has markings of scarcity. And, in popular political parlance, individual honesty on its own has been marketed as a superior value than even the fight against hunger, poverty, inequality, greed, conspicuous consumption and even corruption.

This situation, defined by the public recognition of the circumscribed value of honesty, acts as an invitation to those who have proved their worth in their respective professions ranging from cinema to sports to social activism. These 'celebrities' with their reservoir of social credit drift into politics. The mortality rate of the 'celebrities' in politics is alarming, but there are exceptions also, particularly in South India.

The recent emergence of the Aam Admi Party in politics is a commentary on this political culture and the absence of political ideology. It has the dual advantage of being a product of a mass movement and aggressive appropriator of the space created by the propagation of 'honesty' as a supreme value rather than historical struggle against capital accumulation, inequalities, hunger and poverty. It has used the small screen to make their concerns appear pro-people. In other words, the civilisational reservoir is being used to supposedly make individuals more humane, moral and honest without questioning the basis of their miseries. The commercial interests would be the main beneficiaries of this morality of austerity, thrift and healthy life for those who do not have the means to consume and accumulate as it will facilitate them to multiply and accumulate wealth.

Third Phase 2014 Onwards

In this phase, the Nehruvian institutional secularism was replaced by the indigenous (Hindu) conception of nationhood labelling it as pseudo-secularism. And, the abdication of the State's responsibility to provide for the people's well-being and transform the State capitalism into market-driven economic and social growth mechanism. Unlike the earlier phase, it was made clear that the apologetic capitalism and pseudo-secularism will not be practised. The electoral promises made by the BJP and their ideological pronouncements became consistent. The BJP president J.P. Nadda, addressing the devotees of the Swami Narayan sect at a function in Vadodara, said, 'Politics needs religion the most. One question is frequently asked in society. What is the relation between religion and politics? I firmly believe that politics would become wisdom-less without the presence of religion. There is no meaning of politics without religion. They both go together.' He said,

> Samaaj mein yeh prashan baar baar khada hota hai ki rajniti ka dharma se sambandh kya hai? Mera ye manana hai ki ranjniti dharma ke bagair vivekheen hai, uska koi arth nahi hai. Rajniti hamesha dharma ke sath chalti hai ("Politics Meaningless" 2020).

And, on the economic policies, the Finance Minister Nirmala Sitharaman at the time of the presentation of the Budget on February 1, 2020, stated that 'the compulsion to invest in exemptions was outdated, now that the country had given up on the socialist model of the economy, the government was now giving the taxpayer the option to do what he wished with the money in his hands after paying taxes' (Dikshit 2020).

The paradox between the Nehruvian institutionalised secularism, and unified indigenous (Hindu) nationhood seems to have been resolved by the dominant politics in favour of the latter. Similarly, the dichotomy between capitalist practice and socialist pretence has been replaced by a market-driven economy and politics. The hallmark of this phase is the general acceptance of a right-wing political agenda.

Historically, several leaders and political parties have used the religious symbols and spaces to further their politics like Jamaat-e-Islami, the Muslim League, the Bharatiya Jan Sangh, the Akali Dal, the Hindu Mahasabha. They have argued that the division of politics on religious lines would help the religious groups to represent their interests better than in secular politics.

Here is a rider. The use of (Hindu) civilisational reservoir, may or may not be communal, but the real issues are; What is the vision or ideology of their politics to transform the people's lives? As it appears, their politics is to make the conditions of exploitation bearable and sap the will of the people to launch a struggle for building a just and secular society.

Electoral politics in this phase clearly demonstrated that the ideologies are relevant to win elections. And, as such, an effortless anti-incumbency campaign may not, on its own dislodge the incumbent government. Political parties have vacillated between the religious and caste identities and their claims to build a secular polity. And, regional, caste and tribal identities are being increasingly invoked to expand the electoral constituencies.

The whole concept of civilisation has been treated to convey a restrictive meaning. 'The civilisation and culture both refer to the overall way of life of a people, and a civilisation is a culture writ large. They both involve the values, norms, institutions, and modes of thinking to which successive generations in a given society have attached primary importance' (Huntington 1996: 45). The overall approach has been to employ a cocktail of civilisational symbols with a Hindutva flavour. The usage of civilisational symbols with (Hindu) flavour was strategically packaged as more than a religion, as a core of Indian civilisation. The political discourse very aptly located itself in the majoritarian way of life depicting the range of values, norms, and institutions of a large majority of the population. Slogans like 'development for all,' 'national security', etc., were presented as universal, purer and unadulterated, located in caste, religion, gender and ethnicity. There has been a selective appropriation of the universal symbols like Ganga (river), Gita (scripture), Navratras (ritual), etc., to provide content to the (Hindu) civilisational symbols as inclusive and, in turn, blurred the structural realities of caste and religion. Religious, linguistic, caste and regional factors became so mixed up that none of these emerged as a single factor in the electoral mobilisation. Elections being sites of contestations for social dominance, it has to be seen how far it allows to manufacture the contextual coalitions of caste or religious affiliations.

Further, the electoral discourse has focused mainly on blurring the structural inequalities. The common deficient experience becomes consistent with the 'welfare of all' thrust of the electoral mobilisations. It is this experience of exclusion that has been made central to the electoral discourse and not the exclusion of the marginalised sections from the market and the dominant politics. It can be inferred that the new nation-building project is excessively relying on blurring the structural inequalities through the Hindu civilisation symbolisms for building global-friendly capitalism.

However, relevant questions arise:

- How are the Nehruvian Nation Building project and Modi's New India project different? And, what implications does it have for the multi-cultural ethos and representation and recognition of the rights of the minorities?

- How far will this cocktail of symbolism facilitate a catch-all approach? And, how far will the 'deficient citizenship' mobilised around slogans like 'justice for all,' successfully appropriated be able to withstand the strong undercurrent of discontent emanating from the structural inequalities?
- Have the elections been reduced to winning and losing and no longer about shaping the political discourse for building more democratic, justice-oriented, equitable and inclusive polity and society?

Distinct Features of the Electoral Politics: 2014 Onwards

These trends can be conceptualised in terms of fault lines, i.e. location of the Hindu civilisational symbols in ethnic particularism, citizenship versus deficient citizenship, the convergence of market fundamentalism with religious fundamentalism, and centralisation of power and bargaining federalism (dispossession of farmers' land for the State-led projects to the dispossession of land for the accumulation of wealth for the private players). But, before proceeding further, a glance at the distinct features of the recent Lok Sabha Election, 2019 will help to establish a crystal clear understanding about the same.

Presidential Form of Elections

In the 2019 elections, for the first time in the Indian electoral history, an interesting dimension was added, that is, the tension between the Presidential form and the regional formations (Mahagathbandhan). The two national parties fought it as a Presidential election by presenting their leaders as national. The Bharatiya Janata Party went even a step further by exhorting the people that every vote cast for the BJP is a vote for Mr. Narendra Modi. Interestingly, in most of the election rallies, while addressing the people, Mr. Modi—does not even mention the names of the local leaders. In other words, the electorates are directly voting for their would-be Prime Minister. The speeches delivered by PM Modi at different places while addressing the rallies also show how the importance was given to the local socio-cultural symbols and ideals followed by an emphasis on the link of Modi and his political party with the same. The speeches clearly show the resemblance with a list of public holidays inscribed on the State-government calendars as Mr. Modi mentioned every historical event, anniversary by naming the local sages and saints at the beginning of every speech and relating himself with those symbols, ideals, principles and morals. Not only the speeches but the party manifesto too was coloured in the same pattern as the cover of the 2019 election manifesto has only Modi's photograph, whereas 2014 had the photographs of many party stalwarts. Speaking of the visual design, the 2014 manifesto has only two photographs (of Dr. Shyama Prasad Mukherjee and Pt. Deen Dayal Upadhyaya on the opening page), whereas, in the 2019 manifesto, it had 14 photographs (five photographs of PM Modi, one each of Rajnath Singh and Amit Shah, photos of the party-logo, three random public photographs and one photograph each of Dr. Shyama Prasad Mukherjee. The photographs of Pt. Deen Dayal Upadhyaya, and Mr. Atal Bihari Vajpayee appeared on the back cover. The present election is all of this, but it is also something more. Is the competition amongst the personalities a sign of the increasing competitiveness of the ideologies and the participation a representation of the deepening of democracy?

Participation and Competitiveness

Elections have become relatively more participatory, competitive, and entail the likelihood of a change in the government. In terms of participation, the number of registered voters has increased from 173 million in 1951 to 900 million in the 2019 Lok Sabha elections. However, the voters' turnout has been fluctuating depending on the political climate. As compared to other functional and genuine democracies, the voter turnout is fairly high and representative in India.

Out of the seventeen Lok Sabha elections, in eight elections, it was less than 60 per cent, and in the remaining elections, it was above 60 per cent, with the highest turnout of 67.4 per cent in the 2019 elections (See Table 1.3, Annexures-II).

A relatively high turnout has been possible, besides the ideological factors, due to electoral reforms like awareness campaigns for the voters, efficient polling booth management leading to the elimination of rigging and booth capturing, increasing accessibility, and so on (see Quraishi 2019: 111-121).[8] To illustrate, the poorer sections, the Scheduled Castes and the Scheduled Tribes, the minorities and the women were either not allowed to go to the polling booths, and their votes were forged, or they were threatened to vote for a particular candidate. The vulnerability mapping (see Quraishi 2019: 113)[9] undertaken by the Election Commission could prove to be effective in a limited sense in checking these practices.

Competitiveness and Crowding of Electoral Space

Another qualitative shift in the elections is that these have become more competitive. For instance, elections have been transformed from the single-party dominance to multi-party contests leading to a crowding of the electoral space. In 2019, six national political parties and 40 State/regional parties were in the contest.

And most importantly, since 1951, the effective number of the political parties by votes and seats have multiplied. In 1951, the effective number of the parties by votes was 4.53, which peaked to 7.98 in 2009 and declined to 5.27 in

2019. The effective number of parties by seats was 1.80 in 1951, which increased to 3.45 in 2014 and declined to 3.03 in 2019.

Table 1.4 Political Parties Participated, and Seats Won in Lok Sabha Elections, 1951, 1989, 2009, 2014 and 2019

Party Type/ Year	*No. of Party*					*Seats Won*				
	1951	*1989*	*2009*	*2014*	*2019*	*1951*	*1989*	*2009*	*2014*	*2019*
National Party	14	8	7	6	6	417	475	372	342	375
State Party	39	20	34	39	40	34	33	148	185	158
Others (Registered/ Not-Registered/ Independent)	1	86	323	420	628	38	21	23	16	9
Total	54	114	364	465	674	489	529	543	543	542/ 543

Source: Statistical Reports of General Election to Lok Sabha, 1951, 1989, 2009, 2014, and 2019. Election Commission of India.

Uncontested seats too have drastically come down to nil in the 2014 elections from ten in 1951 elections. The average number of candidates per constituency in 1951 was 4.67, which multiplied to 11.64 in 1989, and 14.8 in 2019. This clearly shows that there is a movement leading to multiplication of choices for the voters. Elections, in a way, performed an effective choice maximisation function. The moot question remains, will these choices make a difference to the quality of life of the people living on the margins?

The crowding of the electoral space is more due to the multiplication of the non-ideological political parties and independent candidates. The main function of the political parties in a democracy is to aggregate the ideas, values and purposes for the formation of a coalition of potential political groupings. In a way, the dilution of the ideological boundaries led to free mobility of the leaders from one political party to another political party. To illustrate, in Maharashtra, the political drama after the 2019 Assembly Elections stood as a witness to this phenomenon. A group of the members of the Legislative Assembly defected from the National Congress Party (NCP) to the BJP and, in a midnight operation, formed the government. Mr. Ajit Pawar, the leader of the breakaway group, took the oath of Deputy Chief Minister. After a few days, he, along with other defectors, returned to the NCP and the government collapsed. A new formation consisting of the Shiv Sena, the NCP and the Congress formed a coalition government with Mr. Ajit Pawar as the Deputy Chief Minister. The relevant question arises, is crowding of the electoral space providing ideologically competitive choices or only multiplication of the numbers?

Figure 1.1 Effective Number of Parties in Lower House Elections

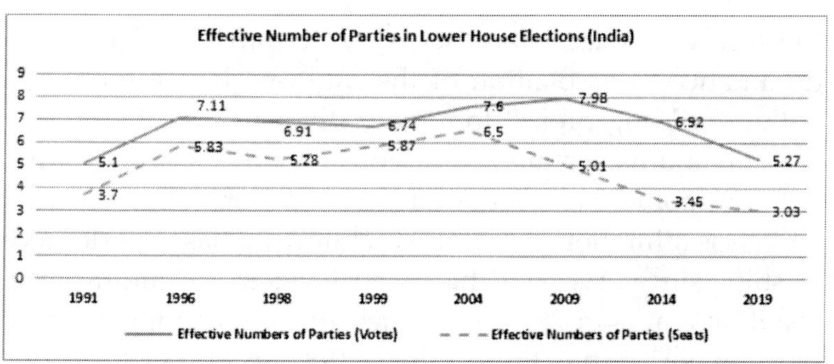

Source: *Statistical Reports of Lower House Elections, 1951, 1996, 1998, 1998, 2004, 2009, 2014, and 2019*. Election Commission of India.

The answer is obvious.

The politics has also surrendered to the market, in which the legislatures are traded. There is a stringent anti-defection law (see "The Constitution (Fifty-Second

Amendment) Act" 1985 (Anti-Defection Act)),[10] but it has been rendered ineffective. History has shown that the laws, if not backed by strong ideological persuasions may crowd the political space, but they may not offer any quality of choices to the voters.

The availability of the electoral choices representing the religious, caste and regional faultlines, but led by the personalities may increase the participation and make the electoral competition more intense. An analysis of the reach of the various political formations will help us to understand the dominant ideas and values having a larger sweep across the faultlines. It may also be a pointer towards the re-emergence of the dominant one-party system in opposition to the coalition of political parties. Is it a cyclical movement from one party dominant to the coalition of the parties and again to one party dominant or it may throw up the two party-system as it exists in some of the States in India?

Cyclical Electoral Architecture

Electoral architecture represents a shift from the single-party dominance to a coalition of the multi-parties; a monolith nation-building project to a more diversity sensitive party system, and has created conditions for greater accessibility for the people irrespective of their gender, religion, caste and class affiliations. Electoral architecture has experienced a shift since 1989; it has transformed to multi-party coalitions, and in 2019, it seemed to be returning to one-party majority rule. From 1951 to 1984 (except in 1977) the Congress Party was dominant. In the first three Lok Sabha elections, the Congress Party secured more than 60 per cent of the seats except in 1967 when it secured around 54 per cent seats.

From 1989 to 2009, in the seven elections, a coalition of the political parties ruled the country. Interestingly, in 2014

Table 1.5 Average Number of Candidates per Constituency

State	1951		State	1989		2009		2014		2019	
	Total Seats	*ACC**		*Total Seats*	*ACC**	*Total Seats*	*ACC**	*Total Seats*	*ACC**	*Total Seats*	*ACC**
Ajmer	2	4	Andhra Pradesh	42	6	42	13	42	14	25	13
Assam	10	4	Arunachal Pradesh	2	3	2	4	2	5	2	6
Bhopal	2	3	Assam			14	11	14	11	14	10
Bihar	44	5	Bihar	54	13	40	16	40	15	40	16
Bilaspur	1	1	Chhattisgarh			11	16	11	19	11	15
Mumbai	37	4	Goa	2	13	2	9	2	9	2	6
Coorg	1	2	Gujarat	26	10	26	13	26	12	26	14
Delhi	3	6	Haryana	10	32	10	21	10	23	10	22
Himachal Pradesh	2	5	Himachal Pradesh	4	8	4	7	4	9	4	11
Hyderabad	21	3	Jammu & Kashmir	6	11	6	13	6	12	6	13
Kutch	2	3	Jharkhand			14	17	14	17	14	16
Madhya Bharat	9	4	Karnataka	28	9	28	15	28	15	28	17
Madhya Pradesh	23	5	Kerala	20	11	20	10	20	13	20	11

State	1951		State	1989		2009		2014		2019	
	Total Seats	*ACC**		*Total Seats*	*ACC**	*Total Seats*	*ACC**	*Total Seats*	*ACC**	*Total Seats*	*ACC**
Chennai	62	5	Madhya Pradesh	40	12	29	14	29	13	29	15
Manipur	2	7	Maharashtra	48	12	48	17	48	18	48	18
Mysore	9	4	Manipur	2	7	2	8	2	9	2	10
Odisha	16	4	Meghalaya	2	3	2	5	2	5	2	5
PEPSU**	4	8	Mizoram	1	4	1	4	1	3	1	6
Punjab	15	7	Nagaland	1	2	1	3	1	3	1	4
Rajasthan	18	4	Odisha	21	6	21	7	21	9	21	8
Saurashtra	6	3	Punjab	13	17	13	16	13	19	13	21
Travancore Cochin	11	4	Rajasthan	25	12	25	13	25	12	25	10
Tripura	2	4	Sikkim	1	4	1	7	1	6	1	11
Uttar Pradesh	69	5	Tamil Nadu	39	13	39	21	39	21	38	22
Vindhya Pradesh	4	6	Telangana							17	26
West Bengal	26	6	Tripura	2	6	2	9	2	12	2	12
Grand Total	401	**4.67**	Uttar Pradesh	85	13	80	17	80	16	80	12

State	1951		State	1989		2009		2014		2019	
	Total Seats	*ACC**		*Total Seats*	*ACC**	*Total Seats*	*ACC**	*Total Seats*	*ACC**	*Total Seats*	*ACC**
			Uttarakhand			5	15	5	14	5	10
			West Bengal	42	8	42	8	42	11	42	11
			A & N Islands	1	7	1	11	1	15	1	15
			Chandigarh	1	27	1	14	1	17	1	36
ACC*; Average number of candidates per constituency			D & N Haveli	1	5	1	5	1	11	1	11
			Daman & Diu	1	5	1	7	1	4	1	4
PEPSU**; Patiala and East Punjab States Union			NCT of Delhi	7	34	7	22	7	21	7	23
			Lakshadweep	1	2	1	4	1	6	1	6
			Puducherry	1	11	1	28	1	30	1	18
			Grand Total	529	**11.64**	543	**14.86**	543	**15.2**	542	14.8

Source: *Statistical Reports of General Elections to Lok Sabha, 1951, 1989, 2009, 2014, and 2019*. Election Commission of India.

Map 1.1: General Election 2014–Party-wise Parliament Constituencies Won

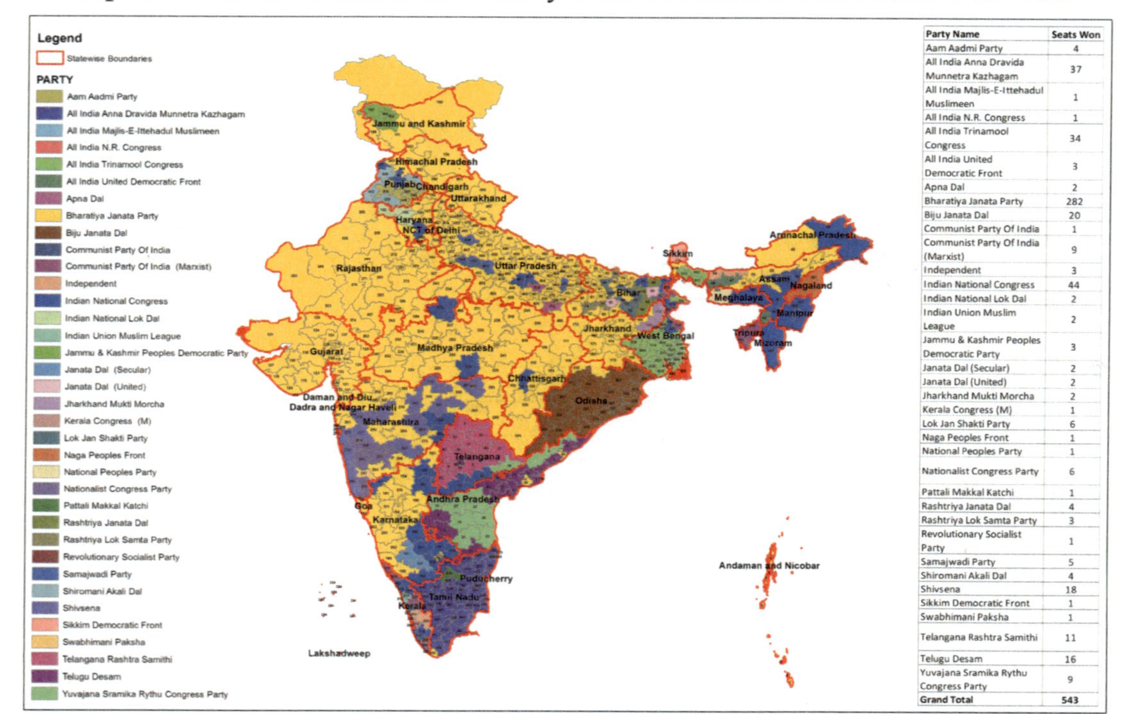

Party Name	Seats Won
Aam Aadmi Party	4
All India Anna Dravida Munnetra Kazhagam	37
All India Majlis-E-Ittehadul Muslimeen	1
All India N.R. Congress	1
All India Trinamool Congress	34
All India United Democratic Front	3
Apna Dal	2
Bharatiya Janata Party	282
Biju Janata Dal	20
Communist Party Of India	1
Communist Party Of India (Marxist)	9
Independent	3
Indian National Congress	44
Indian National Lok Dal	2
Indian Union Muslim League	2
Jammu & Kashmir Peoples Democratic Party	3
Janata Dal (Secular)	2
Janata Dal (United)	2
Jharkhand Mukti Morcha	2
Kerala Congress (M)	1
Lok Jan Shakti Party	6
Naga Peoples Front	1
National Peoples Party	1
Nationalist Congress Party	6
Pattali Makkal Katchi	1
Rashtriya Janata Dal	4
Rashtriya Lok Samta Party	3
Revolutionary Socialist Party	1
Samajwadi Party	5
Shiromani Akali Dal	4
Shivsena	18
Sikkim Democratic Front	1
Swabhimani Paksha	1
Telangana Rashtra Samithi	11
Telugu Desam	16
Yuvajana Sramika Rythu Congress Party	9
Grand Total	**543**

Map 1.2: General Election 2019–Party-wise Parliament Constituencies Won

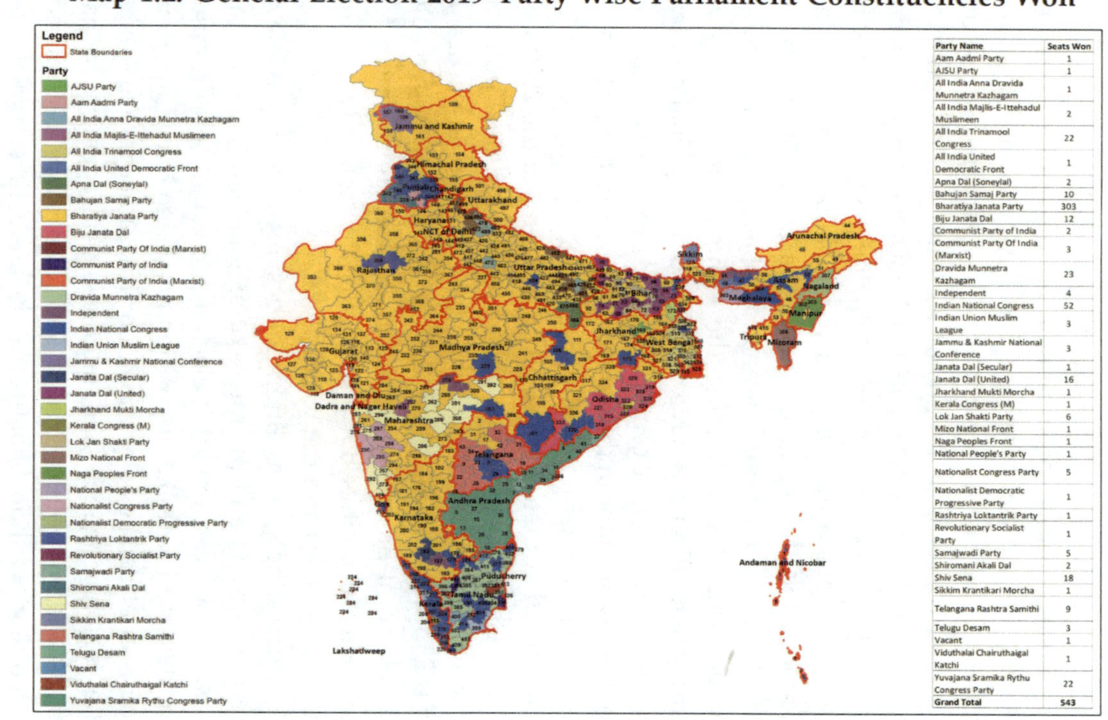

Party Name	Seats Won
Aam Admi Party	1
AJSU Party	1
All India Anna Dravida Munnetra Kazhagam	1
All India Majlis-E-Ittehadul Muslimeen	2
All India Trinamool Congress	22
All India United Democratic Front	1
Apna Dal (Soneylal)	2
Bahujan Samaj Party	10
Bharatiya Janata Party	303
Biju Janata Dal	12
Communist Party of India	2
Communist Party Of India (Marxist)	3
Dravida Munnetra Kazhagam	23
Independent	4
Indian National Congress	52
Indian Union Muslim League	3
Jammu & Kashmir National Conference	3
Janata Dal (Secular)	1
Janata Dal (United)	16
Jharkhand Mukti Morcha	1
Kerala Congress (M)	1
Lok Jan Shakti Party	6
Mizo National Front	1
Naga Peoples Front	1
National People's Party	1
Nationalist Congress Party	5
Nationalist Democratic Progressive Party	1
Rashtriya Loktantrik Party	1
Revolutionary Socialist Party	1
Samajwadi Party	5
Shiromani Akali Dal	2
Shiv Sena	18
Sikkim Krantikari Morcha	1
Telangana Rashtra Samithi	9
Telugu Desam	3
Vacant	1
Viduthalai Chairuthaigal Katchi	1
Yuvajana Sramika Rythu Congress Party	22
Grand Total	**543**

and 2019 Lok Sabha elections, the BJP secured a majority on their own. In the 2014 and 2019 elections, the BJP secured 53 per cent and 56 per cent seats respectively (See Table 1.5 and for details see Table 1.5A, Annexures-II).

Elections have been fought by the national parties raising national concerns and locating these in a regional context, whereas the regional parties attempted to use the regional concerns as a bargain with the national political parties. This has worked in two ways: on the one hand, it has provided greater access to the regional parties to share the spoils of power reducing the alliance between the national and the regional political parties as 'coalition for patronage' and, on the other hand, it has made the regional parties stand on redefining the Centre-State relations as ambivalent. Elections have catapulted the regional political parties to the political centre stage and provided articulation to their aspirations in the political discourse. To illustrate, in 1951, the national political parties polled 76 per cent votes and the other State parties, just 8 per cent. In the 2019 Lok Sabha elections, the votes polled for the national political parties was 68.7 per cent, while for the regional parties, it was 23.1 per cent (See Table 1.3, Annexures II). As a result, the electoral process not only created an environment for competitive politics but also created tension between the national parties and the regional parties.

Interestingly, in coalition politics, regional groups have become strong, and the forces of regionalism have become weak. However, the 2019 elections, created opportunities for the small regional opposition parties to have important ministerial berths as rewards, but the same has weakened the regional agenda and interests. Consequently, it has made Indian politics less federal and more centralised, extending ad hoc benefits to those regions, which are strategic partners in the coalition.

On the other hand, the tension between the national

Map 1.3: General Election 2014–Performance of National and State Parties

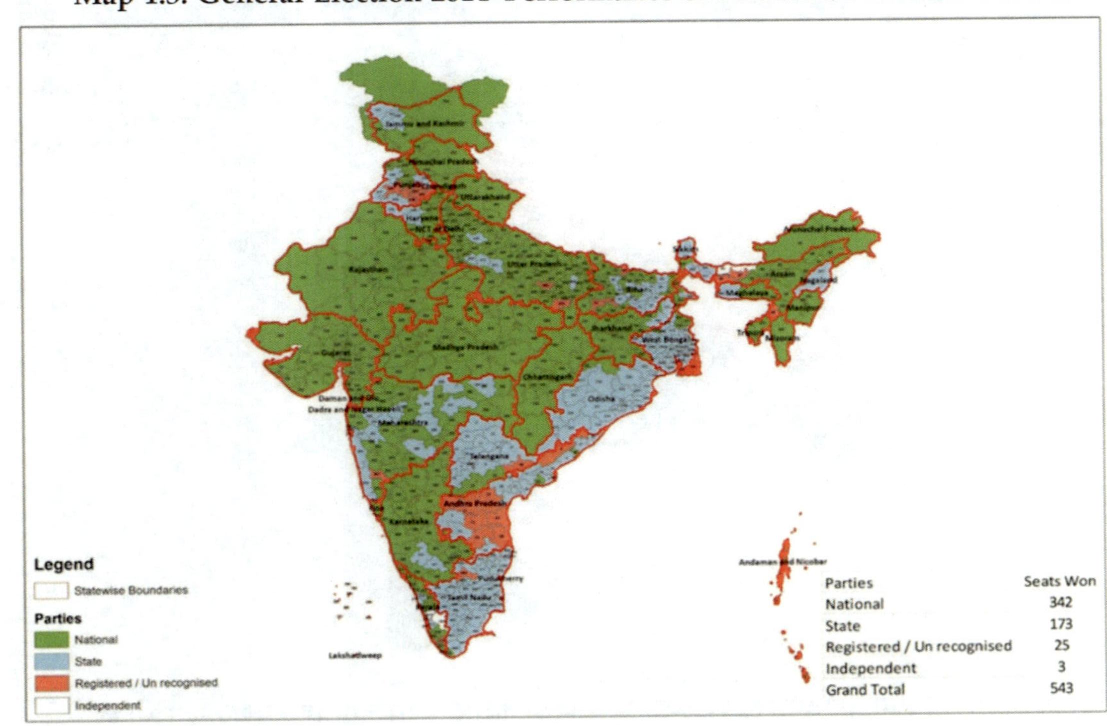

Parties	Seats Won
National	342
State	173
Registered / Un recognised	25
Independent	3
Grand Total	543

Map 1.4: General Election 2019–Performance of National and State Parties

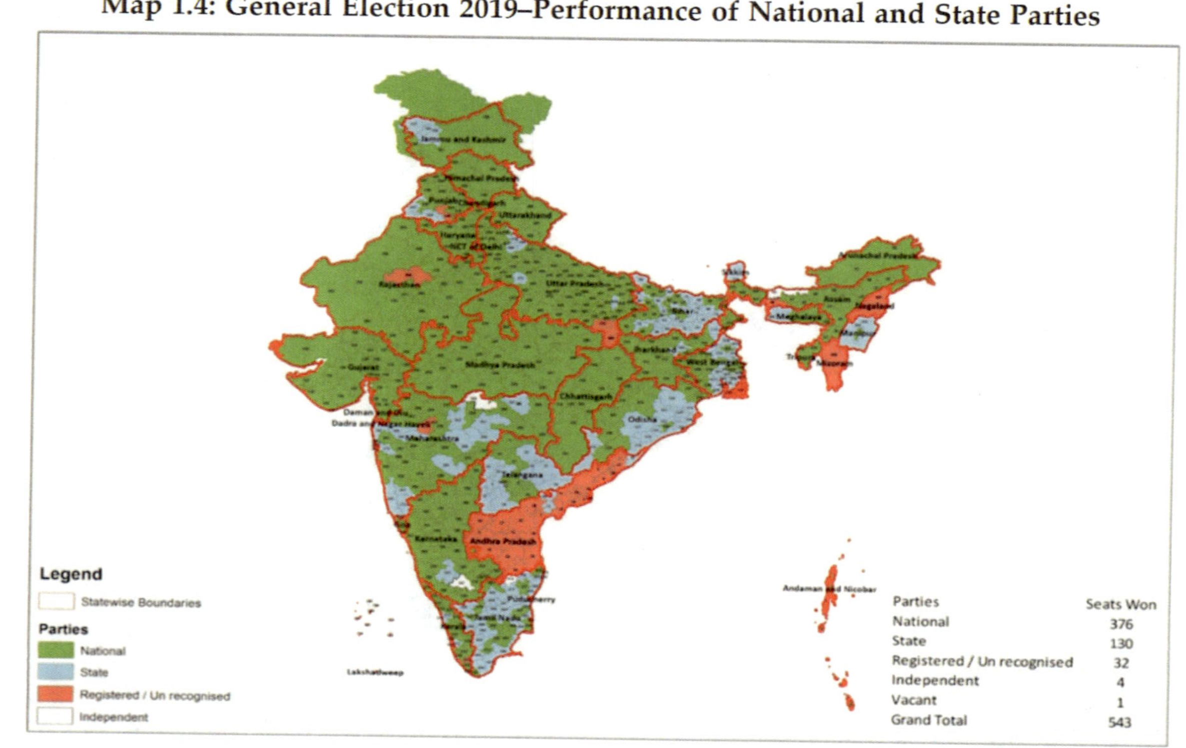

political parties and those regional parties who attributed a central role to the regional agenda and used it as a condition to enter into any alliance. As mentioned earlier, it is these regional parties who could withstand the challenge posed by the national political parties in the 2019 elections. These parties maintained their dominance in the States of Andhra Pradesh, Tamil Nadu, Odisha, Puducherry, Mizoram, Nagaland, West Bengal and Jammu & Kashmir. The parties like Samajwadi Party (SP),[11] Telugu Desam Party (TDP),[12] Tamil Maanila Congress (TMC 'M'),[13] Dravida Munnetra Kazhagam (DMK),[14] All India Anna Dravida Munnetra Kazhagam (AIDMK),[15] Rashtriya Janata Dal (RJD),[16] Janata Dal (United) [JD(U)],[17] Biju Janata Dal (BJD),[18] All India Trinamool Congress (AITC),[19] Yuvajana Sramika Rythu Congress Party (YSRCP),[20] and Shiv Sena (SHS)[21], etc., largely maintained their regional identity and functioned in the framework of bargaining federalism (See Table 1.6, Annexures II). Whereas, the regional parties in the northern States like, Bahujan Samaj Party (BSP),[22] Janata Dal (United), Shiromani Akali Dal (SAD), etc., function in the domain of cooperative federalism. (See Table 1.7, Annexures II).

The 2019 post-election assessment in India has shown that there has been an absence of debate on the nature of development and form of governance at the time of elections. One might like to add that Lazy Intellectualism conceded the framework of development and good governance without ascertaining details from the incumbent regime. The difference lies in the details, notwithstanding the consensus on the assumptions.

Complementarities and Dichotomies in Politics

- ***Consensus on the Path of the Development***

The massive mandate attained by blurring the structural inequalities could not match the resistance to the proposed neoliberal reforms. Indian democracy operates in a much larger space as compared to electoral politics. In other words, electoral arithmetic is inadequate to captivate the democratic impulse riddled with multiple inequalities. But, can the elections be ever indifferent to the reality of the people's fight for mere survival, demand for dignity in governance and protection from abuse?

The mainstream political parties with the Left parties on the margins have reached a consensus on the path of development and economic reforms agenda, with their emphasis on globalisation, liberalisation, and privatisation, notwithstanding the occasional noises about Swadeshi. Indian politics has overlooked its promise to build a socialistic society and committed itself to build market-friendly capitalism. And, in view of the political consensus on economic development, it has been concluded, it seems, that there was an end of political ideology. This conclusion proved to be political naivety with the articulations ranging from cultural nationalism to the non-existence of political alternatives. C. Wright Mills (1963: 249-251) described 'end of ideology' as 'ideology of political complacency, which seems the only way now open for many writers to acquiesce in or justify the status quo.' The main thrust is to conclude that there are no alternatives. But, at the same time, to ward off discontent leading to the crises caused by the production of private goods and its consumption with an emphasis on the growth rate rather than well-being. In view of the glaring social inequality, the States attempt to make necessary ideological and institutional adjustments under the label of welfare capitalism.

In this, the socio-economic structures are taken as given, and the public policies are framed to maintain equilibrium and to preserve the dominant institutions, interests and elites. And, for this, the States excessively rely on 'populism' and 'majoritarianism'. In their interactive relationship, both of these are a movement and an ideology. Populism is not an analytical category, but descriptive as it operates in divergent settings differently. The thrust of populism is to address the people and not the problems without disturbing the structural basis. Its asynchrony ranges from caste, religion, gender and religion located in the feudal attitude, capitalist practices and socialistic rhetoric. This may be in response to the spontaneous protests channelised through the existing institutions as through the amended instrument of law. In the midst of the revolution of the rising expectations with the mass media nurturing the aspirational class, populism becomes a potent tool to connect with this class. In the Indian context, three dimensions of populist politics are practised.

- ***Populism: From Diversities to People***

The tension between diversities of caste, religion, gender, ethnicity and regions are blurred by the articulation of issues and interests with reference to general category people. People are referred to as not having any specific and distinct characteristics existing between various diversities. The hegemonic character of the ruling class is maintained and preserved by using popular discourse with the prefix people, to blur the real issues. For instance, Indira Gandhi in the 1980s used to refer to the struggle in Kashmir as Dharma Yudh in '*Mere teen crore Gujarati bhaiyo aur behno*– we have brought crores of investment in Gujarat to provide you employment' whereas, the reality was that the hunger index was the highest in Gujarat. Most of the growth was jobless ("crores of employment opportunities"). And economic populism was practised through various initiatives like bank nationalisation in 1969, *Garibi Hatao* slogan in 1971 and inclusion of the word socialism in the preamble of the Indian Constitution, all for the poor by the then supreme leader of the Congress Party Indira Gandhi and now, for instance, it has been provided continuity by the Narendra Modi government with demonstrations to fight corruption and opening up of bank accounts of the poor to redistribute income.

In this, the leaders build a direct connection with the people overlooking institutions, local political leadership and regions. And, they present these diversities as integral to homogeneous whole. In the process, the antagonism is transformed into a simple difference with the underlying assumption that this difference will not make any difference to the structural conditions.

- ***Populism: Leader's Enemies as People's Enemies***

The leader in a populist mould defines his enemies as the people's enemy and the nation's enemy. The effort involved is to present himself as an authentic representative of the people and of the national interest. There is a long tradition of the populist leaders at the regional level, mainly in South India, and at the national level, the prominent among them have been Indira Gandhi and recently, Narendra Modi, who provided continuity to this. In the 1970s, the popular slogan was—'*Woh kehtain hain Indira hatao, aur main kehti hun garibi hatao*'. Similarly, in 2020 Mr. Modi retorted that '*Woh kehte hain Modi ko dande marenge, main kehta hun auraten aur bachche mujhe bacha lenge;*[23] *main kehta hun bhrashtachar hatao, woh kehte hain Modi hatao.*'

- ***Populism: From Doles to Subsidies***

The ability of a leader can be assessed by his ability to impose a conception of justice, egalitarianism and survival need through populist measures to neutralise the people's protest and antagonism against those who are the main beneficiaries of crony capitalism.

The political articulations in political discourse largely remain within the domain of the superstructural level. Firstly, these are confined to doles and subsidies—to put it differently the populist economic measures. These measures function within the range of freebies, doles and subsidies. The varieties of populist measures are used differently and are separated in time, space and culture. For example, subsidies can be given as doles and vice versa. There is something abstract about them as it involves dealing with the coexistence of the elements belonging to the feudal, capitalist and socialist. As a form of asynchrony, for instance, doles are given to match the cultural predisposition, but in response to the advance stage of development. To put it in other words, doles are a feudal response to the crisis of capitalism and subsidies are a capitalist response to the crisis of capitalism. Secondly, it addresses the ideological domain to reach out to the majority of the people through political positioning. For instance, taking a political position on nationalism—in support or opposition to the Balakot military strikes against Pakistan, Citizen Amendment Act 2019, the practice of Triple Talaq amongst the Muslims, abrogation of Article 370 of the Indian Constitution, etc. Thirdly, to introduce flexibility by adding the pretence of being welfare-oriented and secular to economic dole-oriented politics and religious and nationalist majoritarianism.

In other words, reach out to the people irrespective of their religion, caste, ethnicity and regional affiliations with a slogan like *'Congress ka haath, aam admi ke saath'* in 2004, *'Jai Jawan, Jai Kisan'* (Hail Soldiers, Hail Farmers) in 1965 marked by food shortages and war with Pakistan, which was tweaked later by the BJP in the post-nuclear tests in 1988 as *'Jai Jawan, Jai Kisan, Jai Vigyan'* (Hail Soldiers, Hail Farmers, Hail Science) in 2011, *'Maa, Maati, Manush'* (Mother, Motherland and People) slogan given by the Trinamool Congress of West Bengal.

Populism is practised to maintain the hegemony of the dominant class by articulating different versions of ideas and values to reach out to the rest of society. It is couched under the garb of the uniform and homogeneous conception of the world view to neutralise the potential antagonism against the dominant interests. The main thrust is to reinvent the State from time to time to integrate the dominated sections through modifications in the super-structural components like redistribution of wealth after it has been generated rather than organically build capacity and institutional mechanisms for the poor to earn an income for themselves.

And, historically in India, all the parties practised populism, of course, with variations. For instance, political parties promise doles and subsidies at the time of elections, and after winning the elections, these parties push for economic reforms.

The overall approach has been to use a cocktail of doles and promises containing something for everyone's taste. So, we have in elections a sort of ***Menu-festo*** rather than Manifesto. There is a menu card for the farmers, traders, students, Dalits, industrialists, women, etc., to cater to everyone's taste replacing Manifesto which is by definition a declaration of the principles, policies, intentions and, of course, ideological commitment. The credit for this invention goes to AAP. It is a reinforcement of the thought that it is the voters' perception, which constitutes reality. It does not matter who is the leader and what he believes in. What matters is how is he perceived by the voters. The focus is to market that image of a leader which the voters want the most.

At the level of populist tactics, there has been competition amongst the political parties to poach the singers, comedians, journalists, human rights activists to look credible. Earlier, these celebrities were used to gather crowds for the politicians, and now many of them have transformed themselves as politicians. Interestingly, the political parties have hired professional managers to connect them with the people. Elections are being treated as events, where the voters have to be managed, and the candidates are presented as the products. It has liberated the political parties from holding any ideological position at the time of elections.

As a consequence, there are claims and counterclaims; a showcasing of performance versus the promise of a golden performance. A snapshot to impress the voters that each party represents, if not the antithesis of the other, at least a different agenda and style of governance. But, scratch the paint of rhetoric and the work of the event managers, you will notice that each shows the carbon copy of others. For instance, to gain the trust of the masses, the politicians are using tactics like, positioning themselves along with majoritarianism. As keeping in mind the Delhi elections, Kejriwal welcomed the central government's decision to scrap Article 370 and said, 'We support the government on its decisions on Jammu and Kashmir. We hope this will bring peace and development in the State' (India Today Web Desk 2019: "Arvind Kejriwal"), Ex-Chief Minister of Haryana Bhupinder Singh Hooda also criticised his party and said, 'When the government does something right, I always support it. Many of my colleagues opposed the Centre's decision to abrogate Article 370. They have lost their way. It is not the same Congress as it used to be' (India Today Web Desk 2019: "Congress has lost"), and so did the former Congress MP, Jyotiraditya Scindia by tweeting that, 'I support the move on #Jammu Kashmir & #Ladakh and its full integration into a union of India. Would have been better if the Constitutional process had been followed. No questions could have been raised then. Nevertheless, this is in our country's interest, and I support this.' (India Today Web Desk 2019: "Congress's Jyotiraditya Scindia"). Not only that the boundaries of populism have encompassed all shades of political of dispensation, but even the language of politics has been devoid of any vision and civil content and, has also been debased to demonise the competing leader.

Language of Politics

The excessive reliance on winnability through any means, be it, money power, communal polarisation and violative language. Politics has plunged to a new low. The new normal in politics does not entail a sense of morality, fairness and dignity towards the political competitors, opponents and enemies. Mudslinging theatrics in the colosseum might seem old, as the rival parties competed in the 2019 Lok Sabha elections, but the rules of the vote bank's histrionics have evolved somewhat further than the 2014 campaigning election by imbibing vices rather than virtues.

One new trend is the use of abstract language and catchy phrases, such as, 'being silent like Bhishma Pitamah', 'crossing lakshman rekha', or 'Draupadi being disrobed', etc., which obscures the real issue that needs attention ("After Yogi, Mayawati" 2019). The trend reminds one of the 1980s' Bollywood theatrics, wherein in one movie, a character names the luxuries he enjoys, while the other reacts with '*Mere paas maa hai*' (means, I have the mother) (Rai and Chopra 1975) thus obscuring the situational context. For instance, when the BJP obscured the Supreme Court order passed earlier, as a clean chit to the government on the Rafale controversy, the Congress president Rahul Gandhi interpreted the next order as an indictment of the government. Well, the Apex Court did serve a notice to Rahul, pointing out that it never said anything about Modi ("Supreme Court serves" 2019).

Language of Power

A two-way approach has been used by competing political parties. One is using abstract language to brand each other corrupt, immoral and unethical. In the other, power is being wielded through having income tax raids on the opponents nearer the elections time. The I-T department conducted raids on the contractors affiliated with the leaders of the JDS-Congress coalition in Karnataka, Madhya Pradesh CM's close aides in Indore and Delhi, 74 locations, including, DMK leader Kanimozhi in Tamil Nadu, close aides of Mayawati, a former bureaucrat, an accountant of the All India Congress Committee in Delhi, and more (Rajeevan and Balakrishnan 2019; Trivedi 2019). Opposition parties termed these as threats and revenge raids. Responding to this, the Election Commission feigned impeccability, saying that "an advisory on carrying out I-T raids ahead of the 2019 elections was aimed at taking ruthless action against corruption, but the raids were carried out without bias" (Kumar 2019). Is it not a coincidence that the raids are conducted only on the opposition party members?

Dehumanised Political Discourse

The language of political dialogue has become dehumanised exclusively to break the morale of the opponents. It is a proven fact that negativity impacts the brain faster than positivity. The unspoken pact in politics, till recently, was not to lose civility in political discourse. But, those were the times. Now, we have Arvind Kejriwal, who in 2012, used 'Dalal' (broker) to describe the then Delhi CM, Sheila Dikshit (Sawant 2012) and labelled Arun Jaitley a 'crook' ("Arun Jaitley again" 2017). Furthermore, the politicians equating the opponents with the animals exposes their incapacity to manage their own affairs. Narendra Modi described Sonia Gandhi as a 'Jersey cow' and Rahul as her 'hybrid bachhada' (calf) (Anandan 2009). Smriti Irani compared Rahul to Chhota Bheem, a popular dwarfed cartoon character ("Smriti Irani mocks" 2018). PM Modi was described as a 'monkey bitten by a dog' by Arjun Modwadia–Congress leader from Gujarat ("Arjun

Modhwadia gets" 2012), and was also likened to a virus called Namonitis by a senior Congress leader Renuka Chowdhry ("Narendra Modi is like a virus" 2013), or called 'Kutte ke bachhe ka bada bhai' (elder brother of a puppy) by Samajwadi leader Azam Khan ("Azam Khan calls" 2014). This sends a message that opposing Modi is not tantamount to harming a human being. Even Priyanka Gandhi exclaimed that the BJP leaders were scampering like 'panic-stricken rats' ("BJP Scrambling" 2014). Amit Shah, in a rally, said, "Attempts are being made for the opposition unity for the 2019 elections. When huge floods occur, everything is washed away. Due to Modi floods, all cats, dogs, snakes and mongooses are joining hands to contest polls" ("Opposition united like cats" 2018). And, the then Maharashtra CM, Devendra Fadnavis compared the opposition to wolves (Ghadyalpatil 2018). Kailash Vijayvargiya, BJP leader from MP, compared the opposition unity to a 'pack of dogs' ("BJP leader Kailash" 2017). This amply indicates that dehumanisation has almost emerged as the new norm in politics.

Sexist Slurs

Further, sexist expressions are being used as a form of psychological violence against opponents. Akhilesh Yadav, former CM of Uttar Pradesh, commented on the BSP leader Mayawati, during a joint press conference with Rahul Gandhi, saying, "How could we have given space to her (Mayawati)? She takes so much space; even her party symbol is that of an elephant" ("Akhilesh Yadav 'sexist' remark" 2017). The 2019 Lok Sabha elections too are not bereft of such blatant sexism. BJP leader Kailash Vijayvargiya's called women candidates from the Congress party as 'chocolate faces' and the Congress leader, Sajjan Singh Verma's term 'bardancers' pointed at BJP's Mathura candidate Hema Malini. Jayadeep Kawade of the People's

Republican Party said of Smriti Irani, "She wears a bindi, and someone said the size of a woman's bindi grows as she changes her husband." And recently, Azam Khan's jibe 'wearing khaki underwear' at BJP leader Jaya Prada is in the same vein ("Lok Sabha elections" 2019).

These remarks are becoming frequent irrespective of the fact that the Election Commission of India (ECI) banned Azam Khan (72 hours), Yogi Adityanath, Chief Minister of Uttar Pradesh (72 hours), BSP supremo Mayawati (48 hours) and Maneka Gandhi (48 hours) for their sexist and communal remarks ("After Yogi" 2019). These incidents cannot be seen as the 'heat of the moment stuff' as one would like to justify later on. Sexual objectification of women only leads to a disconnect with their humane, pro-people, compassionate and intellectual capabilities. And, presenting the enemies as anti-national is to represent them as less than human, and undeserving of any rights. These labels lead to the moral and political exclusion of the patriotic individuals, and those who target them assume the position of the saviours of the great nation.

The discourse has degenerated to no holds barred infighting amongst those competing for the spoils of power even to the extent of violating the rules of their own game. The logical consequence of this is to morally exclude a large section from the fair play, compassion and justice. Therefore, the language of dehumanisation, a derivation of the language of power, must be replaced by a language of justice. If politics cannot offer the citizen's well-being, at least, it should not rob them of civility. There is a need to make the appointments in the EC more transparent and provide the teeth to maintain the legitimacy of the political system. Political engagement has been sullied by dehumanising, sexist and communal speeches, and such incidents must not be justified as the 'heat of the moment stuff' (Kumar 2019). The cocktail of the language of politics, populism, and consensus on the path of development directed to blur the various faultlines led to breaking of ethnic diversities into smaller categories, for instance, in the case of castes into sub-castes and manufacturing alliances of various sub-castes under the umbrella of cultural nationalism.

Caste Arithmetic Remained Elusive

Elections are the sites of contestations not merely for power politics, but also for social dominance. It will be interesting to see how far the 2019 elections have been able to manufacture contextual coalition of the castes to outcompete other formations.

The preliminary investigation suggests that the simple caste arithmetic has ceased to be functional.

> When we appreciate the two overwhelming truths, namely that castes mutually repel each other and that demographically no castes have numerical dominance by far, certain issues suddenly become clear. Today in the caste order where identities align, there are no ideological friends. Only enemies and rivals. In which case, when different castes come together for political reasons, it is not caste logic that is drawing these close, but something outside it (Gupta 2019: 28).

Similarly, caste, as a political capital, has found varied responses blended in the regional flavours covering a vast political spectrum:

(i) The content of the emerging identity assertions amongst the various sub-castes for de facto recognition of their rights, occupational mobility, status parity and even parallel religious symbols has transformed the terms of electoral discourse.

(ii) Further, the ideological content of the political parties using caste arithmetic has been unable to capture the regional, cultural and economic specificities. The purity-pollution and *Manuwad,* as the main ideological planks, do not find expression in the socio-cultural domain in its fundamental form as it exists.

Therefore, it would be appropriate to revisit and examine the emerging sub-caste assertions articulated through caste-based political formations in terms of electoral performance. This has been discussed in detail in the chapter on Dalit Identity Architecture. Given the consensus amongst the political parties on a neoliberal path of development in the absence of an alternate vision, electoral discourse conveniently located itself in the crony capitalism, unemployment, poverty and inequalities in policy paralysis (Kumar 2017).

BJP and RSS

The consensus amongst the political parties on globalisation, privatisation, and liberalisation posed a major dilemma for the Rashtriya Swayamsevak Sangh (RSS), including BJP, which used to stand for protection to the local industry, through its other front organisation Swadeshi Jagaran Manch. It posed a question as to who was in a commanding position, the Modi-led BJP or the RSS? In Indian politics, which is largely functional in the right-wing majoritarian domain, the role of the RSS, particularly with the BJP being the main ruling party, was considered to be the moral stepchild of the RSS. The relevant question arises, how far is the BJP conforming to the RSS ideology or has it carved out its own path? It would be worthwhile to find out the veracity of the claim that the RSS maintains a distance from its various offshoots to maintain its moral hegemony and superior hierarchy.

The RSS Chief Mohan, Bhagwat, clarified that the RSS is a socio-cultural organisation and its members are in every sphere of the socio-cultural and political activity. The main objective of the RSS was to convert the Hindus into a cohesive group with adequate emphasis on the cultural aspects. The members of the RSS maintained dual membership, for instance, Keshav Baliram Hedgewar, the founder of the RSS, remained a member of the Congress and the Hindu Mahasabha. Historically, for the RSS member, the dual membership has been a norm. To quote Mohan Bhagwat, the RSS 'pramukh':

> There is a general belief that BJP is of the Sangh's. I tell you it is not true. There is no relation between the two, because the sangh is not in politics. If at all the Sangh wanted to be in politics, then why hand over the bridle to others? Swayamsevaks are in all parties. There are more in BJP, but they are also in the Congress and in a communist party in West Bengal. So the BJP is not the Sangh's ("No Relation Between RSS and BJP" 2012).

The RSS's core agenda is to influence all spheres of the society with its ideology of Hindu Rashtra. That paved the way for the emergence of the Bharatiya Jana Sangh and, subsequently, BJP, in 1980. Though the RSS claims to have no political ambitions but providing support at the grassroots level during elections also clarifies the *Parivar's* imperceptible agenda of seeking the share of political power (Nair 2009).[24]

The RSS is an ideology—which defines the boundaries of the way of life, whereas, the BJP is the practice of this ideology in politics. Since politics has primacy, the BJP operates in certain spheres as an autonomous unit, but largely remains within the ideological hegemony of the RSS. This became manifest in 2014 with a strong leader like, Narendra Modi, in command led to the multiplication of the non-RSS members in the BJP. It is pertinent that the support base of the BJP multiplied, but the RSS support has remained stagnant. For instance, in 2003 the RSS had 45,946 Shakhas, and it marginally increased to 56,859 in 2016. However, with the BJP in command, the RSS launched a number of projects in the field of health, education, and welfare of the marginalised sections; these projects increased significantly from 5,000 in 1989 to 1,40,000 in 2012, and an estimated 1,65,000 in 2015 (Anderson and Damle 2018).

Figure 1.2 Annual Growth Rate of RSS Shakhas and Activities (2009-19)

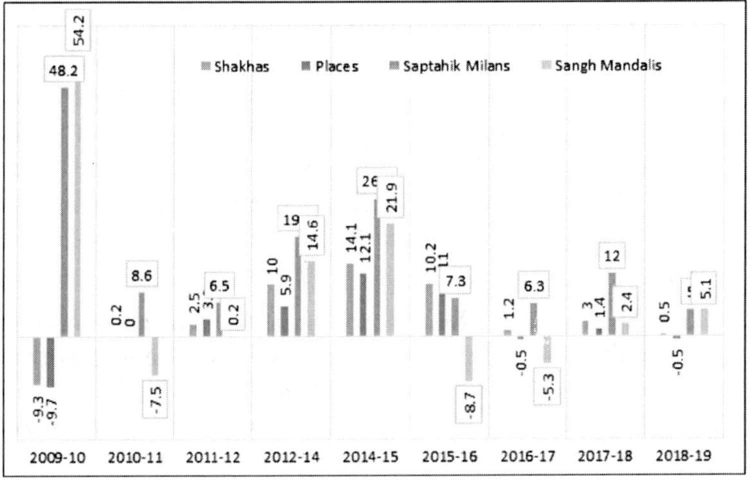

Source: RSS Annual Reports, 2009 to 2019

The RSS cadres used to provide support for the management of elections, but with the introduction of modern technology, digital communication and new management techniques, the BJP leadership captured the leadership role. The technology was excessively used to disseminate ideology rather than relying on the RSS cadres. The gradual expansion of the BJP was incommensurate with the extent of control they have had over the legislature, executive and judiciary. A comparative analysis of the BJP-led rule between 2014 to 2019 and 2019 onwards shows that the BJP strategically carved out political architecture to operationalise its ideological persuasions.

In the 2014 Lok Sabha elections, Narendra Modi as a Prime Ministerial candidate addressed the people with issues exclusively on the economy, governance, India's development record, the high potential of youth employment, etc., And, the Hindutva identity was addressed indirectly as mixing of development, nationalism, and Hindu identity by extensively invoking the Hindu civilisational symbols like, Ganga (river), Gita (a religious script), Sarasvati (Goddess of Education), etc. to unite the Hindus across the board. This was in continuation of the use of these ritualistic religious practices which were common to all the Hindus. Bal Gangadhar Tilak started the practice of holding the Ganpati festival as it was not part of the holy trinity—Brahma, Vishnu and Shiva to unite the Hindus on a common religio-cultural platform (Mukhopadhyay 2019: 57-58).[25]

> The decision to pitchfork Lord Ganesha into the forefront of Hindu religiosity... was a well calculated move, as the elephant-headed God was neither part of the holy trinity—Brahma, Vishnu and Shiva nor the main deity of any particular community in Maharashtra. Shortly after the popularity of the Ganpati festival, Tilak launched the Shivaji festival to arouse nationalistic sentiments amongst Marathi youth. The intention behind such measures were 'to create a pan-Hindu identity to act as a counter divergences between different sects and to induce a sense of collectiveness (Mukhopadhyay 2019: 57-58).

This was in line with the ideology of the RSS. And, on the economic policies, the BJP and RSS were united in opposition to the socialist philosophy but differed on the approach within capitalism. The BJP laid greater emphasis on Make in India, whereas, the disinvestment of the public sector enterprises (PSEs) was termed as 'an imprudent business decision that is against the national interest' by the RSS economic wing ("RSS economic wing" 2019). Historically, the RSS has emphasised economic theory propounded by Deendayal Upadhyaya, that laid greater thrust to make rural India self-sufficient and not in favour of building big dams and industrial complexes. He believed that instead of investing in the public sector, it would be more prudent to encourage the small private enterprises. The first election manifesto of the Jana Sangh in 1951 assigned centrality to the villages as engines of economic growth.

The RSS openly opposes the BJP Government's economic policies, such as foreign direct investment (FDI) liberalisation and all the other anti-Swadeshi policies, but on the other, also plays a 'more assertive mediatory role in handling internal Parivaar debates.' In case of faded boundaries between the two, Anderson and Damle (2018: 136) mentioned that:

> The power balance between the party and the RSS seems to be gradually shifting in favour of the party. One factor in this shift is almost certainly the RSS fear that the charge of Hindu terrorism against it, stemming from a series of bomb explosions in 2006-07, could result in another ban, and thus it must rely on the BJP to shield it from this action.

In 2019, the BJP got a majority in the parliament elections on its own and was in a commanding position in terms of implementation of the various dimensions of cultural nationalism as propounded by the RSS. It has transformed the Nehruvian concept of secular nationalism and mixed economy, to cultural nationalism and market economy with redefining the role of the State to mitigate economic miseries.

Modi's Regional Hindutva and Global Hindutva of RSS

The RSS follows the agenda to homogenise Hinduism at a global level by overcoming its internal social (caste) and regional differences to provide it with a shape of non-complicated, non-sectarian, and enormous Hinduness. For instance, the Vishwa Hindu Parishad (VHP) is one of the examples (Hansen 1993). The popularisation of Hindutva by the RSS and its affiliates to increase its global outreach has used various means. To promote the ideology at the global level, the RSS, after adopting the faces of Swami Vivekananda, Hedgewar, Savarkar, and Golwalkar, is trying to adopt new faces, such as the late Nobel prize-winning author, Sir V.S. Naipaul (also known for his love for Hindutva and hatred for Islam). The Institute for Nurturing Indian Intellect (an RSS-associated organisation) even held a discussion on Naipaul on the occasion of the 27th anniversary of the Babri-Masjid demolition on 6th December at the Delhi Constitution Club (Sampal 2019). The departure from the globalisation of Hindutva, to regionalisation, coincided with the emergence of Mr. Modi as a leader in the most developed State of Gujarat

The BJP in Gujarat has nurtured regional aspirations, patronised new aspirational class filtered through the regionalised version of Hindutva, particularly in post-liberalisation. The whole tenor of electoral mobilisation in Gujarat has been a clever blend of 'Gujarat Ka Gaurav' and Hindutva identity.

Electoral discourse in Gujarat had three dimensions. Firstly, it revolved around mobilisations on regionalised Hindutva identity leading to polarisation in 62 urban constituencies on religious lines, whereas, in the rural areas on the caste-cum-class lines. Secondly, to counter this, Mandal versus Kamandal politics of the 1980s was invoked by co-opting Hardik Patel (reservation for the Patidar caste), Alpesh Thakur (reservation for OBCs) and Jignesh (reservation and welfare for the Dalits). Secondly, both the BJP and the Congress were making rounds of the religious Dhams to overcome these differentiations within the caste groups. Whether it will work to the advantage of original Hindutvawadis or clone Hindutva is not the question. It is nothing else, but competitive communalism. And thirdly, the use of Gaurav of Gujarat as a universal category that appeared to be purer and unadulterated through a clever underplaying of the structural inequalities of caste, religion and ethnicity. And, since the opposition made Modi as the fulcrum of the Gujarat elections, the defeat of the BJP in Gujarat was being propagated as a precursor to Modi's defeat in 2019 elections. Though, that was not to the liking of a number of Gujarati voters as they continue to see Modi as the Gaurav of Gujarat.

Why Has This Happened?

Firstly, the overall approach has been to use the cocktail of 'Hindu civilisational symbols' to blur the structural inequalities. This has led to tension on issues like banning of Pakistani singers, etc.

Secondly, the mobilisation of the emerging aspirational class has been orchestrated from amongst the regional, caste, and tribal groups for the expansion of the electoral base. This has led to tensions between the communities vis-a-vis each other for reconciliation of their competing claims and harmonisation of the citizenship rights and claims of collectivities, for example, the State-wide protest by the Patel caste in Gujarat (see Jaffrelot 2016: 218-232).[26]

These can be understood by analysing the prevalent faultiness in Indian political spectrum.

Faultline I: Location of Hindu Civilisation as Symbols in Ethnic Particularism

This has provided content to broaden the fault lines emerging in Indian politics. The first faultline has emerged from the location of Hindu civilisation in ethnic particularism for blurring inequalities emanating from the development strategy and building universal categories like citizenship for the delivery of State services. This has happened as the Hindu civilisational symbols were extensively used for building universal categories like citizenship. The slogan of 'development for all, along with all' and the issue of national security was presented as universal, more pure, unadulterated—underplaying the structural inequalities located in the caste, religion, gender and ethnicity from a conglomeration of identities to catch all the categories.

Strategic Thrust

Four layers of symbols have been appropriated in the Parliamentary Elections for the consolidation of votes.

(i) Selective Appropriation of Universal Symbols

The usage of (Hindu) civilisational symbols are contextual and dynamic. For instance, 'development for all, along with all' claimed to be universal, more pure, and unadulterated underplaying structural inequalities located in caste, religion, gender, and ethnicity. In other words, the attempt was to reach out to the voters from a conglomeration of the identities to catch-all categories.

In the Parliament elections, the Modi-led BJP selectively appropriated the symbols and icons from Indian history and invoked ideology to make these sound inclusive. Martyrdom and national pride were evoked against "an untrustworthy 'Delhi Empire' that tolerated gruesome acts against the Indian soldiers." And, the use of the symbols including, Ganges (river), Gita (Scripture), and Navratras (ritual), as well as the national icons, such as Madan Mohan Malaviya, Deen Dayal Upadhyay, Sardar Vallabh bhai Patel, have been appropriated to provide content to 'Hindu'/ Indian nationalism to maximise votes (Press Information Bureau 2014).

Whereas the usage of the contextual, for example, in the Bihar Assembly elections, cow as a polarising symbol was used for the consolidation of votes. In several places, PM Modi while delivering speeches used moderated dialogues of historical icons. For instance, using quotes, such as Netaji

Subhas Chandra Bose said '*Tum mujhe khoon do, main tumhe azaadi doonga*' (Give me your blood, and I shall give you freedom) and Mr. Modi moderated it by referring to S.C. Bose that '*Aap mujhe 60 mahine dijiye, main aapko sukh-chain ki zindagi doonga*' (Give me 60 months, and in return, I will deliver you a peaceful and prosperous life) ("Narendra Modi Text Speeches" 2014).

(ii) Filtered Through Religiosity for Sanctification

Furthermore, these symbols were filtered through religiosity to acquire larger acceptability. 'Hindu' symbols were identified with purity. "Uttar Pradesh, the holy land of mother Ganga." It was not the cleanliness of the Ganges that was promised, but its 'purification'. Similarly, the Yamuna River was not to provide safe drinking water, the development terminology, but 'pure water'. Corruption and non-performance were linked to the vilification of the Hindu symbols, even though they themselves have sinned even in the holy name of the Ganges as huge funds sanctioned for cleaning the Ganges have been reportedly misappropriated.

(iii) Regionalisation of Symbols

This Hindu civilisation was located in the regional context to build connections with the people. Rousing of the cultural idioms and regional symbols of pride and group values were raised to seek the reinforcement of the slogan, 'Welfare of all'. And, these symbols were labelled as 'Hindu' and were located in diverse regions in the country to establish their link with the Indian culture.

Haryana is the land of Kurukshetra, and Lord Krishna provides the message of the Gita to the world. Assam is the land of Maa Kamakhya, and Jammu crowds in the rally were attributed to Maa Vaishno Devi's blessings. Respect is paid to the Goddess of Basta Aradhya Devi and Mata Dhantswar in Chhattisgarh. Bengal is remembered for Durga Puja, Rosgulla, and drum beats (dhaak), and songs (saankh) as an integral part of Durga Puja. Gujarat became the 'land of Somnatha', while Bihar's historic and glorious role was hailed during the Ramayana, Mahabharata, Buddhist, and Mauryan era, and during the British period. Uttar Pradesh as the land of Ramrajya was evoked with the strength, traditions, and cultural heritage. "People of this land, your own ancestors realised the ideal of Ramrajya" (Narendra Modi Text Speeches, 2014 onwards). The important thing to note is that the politics of invoking (Hindu) civilisational values, symbols and norms is to reinforce the majoritarian social order. It leaves minimal space for the real issues as it focuses so much on their identity through the day-to-day practices and perceived reality.

(iv) Packaging of the Leader

The role of the leader becomes central with the decline in the conventional party system and excessive use of social media and televised political advertisements. The logical outcome is to package the leader as a civilisational representative by giving negligible attention to the issues relating to distributive justice. The persona of Modi was packaged around these (Hindu) civilisational, symbols, norms, institutions, and values. For instance, Modi and Gujarat were linked with religious connection with the various regions and his lower caste origin. Modi and Gujarat were presented as synonymous with the religious, traditional connections drawn to the rally locations. The Yadavs in Bihar were reminded that the king of Yadavs, Lord Krishna, resided in Dwarka, Gujarat—the home of Modi. Similarly, the people in West Bengal were addressed that each member of the BJP embodies the values of the Bengali diaspora inspired by Swami Vivekananda, people in Udaipur (Rajasthan) were addressed as to how Bheelu

Rana (Commander-in-Chief of Maharana Pratap) carried out the surgical strikes against his enemies (referring to the surgical strikes conducted under the BJP rule on Pakistan in 2016). For instance, in one of his speeches given at Prayagraj (earlier Allahabad), Uttar Pradesh, he says:

> ...Prayagraj and boatmen have an age-old relationship. Even Maryada Purshottam Ram's *Ramayana* will not be complete without the boatmen. The saviour of the world was saved by these sailors. The relationship between you and me is also very strong. You consider yourselves to be servants of Lord Rama while I consider myself to be your Pradhan Sevak or Prime Servant. You consider yourselves to be sons of Mother Ganga while I am at your service at the call of Mother Ganga. Now tell me, isn't there a strong bond between you and me? (Publications Division 2019).

Modi emphasised his own lower caste origin and said that the saints and social reformers in the past belonged to either the Dalits or backward castes. Speaking at a rally in Muzaffarpur in Bihar on March 3, 2014, Narendra Modi emphasised his own lower caste origins and said: "The next decade will belong to the Dalits and the backwards" ("Narendra Modi Text Speeches" 2014), and also in a Mahasabha in Kochi, he repeated that the saints and social reformers in the past century had belonged to either the Dalit or backward sections of the society. He wondered why a memorial honouring the contribution of Ayyankali was not built in Kerala ("Narendra Modi Text Speeches" 2014). No doubt, he identified himself humbly as an ordinary man, but from the land of Mahatma Gandhi and Sardar Patel. An analysis of Mr. Modi's speeches during the 16th and 17th Lok Sabha elections shows that these were mainly contextualised in the socio-cultural aspects and of course, garnished with the regional economic scenario. The slogans like, *'Sabka Saath-Sabka Vikaas,'* and *'Suraaj'*, were supplemented with the use of words like *Sevak* (a servant),

Chai-wala (a Tea-seller) and *Chowkidar* (a guard) as an identity connect with the common people. In 2014, the events like *'Chai par Charcha'* which means discussion over a cup of tea were also initiated in 300 cities (1,000 tea stalls in each city) to reach out to the voters using the potent symbolism of Modi's rise from an underprivileged background. Whereas, the use of the identity of 'Chowkidar' was introduced in the 2014 election campaign, but got real success in the election campaign of 2019 with all the leaders of the BJP using 'Chowkidar' as a prefix to their name to symbolise the resolve against corruption, pollution, both social and environmental, and security and safety of the marginalised sections including, Dalits and women. A multi-layered packaging was done starting with the region through linkages with the religious traditions, icons, institutions, followed by claiming a relation with the prominent local, national political icons having roots in that region and a connection with the people. At another level, he located himself with the lower caste and class by highlighting his lower caste and class origin.[27]

Implications

The branding is devoid of any meaningful commitment to remove poverty, reduce inequalities, promote distributive justice and, ensure and deliver rights-based governance. Consequently, religious, linguistic, and regional factors became so mixed up that none of these emerged as a single factor in the electoral mobilisation. One of the reasons is that contemporary politics is reproducing itself within a broad range of the bound and unbound seriality (Anderson 1998: 29-45), centre with or without periphery and, historical (in terms of symbolism) and ahistorical (in ideological persuasions). This brings us to another level, that is, how does this cocktail of symbolisms facilitate a catch-all approach? And also, under what conditions and political contexts will this nuanced usage of (Hindu) civilisation symbolisms degenerate into a clash of civilisation (to use Huntington's (1996) phrase).

Faultline II: Convergence of Market Fundamentalism with Catch-All Hindu Civilisational Symbols

Given the consensus amongst the political parties on a neoliberal path of development and in the absence of an alternate vision, the electoral discourse conveniently located the crony capitalism, unemployment, poverty, and inequalities in the policy paralysis.

Politics is seen as a means to resolve the tensions between the opposing claims of the market, efficiency, and economic growth as against those of social equity and justice. On the one hand, it has guaranteed various rights to meet the challenges and experiences of exclusion and, on the other, accumulation by dispossession has been practised.

The new nation-building project appears to have in its core the land and labour reforms. It has been packaged under the banner '*Make in India*' to build global-friendly capitalism.

For dispossession of land from the farmers, the electoral legitimacy was not sufficient to overcome the opposition. Unlike Nehruvian developmentalism in which the State could mobilise substantial legitimacy for the dispossession of land from the farmers for public sector projects, the present political dispensation could not motivate the farmers to make sacrifices for the new 'nation-building project' by dispossessing land for private accumulation. For India's semi-proletariat, a small piece of land is a survival need and far more preferable than pure landlessness. As a consequence, dispossession requires political will to use its monopoly of the means of violence to acquire land from the farmers for the benefit of the capital.

Another feature for creating a more enabling environment for transacting business is labour reforms. India's national pride to become a manufacturing hub through the 'Make in India' programme has been tied to labour reforms. The pretence is not labour welfare, but 'investment climate and investors' confidence' to rationalise changes in the Workmen's Compensation Act, 1923; the Trade Unions Act, 1926; the Payment of Wages Act, 1936; the Employment of Children Act, 1938; the Factories Act, 1948; the Employees State Insurance Act, 1948; the Plantations Labour Act, 1951; the Mines Act, 1952; the Employees' Provident Fund and Miscellaneous Provisions Act, 1952; the Payment of Bonus Act, 1965; the Payment of Gratuity Act, 1972; the Bonded Labour Act, 1976; Contract Labour (Regulation and Abolition) Act, 1970; Interstate Workmen (Regulation of Employment and Conditions of Service) Act, 1979; Child Labour (Prohibition and Regulation) Act, 1986; Factories (Amendment) Act, 1987; Land Acquisition Bill, etc.

There is a Labour Code on Wages 2019, which is an Act of the Parliament of India that consolidates four central laws—the Minimum Wages Act, 1948; the Payment of Wages Act, 1936; the Payment of Bonus Act, 1965; and the Equal Remuneration Act, 1976.

> The Wage Code removes the schedule of employments, which documents the specific industries that would be covered by existing minimum wage legislations... The industry-level minimum wage has now been replaced by a standardised minimum wage based on either time-based or piece work, which is applicable to all sectors... This means that without the schedule, the minimum wage rates set at the state-level might be based on the wages paid to the poorest workers, thereby bringing down wages in all sectors (Jayaram 2019).

The imperatives of enabling competitiveness, and profitability has to be sustained at all cost—the freedom to hire and fire, casualise labour and reduce the presence of regularised labour, scrap laws on contract labour, take regulators off their back, revoke the answerability of the directors of corporations—as 'occupiers'—in matters of health, safety and welfare in factories, shut and exit from establishments without having to report to the government and get its prior permission, all of this is to be made legal.

In a nutshell, as mentioned before, in view of these structural reforms, the multiplication of deprivations, discrimination leading to multiplication of inequalities, the concealment of these through invoking contradictions existing at the level of superstructure, etc., facilitated the transformation process. The application of ideology may be differential as per the nature of politics. Since 1994, the shift has been to shape the right wing discourse to smudge the deprivations emerging from the structural reforms. The political discourse around Ram Janmabhoomi and Babri Masjid, uniform civil code, criminalisation of the Triple Talaq, and abrogation of the Article 370, etc., acquired political currency and efforts were made to acquire normative dignity.

Firstly, the cultural civilisational advocates relied on the judicial verdict on the Ram Janmabhoomi, and Babri Masjid disputed land that, 'the Temple is a disputed site and alternative land will be provided for the mosque; SC orders the Centre to formulate a scheme within three months and set up a trust to manage the property and construct a temple' ("Chronology of Ayodhya" 2019), to acquire normative supremacy over the secular nationalism.

This, in a way, reinvigorated the agenda of cultural nationalism by not only legitimising the ideology of Hindutva but also provided normative dignity to the claimants (Hindus) and the politics of the BJP.

Secondly, the step towards the adoption of a uniform civil code by the criminalisation of Triple Talaq by law and sending a message that it is not a religion, but the laws of the State that shall govern. This was a comment on the reversal of the Shah Bano Supreme Court verdict by the parliament during the Congress regime. The reversal of this decision was a statement to expose the accusation of the 'minority appeasement' by the Congress Party regime at the expense of the rights of Muslim women.

The Muslim Women's (Protection of Rights on Marriage) Act, 2019 is "an act to protect the rights of married Muslim women and to prohibit divorce by pronouncing talaq by their husbands and to provide for matters connected therewith or incidental thereto" ("The Gazette of India" 2019). The five-judge bench of the Apex Court declared the practice as unconstitutional by 3:2 majority (See Annexure 1.3).

The Home Minister of India on the passing of the Act in July 2019 stated that 'From now on, the door to unlimited possibilities will open for Muslim women, and they would now be able to play an effective role in the creation of "New India" (Press Information Bureau 2019).

Thirdly, in view of the continuous contention between Pakistan and India over the issue of Kashmir, terrorist attacks in the region, etc., the legal abrogation of Article 370 was another step towards defining the core of cultural nationalism. For instance, the Bharatiya Janata Party has consistently reiterated its stand on the abrogation of the Article 370 in both the 15th and 16th Lok Sabha Elections Manifesto (2009 and 2014 respectively), while the Article 35A was included along with Article 370A into the Manifesto of the 17th Lok Sabha Election (2019) and considered the article as 'a psychological barrier for the full integration of the people of Jammu & Kashmir with the national mainstream' ("Bharatiya Janata Party" 2009; 2014; 2019).

The opposition parties accused the BJP of installing the ideals of Hindu majoritarianism as the 'constitutional coup' (Kronstadt 2019).

The explanation given was that the radical step had been taken to ensure full integration of the people of Kashmir and to provide them access to the new opportunities. It will also encourage the outsiders to invest in property or land or industry to create employment opportunities for the locals.

All these activities starting with an invoking of Lord Rama for the consolidation of the Hindu consciousness, for the criminalisation of Triple Talaq and the abrogation of Article 370 dealing with Kashmir through Constitutional Amendments led to the consolidation of cultural nationalism by invoking civilisational discourse. The contemporary context of electoral politics is trying to draw the legitimisation of the Hindutva based on values which are civilisational but happen to be Hindu. For example, the Saraswati, as a symbol of education, is a civilisational value, (but presented as Hindu) that transcends the very thin line between the secular nationalism and cultural nationalism that is being propagated.

Faultline III: Market Fundamentalism and (Cultural) Nationalism

The market-driven politics has redefined and reshaped the discourse on nationalism as well as secularism. It has subsumed not the economic, but also the political sovereignty of the nation-states. The market-driven 'mass culture' instates a dualism in which it creates a demand for consumption catering to the people's wants which may not be to their needs, but is aimed at profit-making and ideological mobilisation of the people through the selective appropriation of the cultural values to enhance their political and social hegemonic power. Every human practice, social relations, cultural spaces, and socio-political institutions are moulded as per the moralities of the market. This leads to the breaking down of the local cultures of religious and ethnic groups and replaces it with cosmopolitan culture. This hybrid 'cosmopolitan culture' in no way reflects the different cultural predispositions and in the process negates the formation of common culture. If the State positions itself to facilitate, rather than intervene, to mitigate the cultural exclusivities and the illusion of being part of the 'cosmopolitan culture', it will lead to self-destructive consequences.

Perhaps, this is the logic of the globalisation of capital. It presents this as an opportunity for developing countries to achieve parity with the developed world. The present government should not be blamed for inviting the 'mighty Americans' to help the Indian State in controlling terrorism. Having compromised economic sovereignty, the developing countries are over enthusiastically surrendering their political sovereignty to the dominant powers. Consequently, both India and Pakistan, rather than protecting themselves from the coalition of globally dominant power regimes and their diktats, have surrendered their political autonomy.

For them, the national interest means to protect the 'territory' and not the political and economic sovereignty of the people. And the 'threat' is perceived from the 'weak' (Pakistan), 'Taliban', 'Jaish-e-Mohammad' and not from the powerful regimes that keep the developing countries on the margins of politics and economy. And, 'security' is to be sought from the military deployment rather than strengthening democracy. The maintenance of domestic peace has also come within the realm of global political decision-making and diktats. It may be politically useful to whip up national sentiments against Pakistan for the terrorist strikes.

More serious is the fact that the senseless terrorist attacks and the war cry against Pakistan are nothing but competitive terrorism which will only reinforce the culture of violence. Whereas, the threat of use of violence is more potent instrument for peace building rather than the actual use of violence per se. Further, the acts of terror groups are responded by attacking the civilian population of the 'enemy country,'and that will not eliminate the cause of terrorism per se, but it may lead to the legitimisation of the acts of terror. The war against terror must not be used as a tool to reinforce the nationalistic fervour. However, in the 2019 Lok Sabha elections, the issue of national security became paramount in elections campaigns.

If a caterer is well acquainted with the kind of appetite that a customer yearns for and, he serves him accordingly; a favourable tip is what he gets. The issue of national security has always been used in a similar manner. The Bharatiya Janata Party has taken a firm stand on the issue of the nation's security and criticised the opposition (UPA) for its soft approach towards the same. For instance, in the 2009 Lok Sabha election manifesto, the BJP was critical of the fact that instead of ensuring the safety of the people, the Congress government scrapped 'The Prevention of Terrorism Act; halted investigations; and, slowed down the prosecution' ("Bharatiya Janata Party" 2009). The similar items like, modernising armed forces, building war memorials, implementation of one rank-one pension, setting up of the defence universities to increase the manpower were put on the itinerary in the 2014 election manifesto ("Bharatiya Janata Party" 2014). A similar apparatus was also used in the 17th Lok Sabha Elections (2019) as the developmental approach of 'Sabka Sath, Sabka Vikaas' was shifted to 'Sashakt Bharat (powerful nation)' and 'Development for all' to 'Jaikara.' As the BJP President, Mr. Shah said that 'this election is not merely to elect a government, it is an election to ensure the country's national security' ("Bharatiya Janata Party" 2019). And, such an environment inspired the UPA for the first time to come out with a 'Plan on National Security' in its 2019 election manifesto (Mukherjee 2019: 287).

Both the attacks (the militant attack on the Indian Army base at Uri in 2016 and the Pulwama attack in which a convoy of the Central Reserve Police Force (CRPF) was attacked by a vehicle-borne suicide bomber in Pulwama district on February 14, 2019, which killed 40 CRPF personnel), and the government's response to the attack (the surgical-strike in 2016 and the Balakot air-strike in 2019), influenced the trajectory of the 17th Lok Sabha Election, 2019. The attacks were condemned, no doubt, but the government's actions regarding the same were severely criticised by the opposition parties as they demanded evidence about the strikes and expressed their serious doubts regarding the same (Pradhan 2018). Though, the government officials maintained it throughout the election period (pre and post) that, 'strikes were not political, and one can't think about it in terms of votes' ("Balakot strike not political" 2019). But, the politicisation of the armed forces was one of the growing concerns during the election campaigning, and it was predetermined that the 2019 election was based on the issue of national security (as the BJP mentioned in the election manifesto and Congress introduced a plan on national security). The debate on the military strategy relating to the national security prompted the Election Commission of India to intervene. In a communication addressed to all the political parties, the Election Commission instructed them to desist from using military photographs or symbols during their campaigns. Despite this advisory, there were transgressions, both minor and major as the electoral spotlight turned to the military," asserts Mukherjee (2019: 287-288).

Mr. Modi's decision to undertake aerial strikes on the Balakot Camp (operated by the terrorist group Jaish-e-Mohammed) earned him the reputation of being a decisive leader (Rukmini 2019: 39). Another fact that was also highlighted that the aerial strikes were glorified by Prime Minister Modi himself by endorsing the movie made on the same (Rej and Sagar (2019: 78). They further argued that by avowing the strikes publicly, Mr. Modi met his two objectives of 'a warning to Pakistan' and 'assuaging his constituents.' They quoted, "the subsequent glorification of an admittedly limited military engagement in sync with the Hindu nationalist identification of national self-image and martial prowess."

Interestingly, the BJP opponents supported or opposed the BJP over the issue of the strikes as per their understanding of the mood of the electorates. The Congress Party president, Rahul Gandhi took a jibe of a '180-degree turn over the Indian Army cross-border, or statement like 'Khoon ki dalaali', meaning thereby that Mr. Modi was attempting to take profit from the soldiers' blood. And, other leaders like, AAP Chief, Arvind Kejriwal, BSP supremo Mayawati, and Nirupam Roy remained ambivalent in their response. In this political discourse, the identification of the enemy was done based on the religion (i.e. Muslims) and the place of origin (i.e. Pakistan).

It may be politically useful to whip up national sentiments against Pakistan, but to fight footloose terrorism, the need has been to improve the level of governance in the country and make the delivery of justice efficient, just and accountable. The counterterrorism laws and enhanced surveillance have to be balanced by enhancing 'the state's ability to uphold the rule of law' and the rights of the groups of citizens. Strict laws may have to be framed, but it is equally important to put stronger measures in place to make the systems accountable.

The question of cultural nationalism was also reflected in the definition of citizenship and located in civilisation which was depicted as a conglomerate of the majority of the people who have a common history with the local origin of their religion and its institutions and subjective identification of the people with it. It has been rightly described by Lucian Pye that the civilisation may pretend to be a State (Huntington 1996: 45). The Citizen Amendment Act, 2019 has brought the religion, citizenship and cultural nationalism into the public space. The Citizenship Act (LVII of 1955) mentions five provisions for acquiring citizenship, i.e. by birth, by descent, by registration, naturalisation, and through the incorporation of the territory into India. The Act was amended in 1986 with the inclusion of Article 6A (special provisions for the citizenship of the persons covered by the Assam Accord); in 2003, with the introduction of the dual or transnational citizenship for the persons of Indian origin in the form of 'Overseas Indian Citizenship'; and in 2016, the Citizenship Amendment Act was put forward by the NDA government with the major objectives of defining the illegal migrant, provision of citizenship by naturalisation, and cancellation of registration of Overseas Citizenship of India.[28] The Act says, "provided that any person belonging to Hindu, Sikh, Buddhist, Jain, Parsi or Christian community from Afghanistan, Bangladesh or Pakistan, who entered India on or before December 31, 2014 and who has been exempted by the Central Government by or under clause (c) of sub-section (2) of Section 3 of the Passport (Entry into India) Act, 1920 or from the application of the provisions of the Foreigners Act, 1946 or any rule or order made thereunder, shall not be treated as an illegal migrant for the purposes of this Act."

But, the ascribed provisions of citizenship, such as inclusiveness remain elusive, particularly when secular nationalism is being redefined (see Roy 2010: 11).[29]

The recent amendment in the Citizenship Act grants citizenship to the persons religiously persecuted which ultimately violates the Constitution of the country and makes these citizens as 'deficient' which further produces a whole new arena of tension.

Whereas the Home Minister of India justified the necessity of the Bill on the basis of Nehru's statement on the aftermath of partition that:

> We feel concerned about our brothers and sisters who have become alienated from us due to new political boundaries and are not able to participate in freedom celebrations. I would like to make it clear that they belong to us and shall always belong to us. Their welfare and difficulties shall always be uppermost in our minds. I would like to assure them that they are free to come here and whenever they choose to come to India, we shall accept them (Babu 2019).

He further mentioned the Nehru-Liaquat Ali agreement and asserted that India had kept the promise to support the minorities, but Pakistan has not. As in Pakistan, 'the number of minorities came down from 23 per cent to 3 per cent. But here Muslims also became Chief Justice of India, Chairman of this House, Chief Election Commissioner, President or Vice President,' stated Shah ("Rajya Sabha" 2019: 570). While Dr. Subramanian Swamy, also quoted Dr. Manmohan Singh in support of the bill that, 'the minorities in countries like Bangladesh, have faced persecution, and it is our moral obligation that if circumstances force people, these unfortunate people, to seek refuge in our country, our approach to granting citizenship to these unfortunate persons should be more liberal.' He further mentioned that the minorities are ill-treated and oppressed in Pakistan, Bangladesh, and Afghanistan ("Rajya Sabha" 2019: 560-61).

The historical correction was made by Independent India to go secular on the aftermath of partition. If Nehru said, what the Home Minister of India implied in support of CAA, then it is BJP's role to settle the matter with the Congress, not with the Constitution. The CAA defies the very first virtue of that historical correction, i.e. by going secular.

Another dimension linked with the illegal citizenship and the background of NRC in Assam is related to the immigration and sovereignty of the country. The illegal immigration from the neighbouring countries has transformed the conventional definition of sovereignty and the States' claims to sovereignty. The claims to sovereignty are seen against the backdrop of the capacity of the States to control immigration. The golden rule of market fundamentalism is the globalisation of the capital and localisation of the human capital, their aspirations, culture, history and language. In this era of the capital, the goods and services are deregulated, and the labour is bound by the rules and regulations. The seeming inability of the States to regulate the mobility of labour and population is seen as evidence of a soft state. In the South-Asian post-colonial countries, territorial integrity has a hyper-national identity context. As a fallout, the globalisation of capital with the active implementation of the State in deepening of the capital base without creating relatively free mobility of labour is providing impetus to self-limiting the group identity formation. This phenomenon has provided an impetus to the "sons of the soil" movements throughout the world. This is visible within and among many countries. For instance, the movements like Punjab for Punjabis (Sikhs), Kashmir for Kashmiris (Muslims), Maharashtra for Marathas (Hindus), etc., have acquired a structural logic because of the resources crunch and intense competition for the jobs due to the process of liberalisation and globalisation within the country.

Another outcome of the right-wing political discourse was an abrogation of Article 370 of the Indian Constitution, criminalisation of the Triple Talaq by law and legitimisation of the Hindutva with the Supreme Court's verdict of the Ram-Janambhoomi-Babri Masjid conflict.

There are certain commonalities of experience of the citizen interaction with the State between the various segments of the society. The religion-based nationalism has been used to define deficient citizenship that is appropriated in the electoral discourse. It is this experience of exclusion that became central to the political discourse and not the exclusion of the marginalised sections from the market and the dominant politics.

Faultline IV: Centralisation with the Active Participation of the States

India is a multi-cultural, ethnic, linguistic and religious society. The plural character of the Indian society, the dynamic nature of the Indian Constitution and the fast-changing socio-economic and political reality have provided a dynamic basis to the Centre-State relations. Federalism, according to the Centre-State Relation Commission 'is not a static paradigm; it is a changing notion'. The Indian Constitution has provided an institutional framework for the cooperative federalism.

> **Box 1.1 Federal Transfer System in India**
>
> There are three institutions for federal transfers in India. First is the Finance Commission, which is involved in tax sharing and grants from the centre to the States. There is a statutory sanction behind these transfers. Then there are Plan grants covering central assistance for the State plans. Plan grants constitute the single largest component of grants transferred from the Centre to the States in recent years, and the priorities in plan expenditure are reflective more of what can be called 'national priorities' compared to the regional or local priorities. Then, finally, there are the non-statutory discretionary transfers by the central government ministries to the States on the non-plan side in the form of centrally sponsored schemes (CSS) that are condition specific purpose grants.

The trend of globalisation has transformed the terms of discourse between the Centre and the States. The nation-state has surrendered to the market in the sphere of both the path and the pace of development. The States are not taken into confidence for the Central Government's keenness to fully integrate the Indian economy with the global market. The Indian States are not involved or even taken into confidence for entering into global agreements like WTO or linking the petroleum prices with the global market, which directly affect the agriculturally dominant States. But the Central Government wants the State Governments to share the negative fallout of their economic policies. The petroleum subsidy is cut to create a favourable investment climate' as per the norms laid down by the global rating companies. The Central Government has decided to bear the cost on its own and transfer a part of it to the States. From where will be met the revenue loss faced by the States and even by the Centre? Over the years, the Central regime has made a significant institutional change (fiscal reforms reflected in the changes in the nature of grants; decline in overall transfers; increasing expenditure responsibilities of the states; increase in committed expenditures; increase in relative command over total resources by the Central Government in relation to its expenditure and withdrawal of loan facilities) which forces the States to 'fend' for themselves. This only means that the States will depend increasingly on private debt to meet its expenditure responsibilities completing the full cycle for the global investors.

In certain spheres, some States that have competitive advantage may benefit in terms of getting higher investment from the multinationals and experience greater autonomy. But, the backward States, even if they achieve constitutional autonomy, will see their backwardness multiplied in real terms as the market forces acquire greater autonomy to transcend the non-friendly federal structures.

The Nation-State has promoted metropolitan regions, encouraged FDI, influenced investment flows, introduced user fees, withdrawn subsidies, modified the income support programmes and altered the institutional structure in all sectors of the economy. In the earlier policy regime, there was an incentive and disincentive system that notionally tended to favour those who were lagging, non-industrialised, and the non-metropolitan regions. That approach has now been largely discarded; the new system (after economic reforms) professes to have minimal geographical orientation.

The scope for the discretion of the States to initiate state-specific development strategy is being minimized even as the Central Government is suggesting implicitly that it knows what is best for the States and that 'one size fits all'. And, to be sure, that view is fallacious.

If we try to characterise the changing context of the Centre-State relations, it would appear that with the emergence of coalition politics, it was assumed that with the regional groups having acquired greater stakes in politics, it would be possible to reverse the trend of over-centralisation that had been nurtured by one party dominance since independence. This has worked in two ways: on the one hand, it has provided greater access to the regional political parties to the national resources, and on the other, made them conscious of the constraints faced by the national government. It is this predicament which has made the regional parties position themselves on redefining the Centre-State relations as, by and large, ambivalent. The greater access of the regional parties to the political power has transformed the content of federalism from anti-centre to cooperative federalism and, in practice, bargaining federalism. The Constitution has provided an institutional framework for the cooperative federalism and the socio-economic and political necessities of the changing times have shaped the politics around the bargaining federalism.

The present political dispensation has added another dimension to centralisation. The federating States are encouraged to pass legislation to reinforce the consensus on the neoliberal path of development. In Gujarat, for instance, the law is being recast to make a place for a 'self-certification-cum-consolidated annual return scheme' which will extend to the Factories Act, the laws governing the minimum wages, bonus and gratuity, and those concerning the contract labour. Establishments within the coverage of these laws are to be exempted from inspections; there will, instead, be 'regular audits'. And, those establishments, which comply with the labour standards, will be awarded 'appreciation certificates'; a prize for following the law.

The Rajasthan Amendment Bill went much further on compounding. When an offence is committed, no court is to take cognisance except on the complaint by an inspector (which is the way it was) and 'with the previous sanction in writing by the State Government.' That is, an offence is not an offence till the State Government says it may be so considered.

Madhya Pradesh has been at work straining every nerve to displace Rajasthan as the front-runner in these endeavours. In September 2014, the Madhya Pradesh cabinet gave its approval to the amendments to twenty labour laws. The Labour Commissioner announced that 'lay-offs, retrenchments and even closures will not require any permission' (Trivedi 2014). It will, he is reported as having said, be akin to a 'hire-and-fire' policy in establishments of a designated size. In small and medium enterprises with less than 50 employees, the employers may terminate any employee without assigning any reason or conducting an enquiry. Similarly, Sood and Nath (2020) elaborate on of such changes in existing labour laws by the Governments of Uttar Pradesh (UP), Madhya Pradesh (MP) and Gujarat. They explained in detail that how in the name of simplification of labour laws, the entire burden of responsibility is shifted to labour's shoulders. For instance, increasing the length of the working day from the 9-hour to 12-hour, replacing overtime to full-time work, ease of hire and fire and not maintaining attendance register, a declining share of wages, increasing contractualisation, rise of informality, poor working conditions, and without insurance incentives for any mishap shows the lowered minimum benchmark of workers. In spite of all these new changes in labour laws, most of the states where these reforms were implemented performed 'either at par or worse than the national average, which in itself is abysmal', states Sood and Nath (2020).

This has blurred the regional disparities. And, the competition among the States is being shaped to reach the milestones which the Central Government is finding difficult to attain on its own.

Implications

The political implications are that the national political parties are required to expand their influence in the regions if they wish to regionalise the new nation-building project. In the 2014 elections, the share of the seats and the votes of the regional parties increased during 2009 to 2014 to 36 per cent from 29 per cent and to 36 per cent from 31 per cent respectively. Whereas, of the national parties, it declined from 69 per cent to 63 per cent and 64 per cent to 60 per cent (See Table 1.3, Annexure II).

In the Assembly elections in Haryana and Delhi, the BJP did not ally with its traditional allies. In an election rally in Tasgaon, Sangli district, Maharashtra, Prime Minister Modi appealed to the voters to give a clear majority to the BJP. To quote, 'Alliances did you no good... No party takes responsibility in an alliance. The BJP will take responsibility if you vote it to power' (Wallace 2015: 225). The BJP is following a two-pronged strategy, i.e. consolidation and expansion to emerge as a national alternative.

This entails regionalisation of its leadership and symbolism. It has undertaken social engineering at the micro-level by recruiting leaders from diverse social groups and articulating local issues in convergence with national politics. It is reconstructing federal polity, not through alliances with the regional parties, but by appropriating regional politics at the national level. This approach may prove to be counterproductive for the BJP as the people tend to vote differently in the national, regional and local elections.

The motive attributed is that the Bharatiya Janata Party wants to hold simultaneous elections to overcome the burden of anti-incumbency that it faces in some of the poll-bound States, and to marginalise the regional political parties. These goals and concealed motives are pursued by using legitimate and illegitimate means like persuasion, perverse incentives, coercion, invoking fear and insecurities. In political analysis, it is not prudent in the political discourse to brand contentions as suspect (which they may be) and summarily be dismissive. There is a need to understand these contentions as they claim to be pro-people and pro-democracy. The post-2014 election assessments have shown that many of these claims were partially correct, and there was a wide gap between the claims and performance.

The inferential logic is that simultaneous elections would surely undermine the federal democratic structure and also push the regional political parties on the margins leading to the subversion of the process of deepening of democracy.

The data (See Tables 1.8a, 1.8b. 1.9a, 1.9b. 1.10a, 1.10b. 1.11a, 1.11b and 1.12a, 1.12b) clearly show that the voters cast their vote as per their felt needs. The elections in Rajasthan, Madhya Pradesh, Jharkhand, Maharashtra, and Delhi have shown that a large number of the voters voted for a different party from the assembly elections while they had voted for some other political party during the Parliamentary elections.

Table 1.8A. Assembly Elections Result Rajasthan, 2018

Assembly Election	*BJP*	*BSP*	*CPM*	*INC*	*RLTP*	*BTP*	*RLD*	*IND*	*Total Vote*
Vote %age	38.77	4.03	1.22	39.30	2.40	0.72	0.33	7.37	100.00
Seats Contested	200	190	28	195	58	11	2	185	2494
Seats Won	73	6	2	100	3	2	1	13	200

Table 1.8B. Parliament Elections Assembly Segments-wise Result Rajasthan, 2018

Parliamentary Assembly Elections	*BJP*	*BSP*	*CPIM*	*INC*	*RLTP*	*BTP*	*RLD*	*IND*	*Total Vote*
Vote %age	58.34	1.07	0.24	34.35	2.03	0.97			100.00
Seats Contested	192	160	32	200	8	32			2198
Seats Won	176	0	0	16	7	1			200

Table 1.9A. Assembly Elections Result Madhya Pradesh, 2018

Assembly Election	*BJP*	*BSP*	*INC*	*SP*	*IND*	*Total Vote*
Vote %age	41.04	5.01	40.91	1.30	4.14	100.00
Seats Contested	230	227	229	52	214	3140
Seats Won	109	2	114	1	4	230

Table 1.9B. Parliament Elections Assembly Segments-wise Result Madhya Pradesh, 2018

Parliamentary Assembly Elections	*BJP*	*BSP*	*INC*	*SP*	*IND*	*Total Vote*
Vote %age	58.17	2.39	34.63	0.22		100.00
Seats Contested	230	198	230	16		3389
Seats Won	208	0	22	0		230

Table 1.10A. Assembly Elections Result Jharkhand, 2019

Assembly Elections	*AJSUP*	*BJP*	*JMM*	*JVM*	*INC*	*CPI(ML) (L)*	*RJD*	*NCP*	*IND*	*Total Vote*
Vote %age	8.10	33.37	18.72	5.45	13.88	1.15	2.75	0.42	4.18	100.00
Seats Contested	53	79	43	81	31	14	7	7	77	1297
Seats Won	2	25	30	3	16	1	1	1	2	81

Table 1.10B. Parliament Elections Assembly Segments-wise Result Jharkhand, 2019

Parliamentary Assembly Elections	*AJSUP*	*BJP*	*JMM*	*JVM*	*INC*	*CPI(ML) (L)*	*RJD*	*NCP*	*IND*	*Total Vote*
Vote %age	4.33	50.95	11.51	5.01	15.63	0.49	2.41			100.00
Seats Contested	6	75	24	12	39	12	11			1399
Seats Won	6	57	7	0	11	0	0			81

Table 1.11a. Assembly Elections Result Maharashtra, 2019

Assembly Elections	*INC*	*NCP*	*SHS*	*BJP*	*PHJSP*	*CPIM*	*SWP*	*AIMIM*	*SP*	*BVA*	*KTSTP*	*JSS*	*PWPI*	*RSPS*	*MNS*	*IND*	*Total Vote*
Vote %age	15.87	16.71	16.41	25.75	0.48	0.37	0.40	1.34	0.22	0.67	0.21	0.36	0.97	0.15	2.25	8.36	100.00
Seats Contested	147	121	126	164	26	11	5	44	7	31	1	4	24	1	101	275	3525
Seats Won	44	54	56	105	2	1	1	2	2	3	1	1	1	1	1	13	288

Table 1.11B. Parliament Elections Assembly Segments-wise Result Maharashtra, 2019

Parliamentary Assembly Elections	*INC*	*NCP*	*SHS*	*BJP*	*PHJSP*	*CPIM*	*SWP*	*AIMIM*	*SP*	*BVA*	*IND*	*MSHP*	*Total Vote*
Vote %age	16.27	15.51	23.29	27.57	0.04	0.21	1.54	0.72	0.02	0.91	2.29	0.52	100.00
Seats Contested	150	114	138	150	6	18	12	6	24	6	792	12	5490
Seats Won	22	23	105	122	0	0	4	2	0	3	6	1	288

Table 1.12A Assembly Elections Result Delhi, 2020

Assembly Election	*AAP*	*BJP*	*INC*	*Total Vote*
Vote %age	53.57	38.51	4.26	100.00
Seats Contested	70	67	66	742
Seats Won	62	8	0	70

Table 1.12B Parliament Elections Assembly Segments-wise Result Delhi, 2019

Parliamentary Assembly Elections	*AAAP*	*BJP*	*INC*	*Total Vote*
Vote %age	18.13	56.52	22.53	100.00
Seats Contested	70	70	70	1710
Seats Won	0	65	5	70

*Data is for major parties only, therefore the sum of all not equal to total

Source: *Statistical Reports of General Election to Lok Sabha and State Assembly, 2018, 2019, and 2020*. Election Commission of India.

To argue that the choice of the voters gets limited because of the simultaneous elections is a premise that is based on the data mentioned above, but that appears to be a spurious correlation. Any serious student of politics understands that the voters are influenced by the hierarchy of multiple factors like non-performance of the political parties and their leaders, credibility of the promises, castes, religion, other local factors, etc. To argue that the simultaneous elections may subvert the process of deepening of democracy as if to be perennially in the election mould is, in a way, healthy for any democracy.

Further, it has been asserted that the regional political parties will be at a disadvantage in the event of simultaneous elections. On the contrary, it can be argued that simultaneous elections may be more diversity sensitive as these elections will have a representation of a large range of the political parties giving widespread choices to the people's heterogeneous needs.

It is a different matter that the arguments for or against holding simultaneous elections in the domain of federalism would amount to overstretching the logic which largely falls in the political economy of the neoliberal path of development.

It is unfortunate that frequent electoral cycle is being touted as a cause of distortions and holding of simultaneous elections as a remedy. This is diversionary. The possible remedy to the frequent election cycle lies in the domain of electoral management. And, a very important factor other than the material and human cost, is the new trend of elections by television. The cycle of continuous elections broadcast on the electronic media creates throughout the country an atmosphere of electoral rhetoric and promises for immediate electoral gains rather than pursuing the sustainable pro-people goals.

It would be appropriate to restrict the continuous electoral cycle by the Election Commission of India (ECI) taking the proactive initiative to form electoral clusters of the States with or without making it to happen along with the Lok Sabha elections, and that might not require any amendments in the Constitution and changes in the People's Representation Act. Electoral management is no substitute for certain crucial and imperative electoral reforms.

The voters' complaint regarding the quality of the candidates, absence of the real issues, the trivialisation of the promises, reducing manifestoes to 'menu-festoes', leaders' disconnect with the people, et al., have nothing to do with the timing of the elections, but the larger issues of democratic political culture and electoral reforms (Kumar 2018).

To Sum Up

The above analysis shows that the promises and performance of the political parties may not be analysed in terms of a gap, but as a paradox. Further, the crisis of leadership has acquired a systematic form leading to a crisis of trust in politics and political leadership. Ideological filters have become convenient labels for acquiring legitimacy in electoral competition, what is otherwise blatantly a legislative power game. But, at the same, the dominant politics is operative within the parameters of cultural nationalism. As is evident, the new nation-building project excessively relies on blurring the structural inequalities through (Hindu) civilisational symbolism for building global-friendly capitalism. The social strife emanating from this may act as a necessary condition to push the neoliberal reforms. Till then, the country may have to live with the noises like, banning of 'beef, Pakistani singers, etc., gagging of the writers and dissenting voices, and move away from the complex, nuanced public conversation to common-sense arguments.

There is no ambiguity in the articulation of the right-wing agenda in the economy, politics and the social domain. It has dissolved the ideological boundaries between the RSS and the BJP. The BJP is in the Command and Modi is in the Lead.

To build a consensus on this new nation-building project, the national agenda has been regionalised, and the States are engaged to create instruments for the Central Government to lead. Some of the political parties also seem to be ideologically supportive of the economic reforms and politically going along with the right-wing cultural nationalism. Economic reforms tend to encourage privatisation of health, employment, and often public facilities, such as electricity, water, transportation, without productively engaging within the economic system. Thus, a clear dichotomy has emerged between populist politics and people's politics. The populist politics is more electoral friendly, and people's politics is impregnated with competitive ideological persuasion. And, the elections are treated like events where the voters are managed through a cocktail of symbols, doles and political rhetoric, whereas the politics of ideology is kept on hold to be executed within the constitutional framework after acquiring the political capacity to amend the same. However, the politics of resistance with competing ideology continues to engage with the dominant ideology as a historical struggle. The steady erosion of the vitality of the institutions has caused immense damage to politics. One of the derivatives is a culture of personalised politics. It leads to the building of a cult of a leader through uncritical idolatry. It hampers the core of democratic politics, i.e. the dialogue leading to consent or dissent in opposition to the enforced consensus. The dissent is purged, and the competing individual leaders are targeted to outcompete them through the process of elimination. Such a political practice gives currency to 'revenge politics', a tribal way of settling scores.

Recently, a political commentator on a visit to Afghanistan narrated his experience about the revenge politics. The narration goes like this. His host was a tribal chief. At night, the room in which he was staying was sprayed with bullets. He rushed to his host and told him that there was a danger to his life. The tribal chief confidently assured him that there was no need to worry and he should go back to his room and relax. 'If these people kill you, in revenge, we will kill two persons of theirs.'

There is a need to move away from building a cult of leader and revenge politics, through making the politics participatory, democratic and not violating the space of politics. And, also create a robust institutional framework to provide the people access to decision-making and ensure accountable governance. The arguments that these institutions are not cost-effective, corrupt and non-functional, therefore masked authoritarianism is said to be a necessary evil. On the contrary, these institutions should be made representative, participatory, less corrupt, more efficient, and accountable.

On a larger plane, the liberal political interventionist strategy within the 'boundaries of the capitalists' path of development may be to reinvent the State, to moderate callousness of the untrammelled market system and redefine politics to position itself in defence of the critical thought and the people living on the margins.

NOTES

1. Notwithstanding the fact that between 1951 and 1971, the Congress Party could never win majority votes and its share could not exceed 45 per cent.
2. In the 2014 and 2019 elections, the vote share of BJP could exceed by 5 per cent. But it could win 282 seats in 2014 and 303 in 2019.
3. 'I believe in a socialistic pattern of society... The basic question before us is to increase production of essential consumer goods and ensure their equitable distribution which will reduce the disparity between the haves and, the have nots. We do not want the new wealth to remain in the hands of a few people' ("Selected Works" 2006: 168).
4. Secular Nationalism: "We call our state a secular one. The word "secular" perhaps is not a very happy one and yet for want of a better, we have used it. What exactly does it mean? It does not mean a society where religion itself is discouraged. It means freedom of religion and conscience, including freedom for those who may have no religion. It means free play for all religions, subject only to their not interfering with each other or with the basic conceptions of our state" (Cited in Chandra et al. 1999: 48).
5. 'During the cold war, global politics became bipolar and the world was divided into three parts. A group of mostly wealthy and democratic societies, led by the United States, was engaged in a pervasive ideological, political, economic, and, at times, military competition with a group of somewhat poorer communist societies associated with and led by the Soviet Union. Much of this conflict occurred in the third world outside these two camps, composed of countries which often were poor, lacked

political stability, were recently independent, and claimed to be non-aligned' (Huntington 1996: 21).

6. Nehru in his address to the nation elaborated the concept on democratic planning. 'Democratic planning means the utilisation of all our available resources and in particular, the maximum quantity of labour willingly gives and rightly directed so as to promote the good of the community and the individual' ("Selected Works" 2005: From the Editorial Note).
7. Both the Finance Secretary, S.P. Shukla and the Chief Economic Advisor, Deepak Nayyar have been opposed to the IMF route, and were not the most ardent champions of liberalisation. Even the then Prime Minister, Narasimha Rao was not much charmed by liberalisation, on the contrary, positioned himself closer to Nehru (Ramesh 2015).
8. Quraishi (2019: 111-121) mentions the strategies the Election Commission of India (ECI) adopted to deal with the concern of voter apathy. On ECI's diamond jubilee in 2010, under the theme of 'Greater Participation for a Stronger Democracy,' to maximise the voter participation, programmes like community outreach and multimedia campaigning were rolled out. Surveys called KABP (Knowledge, Attitude, Behaviour, and Practices) were conducted before the interventions and implementation of any strategy. Measures like vulnerability mapping were devised in order to provide a safe and peaceful polling procedure to minor voters such as women. To encourage voters to participate, national and regional icons were also endorsed, special provision like ramps and Braille for specially-abled people, promoting voter rights of trans-genders, declaring 25th January as National Voters Day, and for the same 25,000 youth ambassadors were appointed in schools, colleges, and university campuses before the 2014 Lok Sabha Elections.
9. Vulnerability Mapping: The fear of violence at polling booths was acting as a biggest barrier and feeder of voter apathy. To ensure voters' safety and peaceful conduct of elections, the Election Commission of India launched a big information campaign and vulnerability mapping was one of the steps among these strategies. The vulnerability mapping is a strategy of mapping out 'all the districts to find out areas that suffered from threat and intimidation by criminals, and a series of measures to ensure peace' (Quraishi 2019: 113).
10. The Constitution (Fifty-Second Amendment) Act, 1985 (Anti-

Defection Act): To outlaw defections, the government introduced the Constitution (52nd Amendment) Act in 1985 which added a new Schedule (10th Schedule) with provisions as to disqualification on the ground of defection and also amended Articles 101, 102, 190, and 191 with reference to vacant seats and rejection for Parliament membership. The act consists of:

> "An elected member of Parliament or a State Legislature, who has been elected as a candidate set up by a political party and a nominated member of Parliament or a State Legislature who is a member of a political party at the time he takes his seat or who becomes a member of a political party within six months after he takes his seat would be disqualified on the ground of defection if he voluntarily relinquishes his membership of such political party or votes or abstains from voting in such a House contrary to any direction of such party or is expelled from such party.
>
> An independent Member of Parliament or a State Legislature shall also be disqualified if he joins any political party after his election.
>
> A nominated member of Parliament or a State Legislature who is not a member of a political party at the time of his nomination and who has not become a member of any political party before the expiry of six months from the date on which he takes his seat shall be disqualified if he joins any political party after the expiry of the said period of six months.
>
> It also makes suitable provisions with respect to splits in, and mergers of, political parties."

11. Influenced by the Socialist leader Ram Manohar Lohia, the Samajwadi Party (SP) was founded by Mulayam Singh Yadav after splitting from the Janata Dal (People's Party) in 1992. The party adheres to the principle of equality and sought to mobilise the marginalised sections of the society such as Muslims, SCs, STs, and other backward classes. The SP expands highly during post-Babari mosque demolition phase as it supports the Muslim agenda. Mulayam Singh Yadav is succeeded by Akhilesh Yadav, although the party remained confined to a state party (Routray 2014: Samajwadi Party).
12. A regional political party of Andhra Pradesh, founded by a former cinema actor and director, Nandamuri Taraka Rama Rao (known as NTR) in 1982. Initially the party was announced as a social organisation and within a week it declared itself as a

political Party and emerged as an alternative to the Congress party in Andhra Pradesh. The early era proved fruitful for the party but the later part with demand of Telangana as separate state pushed TDP towards coalitions with BJP, with Congress and again with BJP at present time (Routray 2015: Telugu Desam Party).

13. A regional political party of Tamil Nadu, founded by G.K. Moopnar in 1996 along with other leaders of Tamil Nadu Congress Committee. The party's ideology of pluralist traditions and grassroots democracy revolves around the reviving golden period of Perunthalaivar K. Kamarajar (a freedom fighter, and former CM of Tamil Nadu).
14. C.N. Annadurai after leaving Dravidar Kazhagam led by Periyar, founded the DMK party in 1949 as regional party in the State of Tamil Nadu and Puducherry. Having roots to the South Indian Liberation Federation, DMK became first party to win state election with clear majority apart from Indian National Congress. Since 1969, DMK is headed by M. Karunanidhi till his demise in 2018.
15. ADMK was founded by M.G. Ramachandran (known as MGR, a film star) as a regional party in the state of Tamil Nadu and Puducherry in 1972. The party is an offshoot of DMK led by M. Karunanidhi (then CM of Tamil Nadu). As a Dravidian party, the party also became the first non-Congress Party to be part of Union Cabinet. The party was headed by J. Jayalalithaa from 1989 to 2016. The party's agendas mainly focuses on the downtroddens and destitute sections of society.
16. Lalu Prasad Yadav founded the political party, 'Rashtriya Janata Dal (RJD)' in 1997 after ending his ties from JD (United). The party borrowed the ideological approach from its parent organisation, the socialist democratic, and basic tenets as mobilisation of lower-caste Hindus and Muslim minorities. RJD in early elections lost its hold to parent organisations but in later years with coalition politics came into power by forming alliance with Congress Party and Rabri Devi as its own Chief Minister. The RJD's misrule in Bihar weakened the structure of the party and also loosened the ties with its coalitions, i.e. Congress Party (D'Souza 2014: Rashtriya Janata Dal).
17. Janata Dal (United), a regional political party (with an ideology of socialism, secularism, democracy along with the equality approach of mobilising lower-caste Hindus, and Muslim

minorities of east Indian states like Bihar and Jharkhand. The party also has its active involvement in national politics in central government) was founded in 1977 by V.P. Singh and emerged as an coalitions of many small political groups in opposition of Indira Gandhi's rule (Congress Party). The coalition did not last long as the party splits into many other regional parties such Nitish Kumar's Samata party in 1994 followed by Lalu Prasad Yadav's Rashtriya Janata Dal (RJD) in 1997. In 1999, the coalition with BJP led JD (United) further in to split and formation of new party as Janata Dal (Secular) led by H.D. Deve Gowda. The JD(S) remained confined to coalition politics so far but the radical shifts in its populist approach as pro-farmer measures waiving all loans to farmers, fisherman, artisans, and weavers established its majority in the 2008 state elections (D'Souza 2014: Janata Dal 'United').

18. BJD was formed by Naveen Patnaik in 1977 and named after Bijayananda (Biju) Patnaik, a prominent politician and former CM of Odhisha. The party principles and values consists of secularism, and unity in diversity. The party put its faith on achieving good governance through transparency and accountability. The party emerged as a consistent opponent of Indian National Congress and once allied with BJP but broke the alliance on dispute over issue of secularism. Naveen Patnaik as a leader of the party governed the state five times as Chief Minister from 2000 to present.
19. Mamta Benerjee as AITC's founder and leader, formed her own party registered as 'Trinamool Congress' party in 1999. Emerged as a regional party, Election Commission of India recognised the party as a National Party. The party mostly covers the north-eastern states as West Bengal, Manipur, Tripura, and also Kerala.
20. A regional political party of Andhra Pradesh, formed by Y.S. Jaganmohan Reddy after the split from Indian National Congress in 2011. The party didn't succeeded in initial stage but later emerged an alternative and swept the 2019 Andhra Assembly election and 2019 general elections. The party won 151 seats out of 175 seats in the state elections and 22 seats out of 25 seats in parliamentary elections.
21. Shiv Sena (means Army of Lord Shiva), a regional political party with its mass bases in the state of Maharashtra. The party was formed by cartoonist Balasaheb Thackeray in 1966. The party is headed by Udhav Thackeray since 2012 after the demise of

Balasaheb Thackeray and also serving currently as CM. The party is known for its fascist and extremist political ideology with party logo of 'Bow and Arrow.'

22. The BSP, founded by Kashi Ram (a Dalit, and Civil Service worker) in 1984 and succeeded by Kumari Mayawati in 2003. With no specific ideology of its own, the party's tenets mainly focus on the justice for the downtrodden (SCs, STs, & OBCs). The BSP claims to uphold the constitutional rights of the minorities. The coalition with Samajwadi (Socialist) Party (SP) in 1993 for the governance of Uttar Pradesh brought the success for the BSP, but in 1995 BSP left the coalition and with support of BJP, Mayawati became the Chief Minister. But the narrow ideological approach restricted the expansion of the party. In 2007 election, the radical shift in the party by embracing all communities' rather only minorities (appointing General Secretary from Brahman caste) helped BSP to achieve a majority win with full five year term of governance (D'Souza 2016).
23. In a rally in Assam Guwahati on February 4, Mr. Modi referred to Rahul Gandhi a Congress leaders comments that people will beat Mr. Modi with sticks for not providing them jobs. In response to that PM Modi said, 'sometimes people talk of hitting with a stick; but nothing can harm Modi, as he has a protective shield in the form of huge blessings from mothers and sisters' ("Narendra Modi Text Speech" 2020, February 07).
24. Dasgupta cited by Nair (2009), asserts that 'the debate within the BJP was never about its ties with the RSS, but about the extent to which it should enjoy 'functional autonomy.'
25. Bal Gangadhar Tilak was one of the leading lights of the movement which was sweeping across western India and was credited with bringing ritualistic religious practices into public domain. He began the practice of holding Ganapati festivals in civic venues which united Hindus across the spectrum on a common religious cultural platform... (Mukhopadhyay 2019: 57-58).
26. From the 1920s to 1980s, the Patels (a dominant caste of Gujarat), supported, rallied, and remained around the Congress party. But Congress CM Madhav Singh Solanki's pro-other Backward Classes (OBCs) reservation policy made them shift to the Bharatiya Janata Party (BJP). But after local elections in 2015 onwards, the Patels of rural areas turned back to Congress. The reason being told that BJP despite in ruling position for more

than two decades not including Patels caste on the reservation list under the category of OBC. Patels said that the talks with government has failed and now their demand is to scrap the entire system of reservation or by replacing it with reservation based on the grounds of economic and educational backwardness. But as government took the position by declaring that reservations cannot be expand beyond the point. As a result of that, Patel leaders organised a state-wide protest which mobilised half a million people in 2015. (Jaffrelot 2016: 218-232).

27. Along with civilizational symbols, the packaging also include virtues like devotion to his nation and its people, fighting spirit, global leader, commitment to Sabka Sath and Sabka Vikas be it a worker, farmer, young and old, lower and upper caste, and especially those in between his eagerness. To end corruption in governance through technology and strengthening the state apparatus particularly police and army maintain peace and harmony.
28. The Citizenship Amendment Bill became an act on December 12, 2019.
29. Changes in citizenship practices are imbricated in the politics of place-making, deep cartographic anxieties associated with the delineation of the national space, the assertion of specific ethno-spaces, and the exclusive membership that modern state prescribes (Roy 2010: 11).

2
Governance for the Margins: Tensions and Faultlines

Introduction

Governance crisis is all-inclusive. It is reflected in the economy, the practice of democracy, diversity insensitivity and the 'crumbling social value system'. The harmonisation of the economic, social and cultural dimensions with equity and distributive justice depends largely on the ideological and political persuasions. The dynamics of the market and growth processes on their own cannot moderate the widening disparities. Similarly, fiscal management policy interventions on their own are not equipped to make development inclusive, governance citizen-centric and population productive. The interactive relationship between the civil society, the market and the State has always been blurred and negotiated. It is the State which has to reinvent itself to harmonise this relationship and moderate the impact of the market on society.

The interactive relationships, through the prism of ideological persuasion, smudge and reveal the emerging fault lines simultaneously. As politics has a primacy to determine which are the fault lines to be negotiated to provide sustenance to legitimate governance. For instance, international and inter-regional comparisons are used to maintain a power balance in favour of privatisation. The performance of the State on good governance is measured with reference to the capacity to subsume dissent on account of casualisation of labour, regulation of labour mobility and marginalisation of the small farmers and businesses (Sood 2016). The dissent is blurred using data on GDP (not in relation to the citizens' well-being), global ranking, on ease of doing business and linking it with national pride. In a public rally, the Prime Minister said, "India's GDP growth unprecedented with the five-year average of 7.5 per cent" ("Howdy, Modi! event" 2019). The main principles of 'good governance' in its pure form is the privatisation of public goods, including disinvestment of the public sector. The argument advanced is that the State-led mixed economy has been reduced to the pursuit of public good as interpreted by the self-seeking politicians and civil servants. In other words, the State abdicates its responsibility to provide a livelihood to the people on the margins.

To maintain power balance, the State has to move 'unbound seriality' to 'bound serialities' (Anderson 1998: 29-45). The creation of new social categories like, 'aspirational class' or including some sub-castes into the OBCs for addressing perceived commonalities irrespective of divergent social bases. The State articulates itself through political mobilisations to reach out to the conglomeration of groups cross-cutting social collectivities as targets of multiple policies shaping heterogeneous constructs. Very often, in this process, the State and the market are seen as dichotomous, providing visibility to the emerging contradictions. And, the politics excessively rely on blurring the contradictions by revealing mystified reality for the people; this varies as per the ideological persuasions of the political establishment. The reality is so mystified as to present the problems differently.

Each identified problem is located in the matrix of lesser problems, each of which is analysed as a separate module. For instance, if the school dropout rate is high, it may be addressed by providing midday meals rather than linking it with poverty or with the families without a regular source of livelihood. This kind of analysis precludes the structure of economy and politics, beyond examination and, hence, remains non-problematical.

It is argued that exclusion has to be checked, but, at the same time, the incentive for wealth generation must not be compromised. Hence, privatisation has been couched under the banner of the Public-Private Partnership (PPP). In this, public resources are leveraged for private profit. Subsidies are given to private hospitals, and the people are asked to mind their own health. People are told that nothing comes free, and are asked to pay for the life-saving services even if they do not have the opportunities to earn a livelihood. Besides it, they are told to participate in the self-help groups and launch small businesses in the face of intense global competition.

Having mystified the structural inequalities, the commonality of the experience of the citizens of their interaction with the State becomes consistent with the 'welfare of all' thrust of electoral mobilisations. The experience of exclusion has been made central to the political discourse, rather exclusion of the marginalised sections from the market and the dominant politics. The ruling class claim to address this as the common, universal and rational interest of all the members, appeared to be valid as it benefits all the members of society in one way or the other.

And, governance in the process, becomes restrictive to political articulations and administrative calculations. Politics choose different policies to create or strengthen their own political constituency, which continues to support the implementation of these 'inefficient policies'. As discussed earlier, for India's first Prime Minister Jawaharlal Nehru, it was social justice for all expressed through initiatives like land to the tiller which found continuity under Indira

Gandhi, expressed through the slogan, *'Garibi Hatao'* (poverty eradication). However, after the mid-1980s, the dominant political agenda shifted from justice for all to justice for the Backward Castes, Dalits and minorities. The policy of administrative fragmentation of population on the basis of caste and religion, within 'restrictive citizenship', has been the main thrust of the public policy. On the other hand, the slogan, *'Sabka Saath, Sabka Vikas, Sabka Vishwas'* (together with all, development for all, the trust of all) seeks to present the entitlements, rights and claims within the legal framework of the promise of equal citizenship and overlooks the existence of heterogeneity in the society. And, the politics located it in the 'majoritarian' cultural landscape.

The governance domain in response to continuous negotiations of the State with the civil society and the market transformed along with the shift from a mixed economy to a market economy; from secular nationalism to cultural nationalism and, from non-aligned to more integrated globalised systems. The scope of governance, therefore, has to be located in the politico-economic and cultural landscape. This will determine 'how power is distributed and shared, how policies are formulated, priorities set, and the stakeholders made accountable' ("Concept of Governance").

The selection of facts for prioritising interventions is a political decision. Jean Drèze has observed, "More importantly, whether or not something should be done involving value judgements, that no 'Randomised Control Trials' (RCT) or for that matter no evidence, can settle on its own" (Drèze 2019). For instance, the perpetrators of gender violence were differentially dealt with as per their social position. In a village called Fatehpur Kheri in Punjab, a man belonging to the lower caste took sexual advantage of a Jat Sikh girl. The village panchayat not only physically assaulted the boy, but his land was forcibly sold, and he was evicted from the village. In the second case, the upper caste boy violated the lower caste woman. The village panchayat let off the boy with a warning and the girl was reprimanded for inciting the young men. So, even though evidence of the sexual assault was there, yet the policy outcome was dictated by the socio-cultural context.

This poses a question as to how to select facts for prioritising interventions as the needs are heterogeneously rooted in diverse cultures. "The politics of heterogeneity can never claim to yield a general formula for all people at all times: its solutions are always strategic, contextual, historically specific and inevitably provisional" (Chatterjee 2004: 22).

The definitional imperatives of governance are expressed in the legal terms and the constitutional status of granting equal rights to the citizens and, accordingly, shaped the rights-based claims of equality before the law tends to produce homogeneous constructs.

For tardy delivery of the public services, an easy explanation that is offered is the prevalence of corruption, high transaction costs and lack of transparency. An interesting outcome is that even corruption has ceased to perform one of its foremost functions, i.e. facilitation and efficiency. This was exemplified during the preparation for the Commonwealth Games, wherein even large-scale corruption could not induce efficiency. This was substantiated by a field survey in Punjab in 2010, whereby eighty per cent of the respondents observed that there was rampant corruption and, out of these, thirty per cent mentioned that corruption had ceased to deliver. These respondents further affirmed that most of the government departments were corrupt, but despite the corruption, these departments were sluggish in delivery (Kumar 2011, From 'Introduction' to the Report, "Recommendations of the Punjab Governance"). The departments which have been perceived as most corrupt such as police and revenue, were also seen as the most inefficient. The departments of education, health, electricity, etc., were rated as corrupt but efficient (See Table 2.1, 2.2, and 2.3). This index is based on the perception of the beneficiaries, and it is fairly clear that the perception is an attributed value and may not be factually accurate. There are departments like excise, income tax, banks; the exchange is considered to be beneficial and legitimate. And, in line departments like Irrigation, Public Works Department (PWD), the exchange is online, standardised, and these are across board agreement on the norms of exchange. It is in the departments like the police, revenue, electricity and municipal corporations that the exchange is seen as arbitrary, unfairly regulatory and, hence, illegitimate.

Table 2.1 Department-wise Corruption Index in Punjab

Department	*Score*	*Most Corrupt*	*Rank*
Police	11746	58.32	1
Revenue	8872	44.05	2
Electricity	8430	41.86	3
Education	7469	37.09	4
Punsup/FCI	7416	36.82	5
Panchayat/MC	7187	35.69	6
Water	6956	34.54	7
Health	6802	33.77	8
Irrigation	6626	32.90	9
Veterinary	6272	31.14	10
Agriculture	6097	30.27	11
Banks	5744	28.52	12

Table 2.2 Department-wise Corruption and Efficiency Ranks in Punjab

Department	*Score*	*Corrupt & Efficient*	*Rank*
Electricity	7358.00	36.53	1
Health	7316.00	36.33	2
Education	7199.00	35.74	3
Banks	6989.00	34.70	4
Irrigation	6888.00	34.20	5
Veterinary	6798.00	33.75	6
Water and Sanitation	6644.00	32.99	7
Panchayat/MC	6382.00	31.69	8
Agriculture	6367.00	31.61	9
Revenue	6300.00	31.28	10
Police	6230.00	30.93	11
Punsup/FCI	5861.00	29.10	12

Table 2.3 Department-wise Corruption and Inefficiency Ranks in Punjab

Department	*Score*	*Corrupt But Inefficient*	*Rank*
Police	7018.00	34.85	1
Punsup/FCI	6634.00	32.94	2
Electricity	6424.00	31.90	3
Water and Sanitation	6006.00	29.82	4
Panchayat/MC	5955.00	29.57	5
Irrigation	5590.00	27.76	6
Health	5543.00	27.52	7
Agriculture	5514.00	27.38	8
Veterinary	5175.00	25.70	9
Revenue	5123.00	25.44	10
Education	5084.00	25.24	11
Banks	4515.00	22.42	12

Source: IDC Survey, 2010.

Corruption as an ideological plank cannot be the core of politics. And, honesty cannot be marketed as a supreme value. In fact, the bedrock of human interaction is honesty; otherwise, no exchange or dialogue will have a future. It is essential that everybody has to be honest. Marketing of honesty not only saps the revolutionary urges of human beings and legitimises the unequal status quo, but also becomes a currency for retrogression. The problem with the governance is that the rules have been overtly violated and the system has been rendered non-functional.

Governance? For whom and for what? This legitimate question normally gets lost in the processes, procedures and the application of technology. To illustrate, the application of unique ID numbers, no doubt, shall provide efficiency, but only to the existing process of undignified and exploitative exchange between the citizens and the government. These rules of exchange in many spheres do not protect the rights and the entitlements of the people on the margins besides treating a fairly large section of the citizenry in an undignified manner (Kumar 2010, From 'Introduction' to the Report).

Challenges

Colonial Non-Faith Citizen-Government Exchange

Historically, governance has been a prisoner of the colonial non-faith citizen-government exchange. And, the relationship between the State and the nation acquired meaning in the background of the national freedom movement and post-colonial context. The interaction of the State and the nation (*Awam*) continued to remain divergent, even antagonistic, in terms of their manifest forms of assertion for claims, entitlements and rights. And, it is reflected in more than one way. Most of the time, the expression of frustration is directed at the symbols of the State. This divergence is more structural than behavioural.

The institutions, norms and procedures continued to function as colonial constructs, causing a visible disconnect between the people and the State. The political and constitutional changes could not transform the activised nation into a participating civil society, virtually keeping all the existing social institutions outside the State-civil society interactive frame. And, at the same time, the State conferred citizenship on the colonial subjects in a formal sense, but its substance in many ways provided continuity to some of the retrograde colonial practices.

In other words, the substance of citizenship is related to the evolution of the State. The post-colonial State continued to rely on the processes and procedures which are 'extractive', treating the citizens as colonial subjects and nurtured the social institutions of caste, religion, ethnicity, etc., as exclusive categories. The perpetuation of these practices made the whole conception of citizenship as 'deficient' (Kumar 2010, From 'Introduction' to the Report).

> In many cases, classificatory criteria used by the colonial governmental regimes continued into the postcolonial era, shaping the forms of both political demands and development policy. Thus, caste and religion in India, ethnic groups in Southeast Asia, and the tribes in Africa remained the dominant criteria for identifying communities among the populations as objects of policy (Chatterjee 2004: 37).

In this, the populations were treated as targets of 'multiple policies producing heterogeneous constructs of social life'. The classifications and enumerations for the purpose of welfare administration used as tools to draw legitimacy for the political regimes. This, in a way, has, to use Michel Foucault's term, 'Govermentalisation of the State' (Foucault 1991). In other words, it produces a tension between the citizens and the population identified on the basis of unidimensional characteristics like Scheduled Caste or not Scheduled Caste, Hindu or not Hindu, Muslim or not Muslim, Hindi-speaking or not Hindi-speaking, etc. Anderson (1998: 29-45) described it as bound seriality of the governmentality. And, these 'are constricting and perhaps inherently conflictual. They produce the tool of ethnic politics' (Chatterjee 2004: 6). For instance, equality of the citizens is a Constitutional fact, but the 'unbound seriality' mark myriad factors of ethnicity, caste, gender, etc., that are imbued with social differences and hierarchies.

These myriad differences of ethnicity, region, caste, gender, language and hierarchies place some citizens unfavourably compared to the others. To presume that the prism of equality sees no differences may, in fact, discriminate against the Dalits, minorities and other vulnerable groups. For instance, if the policy of gender equality treats both male and female on parity, then the special needs of women, for instance, privacy to report bodily violence like rape or molestation, would not be included as part of a neutral initiative to treat each citizen alike. A homogeneous language, personal laws or cultural practices, etc., tend to elect one choice (generally of the dominant group) while denying others of their socially constructed reality. Not only this, but the recognition of difference also may not be able to prioritise what difference or whose difference needs to be accorded primacy. Do the institutions have parameters on the basis of which one group's differences stand higher in the hierarchy over others? This arises from a conflict between the rights of the collectivities or the individual rights that come into conflict with the collectivity rights.

In the post-colonial societies, the policy choices provided continuity to the 'ethnographic State' with their excessive reliance on the enumerative technology of the census. "If the ethnographic survey announced the pre-eminence of caste for colonial sociology, it was the decennial census that played the most important role not only in providing the 'fact', but also installing caste as the fundamental unit of India's social structures" (Dirks 2001: 49). To illustrate, in each regional context, the caste dynamics are heavily influenced by the formation of distinct institutions. "These forms have acquired multi-dimensional articulations ranging from cultural adaptations to evolving parallelism in terms of cultural forms and nurturing exclusive sites to bargain for equitable representation—to resistance against violation of icons of group honour and use of symbols, language, rituals to reinforce or question purity-pollution paradigm" (Kumar and Dagar 2004: 274-296). In this context, policies were framed, locating in the given social structure and institutions. The perpetuation of the 'extractive institutions' provided continuity to the whole conception of citizenship as 'deficient'.

As has been established in the literature, the boundaries of citizenship are dynamic in nature and evolve historically. At the same time, it is not to overlook the fact that it is inherent in the nature of the State to interact with the citizens as subjects. But, a crucial distinction to be noted is that freedom and autonomy conferred on the citizens vary from the colonial subjects to the subjects in democratic and egalitarian societies (Kumar 2010, From 'Introduction' to the Report).

It is important, moreover, to explore these various strands in their specific historical contexts bearing in mind, however, that at each historical moment, the earlier strands coexist, keeping alive the tensions and uncertainties over the form and context of citizenship (Roy 2010: 13). And, this largely functioned within the domain of politics. Notwithstanding these variations, the social reality being heterogeneous and seeking contextual and historical specific solutions produces tension by being constantly counterpoised to constitutional and legal parameters of equal citizenship rights.

The post-colonial State has failed to transform the status

of the people from the colonial subjects to the citizens. It has been very aptly described by Nicholas Dirks when he termed the colonial States as ethnographic States. 'The ethnographic State was driven by the belief that India could be ruled using anthropological knowledge to understand and control its subjects and to represent and legitimize its own mission' (Dirks 2001: 44). In other words, the States do not seek the participation of the citizens in decision making but claim to provide for the welfare of the population (Kumar 2009, From 'Introduction' to the Report). The foremost ingredient of this has been mistrust in the subjects or populace. It can be exemplified in several ways, but the most visible is the filing of affidavits for almost every interaction with the government.

These affidavits are required in support of the facts given by the applicants for various services provided by the government. In other words, these are affirmations by the applicants, in some cases, supported by the third parties (Kumar 2011). In most of the cases, these affidavits are given on legal papers sworn before a Magistrate or public notary. For instance, affidavits are required even for availing public utilities, such as new connections for electricity, sewerage and water supply. Besides adding to the citizen's harassment and corruption, it has perpetuated the dichotomy between the State and the nation (Kumar 2009, From 'Introduction' to the Report).

Fragmentation of Population: Hoping for Inclusive Outcomes

Further, the administrative fragmentation of the population is not diversity-sensitive and, instead, produces tensions and reinforces social cleavages. To illustrate, in the 1980s, the Punjab Government initiated a programme to empower the women's groups to facilitate the education of the girl child. A scheme was introduced to advance the seed money to the Mahila Mandals (women's groups) to build assets for the generation of income like utensils, 'shamianas'. The objective was that the residents of the village could rent these for the celebration of the festivals, events and host of other functions, and the returns on this investment could be used to empower the girl children. However, in some of the villages, the Dalits were denied access to these assets because of their low caste status. Consequently, the Dalit women set up their own separate Mahila Mandals to cater to their needs. This initiative activised the dormant social cleavages. A good administrative initiative became the victim of lack of diversity-sensitivity (Kumar 2009, From 'Introduction' to the Report). As Deaton and Cartwright (2018) very aptly described, "What works is not equivalent to what should be." While it was hoped that the scheme would empower the women, but that it will also sharpen the caste cleavages in a particular context that could not be captured as the caste cleavages are not so patently visible in Punjab.

A major casualty of this is citizen-centric democratic governance. If the citizens are treated as population and as a target of governance, the democratic processes become redundant, and the citizens' backlash is built up (Kumar 2009, From 'Introduction' to the Report). In 2002, in Ludhiana and Nawanshahr, a system of tracking the pregnant women for stopping them from seeking sex selection tests to abort the female foetus had been introduced. It included registration of all the pregnant women across the private clinics and the government health centres, tracking through visits by the health workers, software for monitoring the ultrasound database under the supervision of the civil surgeon's office under the broad cover of the PNDT Act. As that was violative of the privacy of the citizens and the negation of the preference change mechanism through the transformation of consciousness, it activated social discord in the neighbourhood and provided a license to those who treat women as commodities. The assumption in both cases was that the cultural practices are delinked from the social and material conditions of existence and can be erased with authoritarian governance. Can human life ever be secured by undermining the dignity of the citizens and imposing enforcement mechanisms that violate the very principle of human rights or by creating conducive conditions to evolve and protect human life chances?

Similarly, the Indian Penal Code was conceived by the British to keep the colonial subjects under their control. The IPC proved to be a lethal instrument in the hands of the colonial State for perpetrating repression. It has several repressive laws. For instance, the law of sedition. It is not only sedition laws, but many sections contained in the IPC that are repressive. And the question is, why did the post-colonial State continue to retain these repressive laws? In the words of Meghnad Desai:

> When they (the Indian ruling class) had the chance, they not only retained just the IPC, but the entire collection of laws of repression installed by the British. The rulers may have changed colour, but their suspicion of the mob has not gone... The mob has to be ruled with an iron rod. (Desai 2019)[1].

It was included in the IPC in 1870 as Section 124A. This provision was used against the great freedom fighters like Bal Gangadhar Tilak in 1897, Mahatma Gandhi, Bhagat Singh and many others. It reads, "Whoever by words, either spoken or written or by signs or by visible representations or otherwise, brings or attempts to bring into hatred or contempt or excites or attempts to excite dissatisfaction towards the government established by law in India, shall be punished for sedition" (Section 124A, Indian Penal Code). Even after independence, this law has been extensively used. For instance, in 2019, a Bihar Court directed the filing of an FIR under Section 124A against 49 eminent persons who had expressed their concern on the incidences of lynching in a letter to the Prime Minister (Pandey 2019). Similarly, in 2012, the protesters voicing their protest against the nuclear power plant in Kudankulam were charged for sedition (Janardhanan 2016). In the same year, cartoonist Aseem Trivedi was booked for sedition (Burke 2012). In 2014, the students supporting the Pakistan cricket match in Meerut, the Adivasis of Jharkhand resisting their displacement, the students protesting in Jawaharlal Nehru University, Delhi were charged under the sedition law.

Role Misappropriation and Competitive Institutionalism

Another area of tension due to the 'governmentalisation' of the State is regarding the allocation of roles to the various institutions. The administration happens to be compartmentalised in various departments, and each department has its own priorities. If a particular department's priorities take precedence over the other, that is likely to lead to dissonance within the system. There is no dearth of examples to demonstrate this point.

As mentioned earlier, in 2004-05, in India, a number of the States in their overactive commitment to impose fiscal management came out with a scheme to contract untrained 'teachers' from the same village to cut the government expenditure. As a result, the quality of teaching further deteriorated and, later, all the contractual 'teachers' launched a protest and demanded that they should be trained as teachers and that their services be regularised (Kumar 2011 "Correcting Distortions"). These policy prescriptions, no doubt, have to be commensurate with the vision and values adhered to by the political leadership but at the same time these should be in consonance with the citizen's needs; otherwise, they may turn out to be counterproductive. This scheme was spearheaded by the need for fiscal management framework rather than access to equity concerns in quality education. As a result, the inability to maintain the delicate functional balance between the institutions produced a major crisis in governance.

To further illustrate, in the 1980s in Punjab, when the political process produced a crisis, overactive administration armed itself with the Terrorist and Disruptive Activities (Prevention) Act (TADA). In view of the failure of the overactive administration to contain the crisis, the police were unleashed. When the police produced a bigger crisis, the judiciary was unleashed. These overactive institutions produced distortions equal or worse and also prevented the processes behind the distortions from coming to the surface. As such, it should be understood that if the civil administration becomes non-functional, the remedy is not to unleash the police. The remedy must be sought to make the same functional. For example, if there is a leakage in the revenue collection, the chemists are trading in illegal drugs, and the functionaries are indulging in corruption, the remedy should not be in stepping up the policing. It is possible that the revenues may increase, and so will the extortions (Kumar 2009, From 'Introduction' to the Report).

To illustrate, the sectorally segregated criminal justice delivery system is not only insensitive to the needs of the diversities but functions without accountability for the outcome. For example, the total complaints received by the police in the year 2015 were 1,68,25,687, and out of these, only 44 per cent were registered. It means around 56 per cent of the cases just got dropped. Out of the registered cases, only 37 per cent reached the investigation, and 33 per cent reached the courts (see Table 2.4). The focus is to address the problems leading to displaced accountability. It is organised and segregated in such a way that the registration of crime investigation and preparation of charge-sheeting are with the different departments of the police. The prosecution function is with the prosecution wing, and the disposal of the caseload is with the judiciary. These institutions have their corresponding parameters of performance within an enforcement-oriented framework. In other words, the investigation is an exclusive domain of policing, prosecution falls within the ambit of the Director Prosecution and Litigation, while the conviction trials remain with the courts. The whole process of delivery of justice is so split that each institution performs its own assigned role with no accountability towards the end result. This is the fundamental problem of the criminal justice system.

Table 2.4 Registration and Charge-Sheeting in India

Complaints Received 2015			
Total Complaints received	16825687		
Number of Cases Registered			
Total cases registered	7326099		
Percentage of cases registered	43.54		
Disposal and pendency of cases 2015	*IPC*	*SLL*	*Total*
Total number of cases for investigation 2015	2949400	4376699	7326099
Cases investigated	2107056	4085785	6192841
Percentage of cases investigated	71.44	93.35	84.53
Charge sheets were submitted	1510289	3998040	5508329
Percentage of cases in which charge-sheet given out of total cases investigated	71.68	97.85	88.95

Source: *Crime in India*, National Crime Records Bureau, 2015.

Note: Pending cases of previous year proportionately deducted from cases investigated and charge-sheeted in 2015.

For the police, the assumption is that the lower the reported crime rate (even if the occurrence of crime is high), the more efficient is the policing. For the prosecution and the courts, the measure is a high conviction rate even if the quality of the trial and justice dispensed remains poor.

Thus, "the deeper we delve into the processes of criminal justice and the more we rely on prosecution, court and prison statistics, the more we reduce our chances of saying anything straightforward about the nature and extent of crime" (Muncie 2001: 29).

Political Interference and Not Political Intervention

Interestingly, governance has become a prisoner of the administrative structure; any political statement is seen as interference. It remains interference since no structural transformation takes place so as to legitimise the space for political interventions. This political interference which has become an accepted part of the political culture has produced glaring distortions in the practice of governance, particularly in administrative recruitments, postings, transfers, allocation of works, service delivery, etc., leading to the dilution of hierarchy, dysfunctional internal accountability mechanisms and patronage-centric governance. For example, in Punjab, the average tenure in 2009 of the Station House Officer (SHO) was around six months, which was about seven months in 2004. In the case of the Deputy Superintendent, the same is ten months and one year for the District Police Chief. Political interference in the transfers and postings of the police officers at the cutting edge level has distorted the justice delivery (The World Bank 2004: 46).

What public policy prescriptions can be offered for the serious reflections about the political and ideological predisposition of those in power? For instance, to base the policy prescription on randomised control trials (RCT) aimed at examining, for instance, whether or not the reduction in time consumed in the contested land mutations will lead to efficient justice-delivery or reduction in the judicial workload of the civil administration? But, the most pertinent issue is to find an answer, how to do this? After deliberations, it was proposed to make certain amendments in the Punjab Revenue Act. The amendments primarily provided for (see Kumar 2011, From 'Introduction' to the Report):[2]

(i) In the case of mutations, the powers of Remand to be limited to the appellate authority.
(ii) The powers of revision for the mutation cases vested with FC were transferred to the Commissioners.
(iii) In the case of partition, appeals against the interim orders were barred for the issues of the mode of partition and the exact dimensions of property to be divided, etc. (see Annexure 2.1)

Nearly a year later, the government reverted to the status quo ante on the following grounds:

(a) Revision by the Financial Commissioner is necessary as the FC is the final arbiter for the revenue law and, as such, should continue to be the final authority.
(b) Remand powers may be necessary where the parties are not given a proper opportunity of being heard by the lower courts.
(c) Interim orders on the mode of partition, etc., may be made appealable, as these are important issues in the partition cases. (see Annexure 2.2)

The amendments regarding the mutations were proposed by PGRC keeping the following in view:

(a) Mutations do not confer the title, and the entry of the administrative process of mutation tends to get delayed indefinitely through the long channels of appeals/revision, thus, burdening all the parties with costs of money and time.
(b) Most of the contested cases which come to the FC for revision invariably get challenged in the High Court. Therefore, the revision is not an effective screening method for reducing the pendency of revenue disputes.

(c) The revision powers are mostly used for obtaining/giving stay and delaying implementation even of the genuine decisions indefinitely.

(d) There is minimal evidence of the problems faced due to the changes made, except to the parties (and lawyers) who are aggrieved and would like to delay the mutation entries as long as possible.

(e) There is little reason to believe that the senior officers at the District Collector/Commissioner level will be performing their duties dishonestly when we all talk of decentralisation, justice at the doorstep, and so on.

(f) The parties, in any case, can go to the civil courts and, in fact, they do. The only difference is that the new procedure would have saved several years of delay in the cases where the parties have to wait to exhaust all the revenue channels before they can approach the High Court/civil courts.

(g) The proposal of restricting the remand to the cases where the parties have not been heard properly is impractical as this can only be decided, once an opportunity is given to other parties to produce evidence, the case is fully heard and the lower authorities' view obtained. The rationale of the quasi-judicial hierarchy is that it should not function like a court and settle cases quickly. The provision of remand would defeat this objective, especially keeping in view the experience even of the officials that the remand is simply an instrument of delay; there is hardly any application of mind at the level of the appellate authority in the cases that are remanded—in other words, it is a casual way of disposing of the revenue cases but has unfortunately become almost customary. The restoration of the remand and revision powers to the Financial Commissioners will bring back the usual problems of long delays, stay not being vacated for years and, so on.

It means the perverse incentives, business interests and the land mafia felt threatened by the changes incorporated in pursuance to PGRC's recommendations. The higher revenue officials, advocates, judicial officers and the vested political interests came into play and, within a year, the old system was restored. To deal with such vested interests, merely showing evidence that it is in the public interest is not sufficient. 'Dealing with these choices, conflicts and dilemmas require much more than 'evidence'. "Quite often, public policy is flawed due to wrong priorities rather than lack of evidence" (Drèze 2019).

But, the damage caused to the system remain irreparable. The tendency to empower the institutions with ad hoc licenses has a clear message, i.e. killing the poison with poison and letting the patient die. This has made governance less a matter of politics, more of administrative policy and the discretionary political interference (Kumar 2011 "Correcting Distortions").

Tension Between State Politics and Populist Politics

Tension also persists in governance between what has been labelled as State politics, populist politics and people's politics. Those who govern and those who are governed in a collaborative arrangement became custodians of the State and shaped the terms of political discourse which can be termed as State politics. The people on the margins (constituting a large section of the voters in elections) shaped the electoral discourse which constitutes the core of populist politics. In this discourse, these people are reduced to beneficiaries, clients, recipients, victims, etc. This dichotomous relationship between State politics and populist politics has given rise to the 'dole giver—dole receiver' syndrome (Kumar 2009, From 'Introduction' to the Report).

In this political culture, the rights are given as doles to the poor, and the doles are presented as rights to the privileged. For instance, subsidies to enhance the productivity of the poor are given as doles. These doles are packaged as the spoils to be shared between the dole-giver and the dole-receiver. To illustrate: in the section on Social Security and Welfare Programmes, it has been established as to how the social security programmes such as pensions and *shagun* are given as doles to a large section of the ineligible population. This has become a practice with successive governments (Kumar 2009 "Correcting Distortions"). Consequently, in Punjab State, it leads to wastage to the extent of about Rs. 220 crore and Rs. 40 crore in the case of old-age pension and shagun schemes, respectively (Kumar 2009, From 'Introduction' to the Report: 9). The need is to identify the deserving beneficiaries as also to ensure that its reach is periodically evaluated. In this process, the purpose to build productive capacity and enhance the productivity of the poor gets defeated. Instead of productive engagement of the citizen, a culture of sharing of the spoils is reinforced. And, it also results in denial of the conditions to avail opportunities.

Why are subsidies taken as synonymous with populism? Why are the welfare schemes directed at the poor branded as populist? Why are the political leaders who formulate pro-poor policies accused of being reckless with the State exchequer? Why are subsidies, if directed at the poor, termed as dole-outs? On the contrary, if the subsidies are directed to protect the profits, these are described as 'rescue' packages (Kumar 2010, From 'Introduction' to the Report).

The State has to cater to the needs of those who do not have the capacity to pay to remain in the business of governance and, hence, the doles. It has also to empower those who generate wealth which provides sustenance to those who control the levers of power.

Most importantly, the market only responds to the needs of

> those who have the capacity (or economic/political clout) to pay and not those who do not possess this capacity but need these services desperately. Furthermore, resources generated through sales of the public assets were not always used for development activities but, instead, were utilised either for servicing the accumulated debts (around programmes from which the poor rarely benefited) or poured into the State activities that were of little or marginal relevance to the socio-economic needs of the broader population (Khan 2005: 7).

The promise of politics is to create sufficient conditions and opportunities for the people to be productive rather than giving them subsidies as doles. In other words, inclusive growth cannot be reached by simply distributing the doles after the growth. In fact, the disadvantaged groups have to be empowered to participate in the growth process by having access to the assets, livelihood jobs and investment opportunities to make their survival competitive and equitable and the social existence without any discrimination.

The arguments highlighted above shaped two divergent kinds of discourse, one emanating from the shift in the path of development manifesting in, what has been termed as 'State politics', and another found articulation at the time of elections in the form of 'populist politics'.

The practice of democracy has a select domain restricted to those who govern and those who avail its governance. The two have entered into a collaborative relationship and emerged as the custodians of the State, shaping the terms of political discourse under the banner of 'State politics' (Kumar 2015). The people on the margins remain outside the realm of the democratic process even as per the practice there is need for doles for their survival that are provided by the electoral politics, which becomes their mainstay lending content to what is known as 'populist politics' (see Laclau 1997: 143).[3] It is a descriptive category, which addresses the common interests of the people with divergent social bases. It recognises the existence of multiple elements of the stages of development manifesting in the geographical regions—developed-underdeveloped and central-peripheral. It also responds to the rising expectations of an 'aspirational class' with an intense desire to have the representation in the State structure and market. In other words, populist politics creates a semblance of representation as synonymous with the presence of the citizens, diversities and regions in exclusion to their stake building in the State structure and market. And, populism emanates from the incapacity of the political leadership to provide a structural response to the survival needs and rising expectations of the masses. As a consequence, it is wrapped in ideology with a widespread emotional appeal. The outcome of this is that the ideological difference between the political parties gets blurred while the difference between the 'populist' and 'State politics' become more manifest. This has provided dominant space in the mainstream politics to a coalition of interests in negation to the participation of the citizens, diversities and regions in democratic governance. The politics of presence overtakes the politics of representation (see Hasan 2006).[4]

And, these privileged sections become the custodians of the State and, not only appropriate their claims and even rights as the citizens (which are denied to others) but misappropriate privileges and power. But, intense explorations with the cross-sections of the people has uncovered certain commonalities in their experience of interactions with the State. These commonalities may not constitute the organisation of their collective life, but it reflects the way people connect with the State. Broadly, irrespective of their social positioning—these are values of identity, dignity and productivity. The narratives uncover how the people associate themselves with the State through these values. But, non-realisation of the values like identity, dignity and productivity for a large section of the population results in an experience exclusion. In this sense, they remain 'deficient citizens' (Kumar 2010, From 'Introduction' to the Report). There is a denial of 'personhood' across the board to the citizens, as the colonial construct reinforces the demand for what Hannah Arendt termed as 'the right to have rights' (see Arendt 1986: 296-97).[5] The prerequisite right is based on the realisation of values like identity, dignity and productivity, which in turn, creates a conducive environment for availing of the other political, economic and social rights.

Having failed to moderate the structured inequalities, the common experience of the citizens, interaction with the State was captured to provide meaning to the political slogan, *Sabka Sath, Sabka Vikas* (together with all, development for all). The commonality of the deficient experience across board became the thrust consistent with the welfare of all the electoral mobilisations that appeared to be. This experience has been made central to the political discourse and the exclusions discussed above.

This section deals with the deficiencies as an outcome of these interactions and the reforms proposed and implemented by the government. These were proposed by the Punjab Governance Reforms Commission (PGRC) 2009 to 2017.

Boundary Conditions for Engaged Governance

Trust Deficit

First and foremost the initiative is to be taken to restore the identity of the citizens. Even after seventy years of Independence, the citizens have to prove their identity. The post-colonial State has failed to change the 'restrictive citizenship' to full citizenship. Hence, a major ingredient of the 'restrictive citizenship' is the mistrust. That has been institutionalised to the extent that, even to prove their name, they have to seek affirmation from a gazetted officer of the government. For declarations relating to their profession, income, caste, residential proof, etc., affidavits have to be given on legal papers sworn before a Magistrate or public notary. Even to procure the ration cards, electricity, sewerage and water connection, birth and death certificates, applications for admission to the educational institutions, affidavits attested by the gazetted officer or third party or public notary, or Magistrate have to be produced (see Kumar 2009, From 'Introduction' to the Report).[6] The 'govern-mentality' continues to treat the citizens as colonial subjects. It is, however, interesting to note that most of these affidavits are local inventions and are not required by the law. On the contrary, there are legal provisions for imposing punishment on the citizens for making wrong declarations. For instance, Section 199 of the IPC stipulates that:

> Whoever, in any declaration made or subscribed by him, which declaration any Court of Justice, or any public servant or other person, is bound or authorised by law to receive as evidence of any fact, makes any statement which is false, and which he either knows or believes to be false or does not believe to be true, touching any point material to the object for which the declaration is made or used, shall be punished in the same manner as if he gave false evidence.

And, Section 200 states that:

> Whoever corruptly uses or attempts to use as true any such declaration, knowing the same to be false in any material point, shall be punished in the same manner as if he gave false evidence.

But, 'govern-mentality' of mistrust has resisted any attempt on the part of the governments from reposing any trust in its own citizens by accepting self-declarations as reliable and authentic. It is, therefore, urgent to discontinue the practice of attestations by the third parties and replace the same with self-declarations as a step towards bridging the dichotomy between the State and the nation (Kumar 2010, From 'Introduction' to the Report).

Further, the administrative fragmentation of the population based on caste and religion, within 'restrictive citizenship' has multiplied social cleavages and led to the denial of full citizenship. The decision to conduct a caste-based census is a sign of diversity insensitivity that will only produce fractured identity as a citizen. And, the government's oft-proclaimed inclusive growth will become a prisoner to the exclusive social categories.

The power dynamics has also created a class in possession of the red beacons and security guards as a status symbol with exclusive identity. To illustrate, as the threat of terrorism in Punjab is decreasing in the case of individuals and, is on the increase in so far as the mass of the people and public spaces are concerned, the number of the individual protectees is multiplying. This clearly shows that the security cover has become a status symbol for the power holders and denial of this to the large public depicts a built-in contempt and indifference for the security of the common citizens (Kumar 2010, From 'Introduction' to the Report).

Dignity Deficit

Absence of citizenship status is reflected in everyday interactions of the people with the government and is characterised by the lack of respect and dignity. 'The understanding of citizenship, therefore, needs to be conceptually grounded, keeping in mind the principles of universalisation and those of the dignity of the individual' (Gupta 1999: 2313). To illustrate, it was observed that the citizens value their dignity over and above efficiency, and the same was exemplified by referring to their exchange with the police, revenue and district collector's office that was undignified and corrupt. On the other hand, the exchange with the personnel dealing with health, education, bank and electricity board was termed as dignified, even though corrupt. The citizens appeared to prefer the latter.

Table 2.5 Nature of Exchange Between Citizens and Administration

Exchange Undignified and Corrupt	
Police	58.32
Revenue	44.05
District Collector	41.86
Exchange Corrupt But 'Dignified'	
Electricity Board	36.53
Health	36.33
Education	35.74
Bank	34.70
Irrigation	34.20
Animal Husbandry	33.75

Source: IDC Survey, 2014.

This was more pronounced in the case of the police (58 per cent), revenue department (44 per cent) and district collector's office (41 per cent). The departments like electricity board, health, education, irrigation and veterinary services, were considered corrupt but dignified by one-third of the respondents. In terms of their choice between dignity preservation and monetary loss, they opted for dignity preservation. The monetary exchange was seen as a moral binding on the person responsible for the delivery of service. This is a kind of ethical fallacy. It was believed that monetary (perverse) incentive would be morally binding to deliver the service. So, they preferred dignity preservation over the monetary loss. In other words, material loss is seen as compensation for the dignity gain. A prerequisite condition to claim rights and entitlements as a citizen is to be treated with dignity as a human being. The narrative of the people, irrespective of their caste, religion and social status, uncovers a strong feeling of the loss of the dignity in their interactions with the government, particularly, the police, revenue collection agencies, and district administration. In addition to this, the accentuated perception of the loss of dignity is narrated by the marginalised groups like Dalits, women, minorities, etc., in the context of the structural need for recognition and respect for them as human beings (Kumar 2010, From 'Introduction' to the Report).

However, there are different forms of indignities which are experienced by the people in their everyday interaction with the government. These forms are rooted in the cultural domains in which various institutions have evolved and nurtured. These indignities range from the denial of 'personhood' to coercive extraction of material wealth.

The spatial disconnect experienced by the citizens in the police stations, in particular, and District Collectorates in general, is more pronounced. The visit to these spaces gives a feeling of being in an alien place and a sense of loss of dignity and identity. And, interactions with the police with consequent loss of dignity has been described succinctly in the Fifth Report of the National Police Commission (November 1980). The Commission expressed anguish that the 1902 Fraser Commission's observation that the 'people' now may not dread the police, but they certainly dread getting involved with it in any capacity, continues to be valid. It is, therefore, not surprising that the quote of Sir Phillip Chetwode is displayed in some of the police stations stating that: The safety, honour and welfare of your country come first, always and every time. The honour, welfare and comfort of the men you command, comes next. Your own ease, comfort and safety come last, always and every time (Kumar 2010, From 'Introduction' to the Report).

In this pronouncement, the claim to justice for the community and their right to dignity is not the core of policing. This notion has been integral to even the current police practices that regarded enforcement backed by force as the only appropriate mode to deal with the people. And, the people also avoid the police as they are apprehensive and consider messing up with the police as undignified. 'Their (people) general strategy of survival perfected over generations of experience, is to stay away from any entanglement with the government and its procedures' (Chatterjee 2004: 6).

Productivity Deficit

A third set of the prerequisites relates to the productivity, i.e. to engage the people with the system in a productive manner and provide conducive conditions to nurture the people's capacity to be productive and their ability to exercise some degree of control over their lives. In the post-colonial State, the *Riaya-Mai-Baap* (see Sharma 2008: 131)[7] political culture has been institutionalised to engage the people with the State.

The meaning of citizenship in post-colonial societies remains ambivalent or extremely vague. However, there are certain 'practical values' which have come to be associated with the idea of citizenship. In this sense, there are two sets of values through which the people connect as citizens with the State, i.e. the value of welfare as reflected in the dole-giver and dole-receiver interaction and, second is the value of political power and material wealth. The value of power position and possession of the material wealth enables them to realise their claims. The value of hierarchical power position and material wealth builds a collaborative arrangement between those who govern and those who are governed which has been rightly phrased by David Korten, as 'coalition of indifference' (Korten and

Alfonso 1983: 32).

> For example, in many developing countries, where the predominant need in the health sector is for preventive public health measures (this is what the poor, especially, the rural poor need), quite frequently, the bulk of the resources are allocated to curative health measures (this is what the rich and the advantaged who also constitute the ruling elite, need). In other words, the government responds to the most politically able segments of its 'market' (Khan 2005: 7).

These prerequisites have not been directly addressed in the discourse on the citizens' interaction with the State. It is precisely because of this that the restrictive citizenship has resulted in non-realisation of the entitlements as rights, particularly, for the excluded groups (Kumar 2010, From 'Introduction' to the Report).

Building Partnership: Challenges and the Way Out

The fourth boundary condition is to transform the patron-client relationship between the political class—the public servants and the citizens as Deaton affirms that "without effective States working with active and involved citizens, there is a little chance for the growth that is needed to abolish global poverty" (Khera 2015). The democratic governance necessitates that mere representation and participation have to be extended to active engagement with the decision-making processes within the framework of right based governance.

Nevertheless, the basic principles of 'Engaged Governance', i.e. trust, dignity, productivity and the citizens' engagement and E-governance, i.e. transparency, accountability and efficiency have to be harmonised. And, these have to be made integral to the designed architecture of each service delivery module. They have to be made pro-people by cutting their practical costs, including multiple visits, opportunity costs, fees, which in certain contexts, may be more relevant than even the corruption. The factors like information deficit, absence of transparency, access to grievance redressal mechanisms and greater control (more reports and verifications) to check misuse, may make the process cumbersome and corruptible. The competition to have access to the services coupled with the citizen's engagement may act as a check on the distortions in the service-delivery.

The application of technology must not be at the expense of the citizen's engagement. It can be used to reduce discretion and bring efficiency in the delivery of the services. There can be a two-pronged strategy—(a) to reduce discretion in delivery; (b) to transfer discretionary powers from the gazetted officers to the functionaries at the grassroots level.

Therefore, the use of technology, decentralisation of power and the nature of the citizen's engagement may vary from service to service. In other words, the citizen's engagement with the officials has to be located in the policy regime, market demand and political context.

These can be broadly categorised in three groups.

Supply-Side Service-Delivery Architecture

The supply-side service-delivery architecture has to cater to the needs of the citizens. This will include prerequisites for availing the services, regulatory conditions for compliance and, the public-oriented services.

Need-Based Demand Driven Services

For harassment-free delivery of the services, the citizen has to be enabled with certain documents for having easy access to availing the living services. For example, Scheduled Castes certificate, income certificate, domicile certificate, etc., are enabling services. The services are necessary to avail benefits under various schemes like scholarships for education, loans or subsidies for setting up a business, old age benefits like pension, free travel, higher return on investments, etc. These services are necessary preconditions for claiming rights, benefits and entitlements. These are one-off transactions to establish the eligibility for availing of the benefits for the ease of living, having access to opportunities and to establish their identity. These services are demand-driven without any limitation or quota of supply and are not subject to the competing pressures, the possibility of exclusion and discrimination. In these services, equity and economic efficiency are not the core consideration. The risk of misuse and corrupt practices is moderate as it involves competition with multiple barriers.

'Need-Based' Supply-Driven Services

These services are not demand-driven but are conceived for the larger public good. They are essential keeping in view the scarcity of resources, public order and safety, social harmony and sustainable development. These services flow from public policy regulations, which include the building plans, electricity, water, sewerage connections, driving license, pollution certificates, etc. Such services involve high transaction costs, consumer surplus, and at times, some perverse incentives as well: It requires a high degree of sense of preservation of common resources, sensitisation towards the rights of fellow beings and conservation of resources for future generations. It is in this framework that the self-regulation mechanism may have to be conceived, and the processes are redesigned. The best way to do it is to incentivise self-regulation. Otherwise, the citizens are liable to seek 'short cuts' to regulation compliance. For seeking compliance, exceptions have to be minimalistic, while everyone is eligible to have access to these services and facilities after fulfilling the necessary requirements (for example, the proof of ownership in the case of permission for construction). As these services involve high transaction costs and consumer surplus, they require transparent accountability of the officials and the introduction of checks on the perverse incentives.

Public Policy Regulatory Services

The public policy regulatory services are essential, but, they largely depend on the efficient implementation machine of the State. However, in case it is not implemented, that would involve a high degree of public risk and exchange of surplus between the regulations like prevention of food adulteration, quality education, sanitation, cleanliness, etc. Police service delivery involves high risks in terms of perverse advantages to the officials delivering, and individuals availing these services. The risk of non-compliance is high, making it lucrative for those who are assigned the task of delivering these services. These services are difficult to be outsourced for implementation as it involves high incentive to the agents responsible for the delivery of these services and high costs to the beneficiaries.

The post-colonial State continued to be regulatory and enforcement-oriented. The regulatory enforcement is, of course, guided by the outcome, but only with the processes. For instance, industrial and other commercial establishments may be equipped with the pollution control mechanisms, but may not operate the same. Similarly, the fire safety equipment in public and private structures is displayed and certified but remains largely non-functional. The officials responsible for the inspections to ensure compliance does not have the skill sets, but, of course, do have the perverse incentives to do their job. Inspections under the Electricity Act is yet another example.

The speed with which technological change is happening, for example, even a well-meaning Drug Inspector cannot keep pace with all the clauses of the GMP

(Good Manufacturing Practices) under the Drugs Control Act; these are difficult, if not impossible, to comply with. For instance, in the United States of America (USA), for "squashing down on illicit activity led to the seizure of synthetic drugs, such as methamphetamine, ketamine and mephedrone and that led to the addition of 348 psychoactive substances' ("Prohibition and Drugs" 2014). In so far as law enforcement is concerned, the compliance is fait accompli and gives leverage to the enforcement officials to extract some surplus. What we need is to give greater emphasis to prevent the occurrence of such violations in a manner that is laced with a curative approach.

The digital technology, complex exchange architecture, sophisticated equipment and advanced technology may not match with the prevailing skill set of the average regulators. For example, to issue the fitness certificate in the case of the latest car like BMW or Mercedes, boilers or hazardous machines, may be beyond the comprehension and knowledge of the regulators employed in the government. The knowledge will be certainly deficit as compared to the manufacturer or the supplier. In such cases, a routine clearance with a minimalistic number of simple requirements are violated—a 'default rule' for approval, rather than refusal.

The proclaimed purpose of the regulatory system is to achieve the citizens' well-being. The enforcement of regulations is guided by the principle of imposing penalties rather than to achieve positive outcomes. Both the enforcer and the citizen are playing a hide and seek game with each other. For instance, a police person hides behind the bushes to check the speed of the vehicles while the driver is always alert to prejudge these hideouts. In the case of a factory, the imposition of the rules relating to the spatial use, placement of equipment with an assumption that the factory owner is not interested in the well-being of his workers. Moreover, these may not be a constraint on the production of deficient goods. To illustrate, a drug factory equipped with modern gadgets can as easily (or probably even more easily) produce substandard drugs like any other. To inspect the premises before commissioning would not merely be a ritual and a function of the speed money.

The inspections have differential consequences depending on the scale of business. It has been observed that big business prefers these inspections as the costs are affordable without accountability. Whereas, the small business does not have resources to negotiate procedures and perverse demand of the regulators and are exposed to undue harassment.

The inspections or visits to ascertain the veracity of the claims brought in the colonial administration marked by distrust through the backdoor. These inspections are wasteful, except that they provide space for rent-seeking as the violations, if any, detected later can lead to cancellation of the licences, etc.

To operationalise these services and to meet the trust, dignity and productive deficits, the process may have to be redesigned. Public service is to be delivered as a contract rather than as a favour. For administrative purposes, each service has to be treated as a separate module involving varied levels of risks of (mis)use by the citizens and mis(use) of the discretion by the public officials. Moreover, each service may have a different clientele, structure of transactions, responsiveness, and equity. Therefore, a uniform model may not be feasible for all the services even within a specific category.

Parameters of the Citizen-Centric Governance

From Doles to Right-Based: Deficient Citizens to Full Citizens

The process of exchange between the State and the citizens

continues to be undignified and suffers from a trust deficit. It has not evolved to converge the State's welfare predisposition with the claims, entitlements and the basic rights and causes a visible disconnect. To transform the nature of the exchange between the citizens and the public functionaries from the patron-client or *Riaya-Mai-Baap* to public servant-citizen partnership, a number of Indian States have empowered the citizens through legislation so that their claims could be considered as a right. Above all, the citizens of independent India remained deficient as they were not trusted by the government. The citizens were denied access to key values, such as identity. To prove their identity, they have to get affidavits attested from the government officials. The Punjab Governance Commission in 2010 recommended that the government should abolish this practice (see Chapter 3, Case Study II). The government accepted this recommendation and issued an order dated March 10, 2010 abolishing this practice (See Annexure 2.3).[8] An affidavit, is thus an important prerequisite for most of the need-based services. Generally, affidavits require the stamp paper/stamp fee and need to be sworn before a Magistrate or a Notary Public (Kumar 2016, From 'Introduction' to the Report).

It was proposed that to recognise the identity, and repose trust in the citizen and also make them accountable for their claims and entitlements, the practice of self-declaration, self-certification and self-verification should be adopted. A self-certifying citizen is himself or herself the beneficiary of the wrong statement or facts. In the case of misuse, accountability can be fixed by itself, wherever or whenever detected or investigated.

Since each service has to be treated as a separate module, the implementation has to develop its own matrix. For example, the need-based demand-driven services, supply-driven services and public policy regulatory services have to evolve a layered implementation frame.

The need-based demand-driven services do not directly deliver the benefits and, hence, do not have higher consumer surplus. As a result, it has a low incentive for misuse. Therefore, self-certification and self-verification can be made applicable.

Whereas in supply-driven and public policy regulatory services, the perverse incentives to violate the procedures is high, and, hence, it may encourage the citizens to seek ad hoc solutions and shortcuts. The likelihood of public safety supply-side objectives getting compromised with private interests is high. In these cases, the self-certification has to be supplemented by the practice of third party citizen certification. This may be introduced as a substitute for the official verification, particularly for the documents having more risk of misuse (for example, SC certificates/OBC, etc., used for employment or admissions in the professional colleges). The consumer utility and prospect of gains are high; in such cases, self-certification can be supported by authentication/endorsement by the third parties—citizens. The system of citizen-friendly third-party verification can be adopted in place of verification by the public officials for issuance of SC/BC certificates, old-age pensions and other services of a similar nature but with a higher risk of misuse. The practice of verification by them, therefore, in any case, needs to be discontinued (see Kumar 2013).[9]

To change the 'coalition of indifference' to active stakeholding of the citizens in the delivery of justice and services is perhaps a major challenge. To illustrate, in independent India, the major disconnect, spatial or otherwise, is quite pervasive in the policing. The citizens feel that the police might 'detain, physically assault, insult and coerce' them even if they approach them to register their genuine complaints. This kind of perception, poor management practices, lack of accountability and transparency and often prejudiced response contributed to the underreporting of the crimes besides many other distortions.

To reverse this trend, a unique experiment in community policing at the level of the police stations was evolved by the Institute for Development and Communication in 2004 and was implemented by the Punjab Police in 2004, and in 2011 it was named SAANJH (partnership) to engage the citizens in the decision-making processes to delivery of police services (see Chapter 3, Case Study I). This experiment entails—(a) making the police directly accountable to the citizens; (b) institutionalisation of the community-police partnership through establishment of the police station outreach centres attached to each police station with the active participation of the citizens in the decision making; (c) activated institutional mechanisms to make the police stations responsive to the needs of the marginalised sections, such as Dalits, gender, and to the migrants, workers, children, etc.; (d) build the capacities of the police stations commensurate with the citizens' needs. To assess the efficacy of this experiment, a trend analysis using a difference in a different approach has been used. A proxy variable of the ratio between the registered heinous crimes with the petty crimes from 2005 to 2016 has been calculated to measure the confidence of the people in the policing. In this time series pattern, it was quite evident that the ratio of reporting of petty crime over the heinous crime (after the establishment of the SAANJH in 2011) has been increasing in the State of Punjab (see Table 2.6).

Table 2.6 Ratio of Petty Crimes Over Heinous Crimes in Punjab, 2005-16

Year	*Punjab*
2005	1.28
2006	1.30
2007	1.34
2008	1.38
2009	1.34
2010	1.38
2011	1.34
2012	1.37
2013	1.31
2014	1.89
2015	2.07
2016	2.29

Source: Ratio calculated from secondary data on crime incidences provided by the Punjab Police Headquarters.

Strengthening the Internal Controls Rather Than Multiplying External Oversights

There is a trend in governance to multiply the external oversights for enhancing transparency and accountability. The system has been rendered ineffective, and controls have been outsourced to external institutions and oversights. This has not only made internal functioning inefficient, but it is also a statement of the lack of trust in the internal mechanisms. In other words, anything external is credible. An easy solution to check distortions and violations is found in adding on external oversights rather than eliminating the process distorting procedures and, instead, strengthening internal controls to check perverse incentives and discretions. The assumption is that these external oversights should not be engulfed by the systemic dysfunctional. Most of the functions to be performed by the departments of the government have been either outsourced or are being performed by the external oversights.

The need, therefore, is to redefine the parameters of accountability by strengthening the internal controls and, if required, external oversights to be made integral to the internal mechanisms rather than as binaries.

Undoubtedly, the ambiguity in fixing accountability due to the directions without any statutory backing have to be reduced and, at the same time, statutory autonomy to be institutionalised. For instance, the Government of Punjab has set up three-layered community-police service delivery mechanisms. At the district level, 27 Community Police Resource Centres, at the sub-division, 96 Community Police Suvidha Centres at the sub-division level and, 356 Police Station Outreach Centres at the police station level have been established. These centres act as front-end of the police stations to provide services which should include delivery of the copies of FIRs and untraced reports, no-objection certificates for armed licenses, permission for religious and political processions, verification of tenants, registration of servants, etc., to provide counselling services to resolve disputes relating to domestic violence, dowry and various other crimes against women. In view of this, SAANJH will also have the facility for lodging complaints against the working of the police personnel and transparent disposal of the complaints lodged (Kumar 2011, From 'Introduction' to the Report, "Recommendations of the Punjab Governance"). The proposed system shall check the police misconduct through internal accountability mechanism which is integral to the hierarchical chain of command, thus, making it transparent at the level of the citizens' oversight attached to the community policing centres. The proposed system will not only strengthen the internal control but also, through external oversight which has been authorised to seek re-enquiry if not satisfied, make it transparent.

Discretion Reduction Procedural Changes

The core element of governance is a trust deficit between the citizens and the government. This gives a pretext to the regulatory State functionaries to become arbitrators between the government and the citizens and draw perverse incentives on account of trust deficit. To eliminate the perverse incentives, inefficiencies, and citizens' harassment, the need is to change over to those procedures that are conducive for the reduction of the discretionary practices.

To illustrate, for a dignified interaction with the Revenue Department, easy access to revenue services, online copies of jamabandis, simplified process for the settlement of contested mutations, withdrawal of discretionary powers of the *tehsildar* regarding the calculation of the construction cost and its replacement with a flat rate, etc., are the steps that are required to be initiated. These are dealt with in detail in the PGRC status reports.

In the policing, besides many other distortions, the most cumbersome issue is regarding the non-registration of complaints. A number of initiatives, including technology application, have been taken to check this distortion. The main thrust has been to eliminate the discretion of the police. Further, having a copy of the FIR was made more cumbersome; since it could be revoked only by the judiciary. That would add to the cost of the innocent persons to fight a case in the judiciary even when there was no case.

As such, it was proposed that the complaint of the crime can be lodged in any Community Policing Centre (i.e. SAANJH) against a unique ID number. And, if no action is taken on this complaint within 21 days, the SHO concerned will be held accountable under the Punjab Right to Service Act, 2011. This has made the system transparent and also reduced the discretion of the official concerned.

Similarly, the approval for the construction of the buildings was also at the discretion of the officials; the process was quite complicated.

After submission of the required documents, it has to be inspected by the building staff to see while the compliance of the construction as per the plans filed has been made or in case of change, filing of the revised plans was also required (Kumar 2009, From 'Introduction' to the Report).

The regulatory norms have to be simplified in the case of houses as it is in the interest of the owner to live comfortably and safely. For instance, inspections before the construction and completion of construction at the plinth level have to be dispensed with. The regulations do not put any onus on the architect for compliance with the regulations, whereas the owners who carry the responsibility in law have minimal knowledge of the details and have to depend on professional advice. Things may change dramatically if they are held accountable for compliance with the regulations. There is a need to shift the onus of responsibility on the professionals for compliance with the regulations—using 'third party enforcement' (Kumar 2009, From 'Introduction' to the Report).

Further, to reduce the discretion of the officials and harassment of the citizens, there is no need for both the completion and occupation certificates. Probably, these provisions were necessary when sewerage connections were sanctioned after the issue of the completion certificate, but before the occupation certificate was given (after connection for sewerage). That position, however, is changed now and water supply (in case not applied for earlier), as well as sewerage connections, are given independently, after the issue of completion certificate. There needs to be only one application for the completion certificate, and this should result in the grant of that. (Kumar 2009, From 'Introduction' to the Report).

To reduce the discretion of the officials, professional architects should be made primarily responsible for compliance with the rules.

Incentive Compatible Procedural Change

There is an imperative need to bring about those changes in the procedures and processes that can act as incentives per se. This will lead to a check in the delays.

For instance, in the case of birth certificates in Punjab, on the recommendations of the PGRC, delivery was made compatible with functionality and incentivising the functionaries (see Annexure 2.4). The Auxiliary Nurse Midwifery (ANM)[10] who has the jurisdiction for the revenue villages was declared as the local registrar and ASHA[11] worker as the notifier.

Disaggregate Delivery Mechanism

The main thrust of these reforms is to deliver a particular service through multiple agencies, and each one is to act as an oversight for the other for fixing accountability. To illustrate, in Transport, a disaggregate delivery mechanism may assign the registration of vehicles to the authorised dealers, issuing of the learner driving licence to the principals of the government colleges, and procurement of the fitness certificate of the vehicles from an empanelled service station (Kumar 2011, From 'Introduction' to the Report, "Recommendations of the Punjab Governance"). If incentives and disaggregate delivery mechanisms are institutionalised, the governance will become lean and less cumbersome, and reduce the space for perverse incentives.

Convergence of Engaged Governance with E-Governance

Governance is a composite concept. It is defined as the rules, regulations, procedures and processes operationalised through the institutions; realisation of the entitlements, claims and rights of the citizens. The governance is "the exercise of economic, political and administrative authority to manage a country's affairs at all levels. It consists of the mechanisms, processes and institutions through which the citizens and the groups articulate their interests, exercise their legal rights, meet their obligations and mediate their differences" (United National Economic and Social Council 2006). The main thrust of governance has to address the fault lines of caste, religion region and ethnicity to bring about inclusive growth through empowerment of the people on the margins. "Democratic governance is 'a process of creating and sustaining an environment for inclusive and responsive political processes and settlements.' The institutional and human capacities for governance determine how the effectiveness of public policies and strategies is attained, especially in service delivery" (United Nations System Task Team 2012).

The definition argues that there cannot be a standardised universal recipe for reaching out to the unreached. It also emphasises the need for building connectivity between the institutions of governance and efficient, transparent and accountable delivery of services.

Figure 2.1 Engaged Governance Convergence with E-Governance

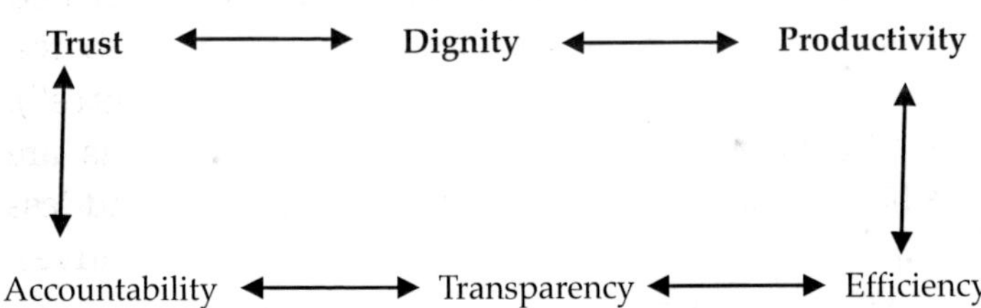

The processes, procedures, and rules have to meet trust, dignity, productivity deficits and, simultaneously, the capacity of the system has to build around the core elements of e-governance, i.e. efficiency, accountability and transparency (Kumar 2011, From 'Introduction' to the Report, "Recommendations of the Punjab Governance"):

(a) To make systems more accountable in terms of costs, conduct and performance.
(b) To enhance efficiency to make it more accessible through the availability of equal services to the people in equal needs (supply-side). And, also to ensure quality and reduce transaction costs through checking the perverse incentives, non-statutory and discretionary powers, amending inappropriate rules leading to inefficiency and corruption.
(c) To make the interaction between the citizens and the government more participatory, leading to transparency.

The convergence of engaged governance with e-governance reflecting corresponding concerns and thrusts breaking these into minute details requires an understanding of each activity as an independent module having specific technological requirement. The efficiency must not be at the cost of dignity, accountability may not compromise with productivity, and transparency has to be for the enhancement of the citizen's trust. The efficiency, accountability, and transparency have to be achieved a priori to meet the deficits of trust, dignity, productivity and citizen's engagement. If these prerequisites are not factored in, it may result in non-realisation of the entitlements as rights, particularly, for the excluded groups.

This has directly impinged upon the citizens' availment of the following rights:

(a) Right to Social Development (e.g. Education, Public Health, Housing).
(b) Right to Social Security and Safety Nets.
(c) Right to Physical Security, Safety and Justice.
(d) Right to Livelihood and Employment

Having recognised the need to transform the status of the subjects from their being colonial to the subjects, the relevance of the across-the-board notion of full citizenship has to be made integral to governance. Further, this notion of full citizenship has to be mediated by overcoming the constraints based on gender, caste, ethnicity and religious identities.

These values and rights can be realised only if the actions reflect the political will and ensure opportunities along with provisions of conditions to avail these and insistence of the institutionalisation of the processes and procedures for the citizens' engagement.

The pursuit of 'engaged governance' has to be based on democratic principles with attributes like participation, representation, distributive justice, accountability and fairness (Kumar 2010, From 'Introduction' to the Report). Engaged governance has been aptly described as,

> an institutional arrangement that links citizens more directly into the decision-making processes of a State so as to enable them to influence the public policies and programmes in a manner that impacts more positively on their social and economic lives (Khan 2005: 20).

The values and rights can be implemented if the structural constraints emanating from the post-colonial nature of the State and society, a priori, to the socio-economic conditions and legal impediments are recognised and moderated. These structural constraints of identity, dignity and productivity have a bearing on the realisation of the principle of equity of access from the supply side consideration. In other words, equal services are to be made available to the citizens in equal need. It also implies to have a critical look at the functioning of the supply side institution of the delivery of services to ensure full citizenship and guarantee rights to the marginalised sections (Kumar 2010, From 'Introduction' to the Report). As Khan (2005) maintains that globalisation and liberalisation might have provided new economic opportunities benefiting many countries, but not all have gained equally or enough. He asserts that the market being as the prime mover ignores the marginalised sections from necessary services. On the whole, globalisation and liberalisation (instead of achieving the expected goals of improved market structure, improved cost-effectiveness in the delivery of services guaranteeing efficient use of the scarce and unevenly distributed resources) are further entrenching marginalisation. The distinction between the variations in the services made available and services availed have to be captured to locate these into systemic inequities suffered by the identifiable groups of the citizens.

The concept of need is ideological as also the capacity to avail these services. In the first stage, the needs should be assessed in the context of the social environment in which the individual lives and, thereafter, the task to formulate the policies relating to availability, quality, costs, information, etc., should be taken up (Kumar 2010, From 'Introduction' to the Report). The needs of the population may be identical, but the social origin may be varied, leading to unequal access to the services.

Similarly, the access to quality of the services which entails costs due to privatisation adversely affected the interests, claims and rights of the people on the margins.

Along with availability, it is utilisation that reflects the process through which 'potential access' is converted into 'realised access'. The 'realised access' will largely depend on the linkages of the delivery policy with the delivery system and its resource structure and strata-wise nature and level of the utilisation of services. Sharma (2008: 63) mentions the term 'two hats', or in other terms, an approach to bridge the gap between authority and people at the margins. The term 'two hats' referred to the dual nature (i.e. having both labels of government and non-government) of any initiative (like SAANJH Kendras) intended to achieve the goals of the citizen-engaged governance. The government label symbolises the source of strength (the potential access) or the capability of having power for necessary decision-making arrangements. The non-government label, on the other hand, indicates a people-centric approach or more connected and citizenry engaged instrument (the realised access) in order to reform the governance processes and meets the deficits of trust, dignity, productivity and citizen engagement or, in simple words, abridges the mistrust between the citizens and the State.

NOTES

1. This in a way was continuation of the Female Infanticide Act VII of 1870. The Act targeted those population groups that practised the 'crime' (see Dagar 2014: 236).
2. This was based on the recommendations made by the Punjab Governance Reforms Commission-PGRC, Fifth Status Report in 2011 (see Kumar 2011, From 'Introduction' to the Report, "Recommendations of the Punjab Governance").
3. What we are witnessing in the world today is a range of accommodated political systems. Even the toughest of them is weak. Even the most monolithic in forms tends to be divided in its practices and diluted in its ideas. A few are totalitarian. Almost all are populist and, in a real sense, mainly pre-democratic rather than anti-democratic. (Laclau 1997: 143 cites Apter).
4. This distinction between the politics of representation and politics of presence has been very aptly described by Zoya Hasan who argued that politics of presence blurs the underrepresentation and the representation of interests of the constituents, specifically the vulnerable sections (see Hasan 2006).
5. In that context, people at the margins may be de jure right to have a right but de facto 'right-less'. To illustrate, Arendt affirms that human rights can be of meaning, if redefined as a right to the human condition (belonging to the human community), and not to be dependent de facto upon some inborn dignity (see Arendt 1986).
6. The Punjab Government by its order discontinued the practice

of submission of affidavits unless it is required by law. A list of affidavits eliminated (submitted by Deputy Commissioner, Sangrur) is being reproduced. (see Kumar 2009, From 'Introduction' to the Report, "Recommendations of the Punjab Governance"). Other districts are in the process of eliminating this practice.

7. Sharma (2008) mentions the views of Vivek Rai (a New Delhi-based civil servant), who labelled development initiatives taken by the government as the state's "dole system," which, he argued, countered the spirit of self-help and, instead, encouraged the "mai-baap syndrome" set in motion by India's erstwhile Mughal and British rulers. He further asserted that the poor people expect the government to take care of them or regard the State as their mai-baap, or mother-father. Rai iterated that the success and sustainability of development rested on the society, and that the State could only serve as "a catalyst, a facilitator." Sharma (2008) notes it as a classic example of the reimagined neoliberal official rhetoric on development and the roles that the State and the civil society ought to play in it (see Sharma 2008: 131).
8. The detailed case study has been presented in the Case Study II. The study was conducted by Pramod Kumar, Chairperson, Sh. R.N. Gupta, IAS (Retd.), Sh. J.R. Kundal, IAS (Retd.). A presentation was also made to the Government of India and this recommendation was accepted and later on implemented in all the States of India (see Annexure 2.5).
9. The view of the government is that by asking for affidavits, the citizens are put to unnecessary harassment and, as such, attestation should be replaced by self-declaration in the majority of cases because there is a provision for stern action under the law for making a wrong declaration. Therefore, it has been decided that no government department or organisation will ask for affidavits from the applicants except in those cases where affidavits are required under law. In place of having affidavits, self-declaration has been accepted and this system will be implemented with effect from April 1, 2010 onwards. It will be ensured by the Deputy Commissioners of the State that the self-declaration forms will be available at all the Suvidha Kendras to the citizens even as the self-declaration will carry a photo of the applicant.

   The government has decided that the applicants, while submitting documents for admission in educational institutions and for seeking employment, will be permitted to submit self-attestation with effect from April 1, 2010 onwards. For admission to the educational institutions and for providing employment, the concerned agencies should accept the self-attested copies from the applicants and the original certificates should be called only from the finally selected candidates (see Kumar 2013, From 'Introduction' to the Report, "Recommendations of the Punjab Governance").

10. Auxiliary Nurse Midwife (ANM) is a village-level female health worker in India who is known as the first contact person between the community and the health services. ANMs are regarded as the grassroot workers in the health organisation pyramid.
11. Accredited Social Health Activist (ASHA)—is an interface between the community and the public health system.

3
Governance for the People: Deficient Citizenship?

Case Study I—Policing the Police: Community Policing Programme in Punjab

Punjab has pioneered what is probably India's finest effort to improve relations between the police and local communities... These centres provide a range of citizen services in a congenial atmosphere. A crime counter provides copies of first information report (FIR) and tracks the status of cases; a victim assistance unit provides professional counselling and support including, advice on how to deal with the criminal justice system; a grievance redressal cell allows the citizens' to file complaints against the police without having to go to a police station. As registered societies, the centres have the right to raise money from external sources, although they are staffed by a mix of NGO activists and police officers (The World Bank 2004: 66).

The SAANJH* is a unique programme launched in the year 2003 in Punjab. This was the first experiment in the country on the institutionalised community policing at

---

* The SAANJH model was conceptualised by Pramod Kumar, in 2003 and assisted by Harsh Chopra. The model was actively implemented by S.K. Sharma IPS (Retd.) Former DGP, Ishwar Singh IPS, ADGP Law and Order, V. Neerja IPS, ADGP Welfare and many others. The technology support was given by Pritpal Singh. This model was also adopted by the Punjab Governance Reforms Commission (PGRC) in its Third Status Report in 2010.

the police station level and above. The main thrust was to reform the police stations as these are the nerve centres of policing.

Community policing is to be seen as integral to policing per se. In other words, there will not be separate community policing officers or functionaries; every police officer shall be sensitised to the community policing perspective, equipped with community policing skills and assigned community policing tasks as per his placement.

However, the broader version of community-policing being policing for and through the community could not bridge the gap between the police and the community. Policing through the community could ensure participation of the members of the community as facilitators in soft policing like traffic management, social fencing, etc. This kind of understanding of community-policing was either reductionist or at the most public relations activity. In other words, community-policing is not merely policing for the community, but along with the community.

This is the integration of engaged governance with the e-governance. This is not a stand-alone model of policing. It also has an institutionalised mechanism for coordination with other departments. These police station outreach centres are meticulously planned and cannot be reshaped or restructured by the individuals. It has 'backbone activities' leading to standardisation and, at the same time, has a provision to initiate activities to suit the local cultural and other specific needs. It performs police service delivery functions, resolves conflicts and disputes, provides legal support and victim relief. It has a centralised police complaint system. Each complaint is given a unique ID number for reference. Above all, it gives the citizens easy and dignified access to police services. It also reinforces the citizens' confidence in democratic policing. Also, it gives a sense of ownership to the citizens of the police station as it is in the case of a school, health centre or public libraries.

Relevance of SAANJH Kendras

- Easy and dignified access of the public to police services
- Improves community-police relations
- Transparency in service and dealings
- Forum to address the rights of all citizens and sections of the community
- Builds confidence of the people in crime management and grievance redressal

Background

The twenty-first century has thrown up major challenges to human security. These have added new dimensions to the principles and scope of accountability of the police systems. With the globalisation of the rights and crimes, the threat posed by terrorism, technological revolution and the emergence of the diaspora, the nature and scope of policing have been transformed. These changes can be captured through the new dimensions and meanings attributed to human rights, maintenance of internal security and policing communities.

With the introduction of new principles of governance in the new era, it would be appropriate to delineate the nature and scope of policing and the corresponding principles of accountability. This will largely depend on what the new era symbolises. What are the main characteristic features of the new global order?

The new global order with its emphasis on globalisation of capital and restricted mobility of labour without ensuring distributive justice has brought into focus issues relating to national and human security. The new global order has nurtured those factors which made both the latent (life-reducing mechanisms such as unemployment, illiteracy, corruption) and manifest violence (ethnic, gender atrocities) more pervasive. Further, the State having abdicated its responsibility to meet the survival needs of the people to the market, its role has been reduced to performing regulatory functions. The regulatory State has to depend excessively on the police to look effective and efficient.

Above all, the technological revolution has made the traditional way of policing ineffective. The criminals are increasingly becoming technology savvy. For instance, cyber crimes are becoming pervasive, and the law enforcement functionaries are severely handicapped to check these. For instance, hackers are not hampered by borders and geographical limitations. These developments require a fresh look at the criminal justice system globally to build its capacity to deliver justice, ensure security and protect the rights of the citizens. The emerging reality has to be contextualised in the nature of the State, be it post-colonial, post-capitalist or post-totalitarian, with a focus on the norms and values that shape police functioning and expectations.

Post-Colonial Indian Context

India gained independence from the British colonialism in 1947. But, its police continued to be governed by the Indian Police Act, 1861, enacted by the British after the people's revolt of 1857. No structural change was brought about in the policing system after independence. The police continued to function as an instrument of the State to provide sustenance to the politicians in power. However, in 1977, the government felt the need for police reforms in response to the partisan role played by the police during the Emergency. A National Police Commission was constituted. It underlined the need to have a relook at the public-police relationship. To quote:

> Far-reaching changes are taking place in our society. Some

> of these are rapid growth in the absolute size of the urban population, increased spatial mobility with faster means of communication and transport, the weakening of joint family and village ties, the growth of an unanchored population in urban areas, the loss of legitimacy of the feudal norms on which village society was based and the growing loss of consensus in social and political values. In a society which is undergoing such changes, tensions are bound to rise between religious communities, between castes and sub-castes of the same community, between management and labour, between urban areas and rural areas, etc. In this situation, crime and disorder increase and affect all segments of society. For dealing with this very complex situation of crime and disorder, we have a criminal justice system which is slow, under-staffed and clogged with heavy backlogs. Under these circumstances, the police cannot control crime without the active goodwill and cooperation of the people.
>
> One objective of public-police relations should be the direct involvement of the people in the prevention and detection of crime and the maintenance of order. People may have to take a much greater interest in protecting their lives and properties without necessarily taking the law into their own hands. They will have to actively cooperate with the police and also participate in organised efforts at self-protection with the support of the police ("Fifth Report of the National Police Commission").

Even after more than 40 years, the recommendations of this Commission have not been implemented. The National Police Commission emphasised that the police should be accountable to the people, the law and its organisational hierarchy. It should function as an impartial force and efficiently protect the citizens' rights. And, it should be insulated from political interference.

In the same vein, the National Human Rights Commission filed a counter affidavit in the Supreme Court, which also says that the police in a democratic society should be low in authority and high on accountability. Disturbed at the disquieting increase in the number of complaints received against the police for violation of human rights, it is felt that 'policing the police is an urgent issue to be addressed seriously'. For this, a number of measures have been suggested in the police reforms commission report. For instance, it suggested that in all cases of custodial deaths or rape, there should be a mandatory judicial enquiry. Similar suggestions are given in the case of fake encounters, disappearances, unauthorised searches, atrocities against women and children, cases of rape, etc. This view was expressed more forcefully in the context of post-terrorism Punjab. There has been a qualitative shift in the interactive relationship between the police-community, judiciary, politics and administrative machinery in Punjab. There is an urgent need to give direction to the recently discovered potentials for building a pro-people force rather than using it for narrow political gains.

> Why have these and many other urgently required steps not been implemented? The answer can be found in the manner the State has been organised, the nation-building project has been implemented, and the democratic institutions have functioned.

The beginning of the twentieth century was a period of consolidation of nationalism into the nation states. After independence, the dichotomy between the State and the nation could not be bridged. The nation—the community—despite being part of the functional democracy, could not establish its ownership over the State. The State continued to remain an alien entity. The logical outcome was an excessive reliance of the State on its security forces to enforce 'order'. In other words, instead of emerging as a nation-state, it became an aggressive State-controlled nation.

The project of nation-building took the initiative away from the community. The State functioned as an enforcement agency and, in the process, got alienated from the people. The police, as the main instrument of enforcement, earned a bad image. The police enforced 'order' without seeking the community support, lending credence to the belief that it was the State against the nation and, in practical terms, it was seen as the police versus the people. This has been reflected through the implementation of the 1861 Police Act and the people's expectations, often belied, from the police. A citizens' survey conducted in 1999 revealed that a majority of the members of the community expected the police to enforce the law effectively (Kumar 2001). This perception converged with the current disposition of a majority of the police personnel (70 per cent) who regarded the authoritarian mode to be the best style of dealing with the public. Consequently, the existing nature of the police-community interaction was guided by an underlying preference for avoiding contact with the police altogether.

The National Police Commission, set up in 1977, has drawn attention to this aspect and stated that the police service could have no future unless it earns respect and confidence of its men and of the public at large. In its Fifth Report (November 1980), the Commission expressed anguish that the 1902 Fraser Commission's observation that 'the 'people' now might not dread the police, but they certainly dreaded getting involved with it in any capacity', continues to be valid. This was mainly the result of the brutal and rude functioning of the police. Various public surveys conducted since the mid-1960s by David Bayley in 1969, by the Indian Institute of Public Opinion in 1978, and by the National Police Commission in 1980, reinforced the view that the constabulary had been rude, threatening, intimidating and brutal in its interaction with the people (Bayley 1969).

In a survey conducted by IDC in 2010, the people expressed the view that they felt deterioration than earlier in the police, as 55 per cent of them said that the police had become more corrupt, 28 per cent perceived the police to be ruder, and, more brutal, by 14 per cent. The police have become non-responsive, 18 per cent said so, and 20 per cent were of the opinion that the police is biased with regard to the social diversities and class positions.

Table 3.1 Deteriorations Perceived in Police

Deterioration		
	Frequency	*Percentage*
Blatant and rude	143	27.88
Bribery and extortions	282	54.97
Compromised in favour of dominant castes and class	104	20.27
Non-responsiveness	91	17.74
Violation of the rights	72	14.04

Source: IDC Field Survey, 2010.

Note: Multiple Responses (the sum total not equal to 100).

One of the reforms that the civil society groups are asking for inclusion in the ongoing police reforms pertains to the prompt registration of the first information report (FIR)[1]. In a survey conducted in 2010, it documented the reasons for non-reporting of the public perception by the citizens and non-registration of the complaints were listed as perceived. A large section believed that the registration of the complaints involves bribes, harassment and loss of dignity in the police stations. Not only the conduct of the police persons, material costs involved but also the complicated procedures leaving a large space for the police discretion acts as a major constraint. Along with the dignity loss, the trust deficit in the police is another dimension of the citizen-police exchange. It is not that the police procedures are complicated, and it involves dignity loss and trust deficit, but the interaction with the police involve social stigma. As a result, while the heinous crimes are selectively reported, the reporting of petty crimes is not considered worth reporting.

Table 3.2 Reporting Crimes to Police

	Frequency	*Percentage*
Fear of harassment dignity and material loss	369	72.00
Lack of faith in the police trust deficit	241	47.00
Social stigma	344	67.00
Complicated procedures procedural inadequacies less serious offences: Considered not worthwhile to report	267	52.00
Registration of cases related to the performance of police	62	12.00

Source: IDC Field Survey, 2010.
Note: Multiple Responses (the sum total not equal to 100).

Police as an Instrument of the Dominant Social Groups

The police are seen as an instrument of the dominant groups and biased against the people living on the margins. A majority of the respondents, i.e. around 80 per cent, believed that the police serve the interests of the powerful and the dominant castes. And, only 18 per cent said that the police serve the community or the common person.

Table 3.3 Whom Does the Police Serve?

	Frequency	*Percentage*
Common citizens	76	14.81
Politicians and bureaucracy	243	47.37
Dominant castes and class	174	33.92
Poor and downtrodden	20	3.90
Total	513	100.00

Source: IDC Field Survey, 2010.

Discriminatory Access to Justice: Women and Lower Castes

Social invisibility attached to the crimes against the women and the lower castes provides a legitimate reason to be indifferent to the violations of the rights of the people on the margins and, instead, serve the interests of the dominant groups. Crimes such as rape, are not reported because the victims fear the social stigma and the caste rapes are not seen as a violation of the rights in a caste hierarchical society. Most of the time, even molestation is not considered as a crime to invite the attention of the police. For instance, in 1994, 30 cases of molestation were reported in Punjab against 11,198 unreported cases (IDC 1994). Similarly, 83 cases of rape were reported as against 5678 unreported cases in the same year. Interestingly, eve-teasing has emerged as a 'new crime' in the police dictionary, with only three cases registered in 1994, whereas unregistered cases revealed in the IDC survey were 27,530.

Table 3.4 Ratio of Reported to Unreported Atrocities in Punjab

Reported	*Unreported*
Rape—1	68
Molestation—1	374
Eve-teasing—1	9177
Dowry death—1	27
Dowry harassment—1	299

Source: IDC Field Survey, 1995.

A survey of the citizens' perceptions of the role of the police in gender-related cases revealed that they considered the police to be biased, prejudiced and indifferent (IDC 1999).

- (i) There was dissatisfaction in the community with the police response to the women since they found the police to be abusive and prejudiced.
- (ii) The police distanced itself from the cases related to the

marital and family disputes, unwilling to intervene in what was termed as the family's private affairs.

(iii) There was also a perception that the police demanded sexual favours from the women victims and, therefore, the women avoided reporting to the police or seeking assistance from it.

(iv) The police, on the other hand, complained that the women lodged fake complaints and were unduly favoured by the law.

(v) The extent of the prejudices against the women was found to be significant. The lack of gender sensitisation was apparent.

One of the personnel deployed in the police station in Punjab even said '*Ae taan aap raat nu kapde lah ke banena pa ke baithe hunde hain. Raat nu ta asi apni janaani nu police station jaan ni dinde.*'

Table 3.5 Domestic Violence: Existing and Expected Role of Police

Existing Response of Police Towards Domestic Violence			*Expected Response of Police Towards Domestic Violence*		
Existing Response	*Frequency*	*Percentage*	*Expected Response*	*Frequency*	*Percentage*
Indifferent	209	40.74	Quality investigation	212	41.33
Violation as routine	54	10.53	Trust building	178	34.70
Private family domain	87	16.96	Diversity representations in police stations	75	14.62
Extremities are responded like rape	40	7.80	Don't know	50	9.75
People refrain from approaching police	74	14.42			
Do not know	50	9.75			

Source: IDC Field Survey, 2010.
Note: Multiple Responses (the sum total not equal to 100).

In a survey conducted in 2010, 41 per cent of the respondents said that the police was indifferent towards the domestic violence cases and did not take it seriously (11 per cent). Seventeen per cent of respondents opined that the police perceived domestic violence as a personal matter of the household, and even some of the complainants also believed this (14 per cent). There was a strong feeling that the investigation was sluggish, delayed and shoddy. And therefore, it was asserted that the quality of the investigation should be improved. This would, in turn, increase the conviction rate and justice delivery. Around 41 per cent felt that proper investigation should be conducted which would reinforce the people's confidence in the police (35 per cent).

Table 3.6 Sexual Violence: Existing and Expected Role of Police

Existing Response of Police Towards Rape/Molestation/Eve-teasing			*Expected Response of Police Towards Rape/Molestation/Eve-teasing*		
Existing response	*Fre-quency*	*Per-centage*	*Expected Response*	*Fre-quency*	*Per-centage*
Women are perpetrators	183	35.67	Transform police prejudices and biases	181	35.28
Re-victimization of women	138	26.90	Sensitise police towards diversities	115	22.42
Law is biased, towards women	72	14.04	Gender issues to be handled by Women Police	165	32.16
Women take un-due advantage	75	14.62	Engagement of civil society representatives	26	5.07
Do not know	42	8.19	Do not know	26	5.07
Police inaction	8	1.56	Rule by law	5	0.97

Source: IDC Field Survey, 2010.
Note: Multiple Responses (the sum total not equal to 100).

In the context of sexual violence, the women were seen as the perpetrators rather than the victims. Around 36 per cent of respondents felt that the police endorse this and believed that it was the women who encouraged violations. Another 27 per cent believed that the police behaviour was prejudiced and in many cases violated the women who really felt victimised once again during the course of the investigation.

It was felt that there was a need to sensitise the police towards the diversity issues (22 per cent) and there was also a need to develop the protocols to check the police biases which were located in the social structure (35 per cent).

Lower Caste Victims of Policing

Most of the surveys of the citizens' perception of their interaction with the lower castes reported that the police was partisan and violated the rights of the vulnerable sections. The members of the Scheduled Castes complained that they were physically assaulted, sexually harassed and socially disgraced by the police.

It is mainly due to their lower caste status, poor economic condition and their inability to bribe, that they are targeted by the police. Most of the violative behaviour of the police remains invisible due to the prevalence and acceptance of the caste system.

Around fifty-two per cent of respondents observed that the police believed that poverty and crime were twins. And, resultantly, thirty-four per cent of respondents inferred that this led to the biased and unfair response of the police.

Most of the people felt that the police should weed out criminality rather labelling the poor and the lower castes as criminals (74 per cent) and not indulge in illegal harassment of the people living on the margins (18 per cent).

Table 3.7 Issues of SCs: Existing and Expected Role of Police

Existing Response of Police Towards SC Issues			*Expected Response of Police Towards SC Issues*		
Existing Response	*Fre-quency*	*Per-cent-age*	*Expected Response*	*Fre-quency*	*Per-cent-age*
Combination of poverty and crime. Dependent on drugs, doles, and no morals	265	51.66	Weeding out of criminality	378	73.68
Biased against lower castes	175	34.11	Stop illegal harass-ment of poor	94	18.32
Have political patronage	32	6.24	Do not know	41	7.99
Do not know	41	7.99	Total	513	100.00
Total	513	100.00			

Source: IDC Field Survey, 2010.

Mobile Population: A Target of Policing

The police are perceived to protect the 'community' from the mobile population, which is excluded from the definition of the community. Their seeming inability to control the migration or to regulate migrants is seen as a failure of the police. If the local communities have ethnic bondage with the immigrant population, the State's efforts to preserve its territorial integrity gets compromised, especially in a hyper-national identity context. In the process, the security forces acquire a licence to violate the citizens' rights in the name of protecting national integrity. In the case of migration within the country, it provides fodder to the radicals to launch the sons of the soil movements. And, the police as a provincial force is seen by a majority of the migrants as a partisan force trying to protect some particular ethnic or religious groups. On the contrary, the local population considered the police to be inefficient in handling migrant issues.

The respondents maintained that the police assume the migrants to be potential criminals and, in contrast, 33 per cent said that the police do not take the potential threat of involvement of the migrants in crime seriously.

Forty-three per cent of respondents expected that the police to stop exploiting the migrants and not be biased against them; a view that was expressed by 37 per cent respondents. That there is a need to be more vigilant about the antecedents of the migrants - was expected by 9 per cent respondents.

Table 3.8 Migrants Issues: Existing and Expected Role of Police

Existing Response of Police Towards Increase in Crime and Migrants			*Expected Response of Police Towards Increase in Crime and Migrants*		
Existing Response	*Fre-quency*	*Per-cent-age*	*Expected Response*	*Fre-quency*	*Per-cent-age*
Migrants are criminals	290	56.53	Treat migrants as citizens	222	43.27
Migrants exploi-tation remains invisible	170	33.14	Over biases, and avoid labelling	191	37.23
Do not know	53	10.33	Verification of their antecedents	48	9.35
Total	513	100.00	Do not know	53	10.33
			Note: Multiple Responses		

Source: IDC Field Survey, 2010.

As discussed above, most of the surveys conducted have stated that the police force is inefficient and corrupt—'they take bribes even for performing legitimate functions'. In its anxiety to shed this image, it is now using the community policing as a face-saving device without putting in place the institutional mechanism. The police enlisted the community's assistance mostly for investigation. In fact, the concept of community participation was restricted to making the community willing witnesses and better informers (this was mentioned as the ideal assistance).

The police complained that the community was not cooperative and, in fact, created hindrances in their functioning. The community perceived the police to be a source of nuisance and even exploitation. A large percentage of the community members believed that the police was inefficient in handling their complaints (Kumar 2001).

An IDC Survey (1999) has shown that a majority of the members of the community resent the role of the information gatherers for crime detection and as facilitators for traffic management and security through neighbourhood watch groups. Community policing is being enforced rather than collectively conceived, implemented and monitored. Community policing experiments were initiated in the 1960s and 1970s in India. Some programmes like crime prevention weeks, setting up of the boys' clubs, the second Saturday sports meet, etc., were positive efforts for establishing police-public contact. The Delhi Police implemented schemes like, Special Police Officers (1985), the Neighbourhood Watch (1989) through neighbourhood watch committees formed in each block, adoption of crime hot spots, and formation of anti-sexual harassment squads, to bring policing closer to the community. To bring the community and the police closer, similar initiatives were taken in many other States—Madhya Pradesh, Tamil Nadu, Maharashtra, Punjab and Karnataka. These included the formation of Mohalla Committees to check communal violence in Bhiwandi (Maharashtra), Citizen Committees in Karnataka, and Village Vigilance Committees in Tamil Nadu. All these efforts were constrained as the community remained on the margin of the policing system. These efforts were directed to provide single window service and to use the community representatives as the facilitators for traffic management and security through neighbourhood watch groups. In other words, it is policing for the community and through the community and not along with the community.

There is a felt need within the police administration to shed this image. Notwithstanding the need for restructuring the criminal justice system, there is also an expressed desire of 'policing the police' and making the community-centric policing initiatives actionable to be made integral to the system of police governance.

Governments that are less democratic, less equipped to provide distributive justice, and more prone to corrupt practices, need the enforcement-oriented police. Therefore, the goal of good governance is to make enforcement-oriented policing less relevant and making its service delivery more distributive, efficient, accountable and less corrupt, if not honest.

Police reforms are expected to involve the community to improve its service delivery and to contain crime. The aim has been to shift the emphasis from an enforcement perspective targeting the community as a potential criminal to crime prevention with community participation. However, a lack of historical and contextual understanding of the power structures operating within the society could result in overlooking the needs of the women, the Scheduled Castes and the migrants.

The success of the policing programmes with the participation of the community is well documented in the community policing programmes the world over. However, there is a need to differentiate between policing for providing efficient services for the community, or delivering services through the community, where the members provide add-on resources to the activities or policing in collaboration with the community.

Why This Experiment?

Radical changes in the governance paradigm necessitated

corresponding changes in policing. The police, as an enforcement agency performed the task of maintaining law, providing security and protecting people's rights with a focus on punishment as a deterrent. The inevitable outcome has been increasing the incidences of violation of the citizens' rights, which the police is expected to protect. In the process, the police got alienated from the people. In the past conflict societies, the alienation acquired an aggravated form. In this background, it was felt that there was a need to make community-policing integral to the existing policing model. It was also felt that there is a need to take into consideration not only the changes at the global level but also to contextualise them into the local conditions.

Post-Terrorism Institution Rebuilding

The need for community outreach was felt like a predominant section of the people was alienated from the police during the terrorism phase in Punjab. It was felt more by the police as the presence of a substantial number of the policemen not only gave the police force high visibility but also allowed the people to have frequent contact with the police. The perception of the police as an enforcement agency, both in the minds of the community and the police, encouraged the police role of crime detection through stringent treatment to the lawbreakers. It amounted to promoting a coercive, abusive and, at times, even brutal police force. The police were, thus beginning to be viewed as a nuisance and the policemen acquiring the image of harassers.

A major lesson learnt was that policing terrorism involves working in partnership with the community and understanding the problem in its totality rather than merely within the law and order framework. Also, to use the techniques and skills that originate from the customs and traditions of the area for combating violent assertions. For this, strategies were to be designed to work in partnership with the police to delegitimise the use of violence, which is essential for the management of violent conflicts. Further, it was felt that democratic methods like, dialogue negotiations, elections, etc., were potent instruments only for reducing hostility and antagonism; while, on the other hand, policing a violent conflict invariably thwarts democratic initiatives. The temptation was to restore peace and order, even at the expense of violating the law. This was really problematic, i.e. how not to indulge in violative activities like tortures, extra-judicial executions, fake encounters, etc. It was in this context that there was a felt need to acquire the knowledge and skills used globally for conflict settlement and management without being violative of the rights of the citizens.

Bridging the Spatial Disconnect

Police Stations (Thanas) are the nerve centres of policing. However, service delivery at the cutting edge level has not been the focus of police reforms. There exists a functional disconnect between the outside space and the police stations. This spatial divide is because the citizens feel that in the police station, they might be 'detained, physically assaulted, insulted and coerced to pay bribes'. This perception, poor management practices, lack of accountability and transparency along with the often prejudiced response, have contributed to the underreporting of crime besides many other distortions. The Police Station evokes a sense of alienation, unlike a school or panchayat office or government dispensary. And, this difference also establishes the fact that an environment can influence the visitor's sense of identity and dignity.

Therefore, the main focus of the police reforms was to involve the community for its improved service delivery and the containment of crime. And, the emphasis was to shift from an enforcement perspective targeting the community as potential criminals to crime prevention with community participation. Police support to the reform initiatives was reflected in a host of community policing initiatives. There was recognition of the alienation from the community, which promoted initiatives in the police ranks to improve service delivery and create a credible image of the police.

From Ad Hoc, Problem Centred, Relational Approach to Institutional Response

The initiatives that were taken, even though, well-intended, but they remained individual oriented in line with what is popularly known as the "Kiran Bedi syndrome" means that an ad hoc nature of these efforts made the service delivery dependent on the preference and capacity of the individual officer.

All interventions remained problem-centred. A number of initiatives, such as those pertaining to land, market encroachment and community disputes were tackled by these interventions, yet these remained focused as isolated incidents. Each problem had a different set of initiatives and support groups to resolve the same. In other words, for each presumed issue, a new programme was formed, and these remained delinked from other similar problems emerging in the area.

Interventions were based on the assumption that interpersonal contact, role models or guidance can effectively intervene to redress the situations. In the context of substance abuse, counselling based on the credibility of the individual police officer is expected to show positive results. A holistic intervention, on the other hand, sought to establish a causal relationship between the criminal activity and the factors leading to it. In other words, the distinction between a terrorist and terrorism would accordingly guide one's policy to deal with this kind of violence. Further, most of the violent clashes between the religious, caste and ethnic groups erupt due to provocations like sexual crimes, processions, etc., and attempts were made to tackle these situations without addressing the causes.

Individual-oriented and ad hoc initiatives limit the community's responsibility and ownership. This puts all responsibility for any problem resolution on the personal intervention of the official concerned. Individual-centred initiatives create scope for political interference. Community involvement and support can help check unnecessary political interference. But, the lack of or biased historical contextual understanding of the power structures operating within the society could result in providing opportunities to those who are 'more equal than others' to dictate their priorities.

Built-in prejudices would have the women, the Scheduled Castes, and the migrants overlooked as partners in this venture. Their participation per se, cannot be taken as synonymous with empowerment. In a given context, a community leader would have no hesitation in proclaiming a raped woman to be a fallen woman, rather than directing efforts to deal with her being victimised and violated yet again. Thus, the aim of community policing is not only that the services are provided to the community through the community, but that the decisions regarding policing are taken along with the community within the legal framework and rights of the humans.

From Trust Deficit, Citizens' as Instruments within the Authoritarian Mode to Democratic Policing

The police complained that the community was not cooperative and, in fact, created hindrances in their functioning. The community perceived the police to be a source of nuisance and even exploitation. Predominant percentage of the community found the police to be inefficient in handling their complaints.

The police enlisted the community's assistance mostly

for investigation. In fact, the concept of community participation was restricted to making the community willing witnesses and better informers (this was mentioned as the ideal assistance). The community also perceived assistance for the investigation to be their prime duty for maintaining order.

The lower ranks were found to be on the exploitative modes with the middle ranks being more dependent on the authoritarian style. The use of democratic styles was nominal.

Given these limitations, the need for a comprehensive, institutionalised model was felt. Not that there was an absence of initiatives to meet these deficits, but these were selective, targeted and individual centred. A brief glance of the initiatives taken will make this point clear.

Process of Institutionalisation of Community Policing Model

Community policing efforts in Punjab have been largely the result of the initiatives taken by the individual officers. These pioneering efforts were not uniform and could not be sustained for long. This was because of the lack of adequate support from the higher command, inadequacy of funds and the lack of an institutionalised structure. Changing public expectations presents tremendous challenges to the way in which the public services are traditionally delivered. Improvements in the delivery of police services can help make the police administration people-friendly and responsive, thereby, satisfying everyone who goes to the police, whether for assistance or for information. And, to ensure that the proposed project is not handicapped by ad hoc initiatives, efforts were made to institutionalise the community policing activities under the banner of the Community Police Programme (later termed as SAANJH).

Inconsistencies and contradictions in the governance

rules necessitated corresponding changes in policing. The police, as an enforcement agency performed the task of maintaining law, providing security and protecting people's rights with a focus on punishment as a deterrent. The inevitable outcome has been the increasing incidences of violation of the citizens' rights, which the police is expected to protect. In the process, the police got alienated from the populace. Given this background, it was felt that there is a need to make the community–policing integral to the existing model. It was also felt that there is a need to take into consideration not only the changes at the global level but also to contextualise them into the local conditions. Thus, in response, community-police interface promoting the concept of people policing aimed at crime prevention rather than detection or enforcement was evolved. The main focus was to move away from ad hoc interventions to an institutionalised administrative edifice with a clearly defined scope, goals, problems, rights and duties.

David Bayley elucidates by saying, that the problem with policing in most countries is that it is centralised at the headquarters and fails to accommodate the diversity of conditions in different localities requiring different approaches. The SAANJH model of the community policing has decentralised power to design strategies from the police headquarters to the police personnel in operational positions, such as SHOs, with the active engagement of the local community. In view of this, it was proposed to set up Community Policing Resource Centres, as per the model prepared by the Institute for Development and Communication (IDC) in the year 2003. The Government of Punjab conveyed its approval vide Memo No. 16/163/2002-4H(5)/415 dated January 28, 2003.

Box 3.1 Evolution of the Model

The model was prepared in close collaboration with the police and civil society activists. In 2001, the Punjab Police collaborated with the Institute for Development and Communication (IDC), to develop an academic understanding of the community policing and evolve a community policing model with a regional approach and signed a Memorandum of Understanding (MoU). IDC conducted field research, seminars and discussions, and came out with an institutionalised community policing model named Community Policing Resource Centres (CPRC) and later titled as SAANJH.

In January 2003, after detailed discussions among the different stakeholders, the Government of Punjab notified the establishment of CPRCs at the district level to provide continuity and sustainability to the ad hoc community policing initiatives. Other objectives were to provide dignified access to the public to avail police services, ensuring greater community participation in police work, and implementing community-oriented schemes in partnership with the civil society. In the initial years, these centres were established at the district level. In the first phase, the scheme was implemented in Moga, Bathinda, Hoshiarpur, Jalandhar, Ludhiana, Patiala and Amritsar districts and, in the second and third phases, the programme was implemented in the remaining districts by 2004.

In 2007, to ensure continuity, a legislative directive for the formation of these centres was incorporated in the Punjab State's Police Act of 2007 (Section 14 Punjab Police Act, 2007).

In the year 2010, the outreach of the CPRC programme was extended, and the sub-division and police station level centres were appended and named Community Policing Suvidha Centres (CPSCs) and Police Station Outreach Centres (PSOCs) respectively.

Community Affairs Division (CAD) headed by an ADGP rank officer and the State Level Coordination and Review Committee (SLCRC) having community representatives at the Punjab Police Headquarter were established to design, develop, implement and monitor the programmes in the area of the community policing and Community Policing Monitoring

Units (CPMUs) at the range level. Besides, CAD and SLCRC were expected to keep oversight over the implementation and execution of the community policing programme in the districts falling under the respective range.

Branding of the community policing programme was envisaged by providing the programme with a unique name. The programme was named SAANJH (means partnership) and the community policing centres at the district, sub-division and police station level were renamed as District SAANJH Kendra, Sub-division SAANJH Kendra and Police Station SAANJH Kendra. The district, sub-division, and police station level SAANJH Committees having community members were also formed to ensure community participation in the management of SAANJH Kendras.

A budget head was created to provide institutionalised infrastructural support to provide physical infrastructure, and IT equipped SAANJH Kendras at sub-divisions and police stations.

In 2010, the Punjab Governance Reforms Commission (PGRC) recommended to the State Government to set up SAANJH (Community Policing Centres) attached to the police stations throughout the State. To address the pivotal concerns regarding Policing in Punjab and to ensure engaged governance through SAANJH, key reforms were recommended by PGRC, and the government implemented the same. These are as follows:

In order to reduce the harassment and corruption and, to form a basis for grievance redressal, for combating inconsistency in reporting complaints and recording FIRs, the community policing system through SAANJH was to provide online registration of the complaints. Issuance of unique number for follow up by the citizen and status of the progress online and was also to have the visitor's enquiry counters.

For ensuring an increase in the confidence of the people in Police, the earlier practice of performance being measured on the number of complaints received was to be replaced by performance measured as per the ratio between petty crimes and heinous crimes.

As the situation stood, the Police routinely did not register complaints, and that led to a great deal of mistrust on the part of the citizenry. The establishment of SAANJH Kendras provided the people with a platform to register gender-related complaints, as also an institutionalised informal justice delivery system in Community Police Centres (CPC). This has put in place a redressal system for domestic violence, dowry demands and other gender-related cases with no stigma attached.

For improving the quality of investigation, a dedicated team for the investigation work in the police stations and one inspector dedicated for the delivery of police services and community policing work—all this was done.

In order to promote gender justice and address the inadequate diversity of representation in the police, a five-year plan to be put in place to enhance 10 per cent of women's representation in the entire strength of the civil and armed police.

To reinforce the idea of community policing, deployment of the CPC staff for security duty to be discontinued.

In order to minimise political intervention and provide continuity, the tenure of the SHO was now fixed for a minimum of one year (Section 15 of the Punjab Police Act). Earlier, the average posting of the district police chief, deputy superintendent of police, police station chief was about or less than one year.

For increasing the trust amongst the citizens and providing them with dignified access to the services, self-declarations and declarations by any two persons of the area, supported by documents to be accepted and forwarded to the concerned agencies for approval. Previously, verification including documents like passport, character certificate, arms license, etc., and testimonies of the neighbour, panchayat member and municipal commissioner were mandatory for most attestations.

Police clearance certificate, issue of residence permits and visa extension for the foreigners, were necessary through the SSP Office. However, all these cases were to be dealt with by the district SAANJH Kendra and action taken was notified online; thus, ensuring a transparent and harassment-free delivery.

Previously, the reporting of the missing persons, missing articles at the police station was not transparent and lacked accountability. Under SAANJH the missing person report was to be entertained at CPC, to be available online, via SMS at the counter of CPC. In addition, weekly updates to be made available to the citizen, thereby reducing harassment by the police and for ensuring a higher level of accountability.

On October 17, 2011, the Government of Punjab formally launched the SAANJH programme by inaugurating 115 state-of-the-art SAANJH Kendras all over the state.

In 2012, the services provided by SAANJH were brought under the purview of the Punjab Right to Services Act, 2011, to ensure time-bound service delivery and accountability by providing provision for appeals and penalty in case of non-delivery of the service within the specified time. In August 2012, the Government of Punjab, Home Affairs and Justice Department implemented facilitation charges on the services provided by the SAANJH Kendras. A total of 27 District SAANJH Kendras, 114 Sub-division SAANJH Kendras and 151 Police Station SAANJH Kendras, i.e. a total of 292 SAANJH Kendras were designated as facilitation fee collection centres. The guidelines regarding fee collection and maintenance of SAANJH funds were developed and implemented. Each SAANJH Kendra has its separate bank account and, being registered as a society, each centre has a service tax and income tax number and is exempted from income tax under Section 12AA of Income Tax Act. In December 2012, the district authorities were barred from deputing SAANJH staff without permission of CAD on any security, law and order and VIP duties, to ensure their availability in SAANJH centres.

In April 2015, SAANJH advisory boards were constituted to widen the scope of community participation from the grassroots level.

In April 2017, the Director-General of the Bureau of Police Research and Development (BPRD), Ministry of Home Affairs, Government of India, appreciated the community policing programme of Punjab.

SAANJH has 27 District SAANJH Kendras at the district level, 114 Sub-division SAANJH Kendras at the sub-division level and 363 Police Station SAANJH Kendras at the police station level, which are functional.

Unique Features of SAANJH

Community policing is not a stand-alone programme. The present model has been conceived as an institutionalised programme which is integral to the regular policing.

The practical explorations and experimentation with the various models of community policing, particularly in a post-conflict situation, has reinforced the understanding that the community-policing is neither a stand-alone programme nor a set of the schemes for promoting community-police interaction for sharing of information, but it is policing per se. In other words, community-policing is not merely policing for the community; it is policing along with the community converged with the existing policing structure, civil society, civil administration and IT applications.

It is to re-establish a link between the police and the community to deliver the services in an efficient, equitable and effective manner. In other words, it is not policing for the community or through the community, but it is policing along with the community.

Convergence with the Police: This model is unique as it has been conceived to make community policing integral to regular policing. It is not a public relations activity or voluntary social work or cosmetic engagement of the community for police work like traffic management, the security of localities, etc. It is policing for crime prevention, investigation and peacebuilding with the active engagement of the community. To converge with the regular policing, SAANJH Kendras were established at each administrative level of the police department, namely, State police headquarters, range offices, district headquarters, police offices at the sub-division level, and at the core level, i.e. police stations. A community affairs division (CAD), an apex State level secretariat, was created at the headquarter level with an Additional Director General of Police (ADGP) rank police officer as its in-charge. At the range level, an officer of the rank of Inspector General of Police (IGP) who along with the range level police administration would also overview and monitor the SAANJH function in their respective range. District SAANJH Kendras (DSK) work from the district police office under the overall supervision of the Commissioner of Police (CP)/Senior Superintendent of Police (SSP) and an SP/DSP rank officer as the District Community Policing Officer (DCPO) to supervise the SAANJH programme at the district level as a nodal officer. The Deputy Superintendent of Police (DSP) and the Station House Officer (SHO) of a police station are liable for the functioning of Sub-division SAANJH Kendra (SDSK) and the Police Station SAANJH Kendra (PSSK) respectively.

This convergence has been constructed from below, i.e. from the police station level upwards to mitigate the spatial disconnect, corruption and ensure harassment-free service delivery, and for building a safe, secure and socially harmonious environment. The first level of convergence of the police with the community has been institutionalised through building a physical infrastructure within the vicinity of the police station, sub-division police office and district level police headquarter, to mitigate the spatial disconnect.

The second level of convergence is to create an infrastructure to deliver services in a transparent and accountable manner. A majority of the population visit the police station to avail themselves these services expecting that these services will be available to them in these centres. Each service has to be treated as a single module with a simplified proforma and prescribed timeline.

The third level of converge is to create institutional mechanisms for the citizen to participate in creating a safe and secure environment by preparing locality security plans. And, also engage the civil society activists, experts and stakeholders, i.e. the police and the parties to the conflict to resolve the conflict and formulate strategies to prevent their recurrence.

These three s's, i.e. spatial connect, service delivery, and a safe and secure environment, constitute the backbone of this institutionalised partnership.

Moreover, at the State, district, and sub-division and at the police station level, there are public committees in which ADGP CAD, CP Commissionerate/SSP District, DSP Sub-division and SHO Police Station are the ex-officio chairpersons of these committees. All these DSKs, SDSKs and PSSKs are staffed with the regular police officers who perform their duties in civil uniform and are trained before their induction in the SAANJH programme. Each SAANJH Kendra staff is headed by a Non-Gazetted Officer assisted by four junior officers.

Institutional Structure of SAANJH Programme

Figure 3.1 Police Organisation and Community-Police Centres (SAANJH Kendras) Structure

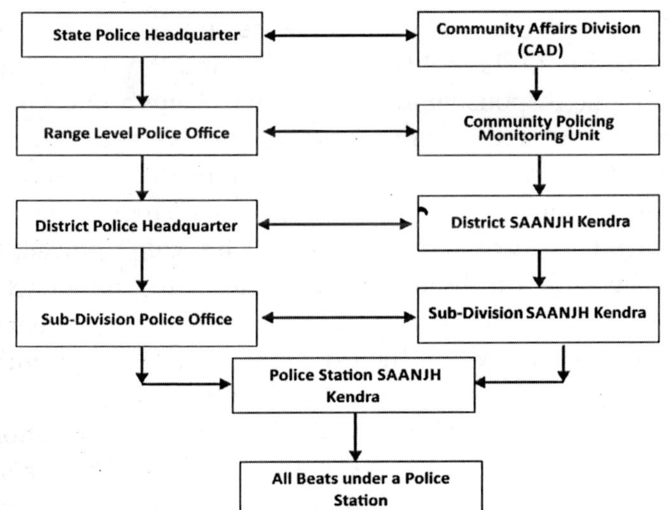

Convergence with the Community: For democratisation of the policing, the foremost requisite is to build a partnership based on collaborative initiatives. This arrangement has been based on comparative advantage and effective division of labour between the police functionaries, volunteers and support structures. This partnership will elicit community participation, mobilisation and support for improving security in the area and spreading awareness about the citizens' rights and also sensitising the community to the rights and concerns of the vulnerable sections. This collaborative relationship between the community representatives, volunteers and the police, necessitates putting in place the democratic platforms and forums to ensure productive participation of each stakeholder.

The participation of the stakeholders has been envisioned in various dimensions ranging from the framing of specific goals, identifying the strategy and monitoring of the programmes. This will provide not only legitimacy but also reinforce the stakeholder's commitment to the programme.

In many societies, there may be initial resistance to participation in the policing activities, and the community may not be responsive to the initiatives being undertaken. However, the community may be responsive to an entirely different area of concern, such as combating drug abuse, girl-child trafficking or safety of older persons. These initiatives can facilitate entry and credibility in the community, and then the same can be used as a platform to promote and mobilise the community.

The rule of law and the principles of good governance seek to involve the community, interest groups and stakeholders from the inception of the functioning of the governance systems. However, this needs to be layered, made responsive and institutionalised. For instance, these levels can be further classified into three stages, reflecting different levels of participation. Ideally, the stages would refer to planning, implementation and monitoring. Laws and policies that already exist can seek participation through an institutionalised community interface. The levels of participation would vary from public awareness, i.e. where the public is informed, to consultations with the interest groups, collaboration with the stakeholders and empowering through multilateral representations. Community participation is central to the SAANJH programme. In the SAANJH programme, the attempt has been made to redefine the boundary conditions for building partnership with the community.

SAANJH Kendras work as Non-Government Organisations (NGO) which are registered under the Societies Registration Act, 1860 and are managed by a governing body called SAANJH Committee, which is inevitable for the functioning of any organisation registered under this Act. District SAANJH Committees, Sub-Division SAANJH Committees and Police Station SAANJH Committees have members from the police department, civil administration and community. The community representatives are non-official members who are appointed, terminated and superannuated as per the prescribed procedure to avoid any ad hoc practices. These members are from amongst the academicians, heads of schools and colleges, human rights activists, lawyers or eminent people from other fields.

Convergence with Civil Administration: Another important prerequisite is to formulate strategies and protocols for networking between the police, civil society and civil administration. Networking for various initiatives is important, whereby they provide linkages in addressing the concept of partnership and ownership to safety in a holistic manner.

Having built up rapport and network through interventions on social issues, simultaneously platform and protocols for the implementation of the core policing by actively engaging the civil administration, and community needs have been put in place. The participation of the civil administration and community for providing access to the police services, resolution of disputes, victim relief and rehabilitation and for crime prevention has been institutionalised.

The SAANJH Committees have an inbuilt representation of the civil administration as in the formation of these committees, the officials of the civil administration are also given representation as to the ex-officio committee members apart from the police. Whereas in the District SAANJH Committees, Civil Surgeon, District Education Officer, District Programme Officer, District Welfare Officer and others are made members; their subordinate counterparts at the Sub-division and line departments, such as Sub-divisional Magistrate, Senior Medical Officer, Child Development Project Officer, Block Development and Panchayat Officer from the Sub-Division and Medical Officer of the Community Health Centre, Circle Supervisor (Aanganwadi) and Head of College/School are made representative members of the civil administration at the local level.

Convergence with Information and Technology: This is the integration of the engaged governance with the e-governance. SAANJH Kendras throughout the State are well equipped with IT infrastructure and networked to a central server. These provide services through the SAANJH portal and various mobile applications. The central server of SAANJH has been established at the Police Lines, Ludhiana, and is the main bedrock of this project. This central server runs all the time. To run, maintain and upgrade the central server, an agreement has been made with the

Traffic Solutions Company, Ludhiana and, presently, 10 engineers, 07 front-end team members, 02 back-end team members and 01 field helper of the company are working on this server. The technical team of the company also visits SAANJH Kendras to assist and resolve the technical issues at the ground level as and when required. SAANJH Kendras, apart from providing services through a single-window system, are providing services in online mode as well. For availing online police services, people-friendly Apps have been developed, and the citizens can avail these services through these Apps.

The convergence of technology has made police functioning transparent and effective. To illustrate, the first information reports (FIRs) are updated online as per the directions of the Supreme Court. Further, as per Rule 23.17 of The Punjab Police Rules, 1934 deals with information sheets of the accused persons which are issued and received by the different police stations manually. Through the 'SAANJH' server, the details pertaining to the information sheets have been digitised and are sent and received online through the 'SAANJH' network. Around 8700 information sheets have been dispatched and received via the SAANJH network since 26.10.2017. This has saved 8700 man-days of the Punjab police and has also saved many financial resources of the State Government, i.e. saving of TA/DA, use of the government transportation, etc., as the manual dispatch and receipt of these information sheets would have taken one complete day of duty of a police official.

These convergences, i.e. with the police, the civil society, technology and civil administration seek to provide holistic answers to complex problems. Undoubtedly, these convergences are important, but there are certain prerequisite activities to be undertaken to make them functional.

Prerequisite Activities for Democratic Policing

Breaking the Spatial Disconnect

The spatial disconnect breeds exclusion. The police station as a space per se is stigmatised. For the woman, visiting the police station exposes her to be labelled as a fallen person, for the Dalits, it robs them of their dignity and for the white-collared, it compromises their social status and so on. The new space created is a step towards a participatory model of partnership between the police and the public.

As discussed earlier, spaces are cultural constructs. The police stations have their own cultural context carefully nurtured by the colonial rule and provided continuity by the post-colonial state and the society. The citizens resist visiting the police stations due to the stigma attached to the police stations as these are perceived to be the space frequented by criminals, antisocial elements and by those who are a potential threat and/or the violators of the accepted social norms. Merely the architecturally designed modern police stations may not de-stigmatise a police station. It will continue to be socially exclusive. Therefore, it was proposed to create the new space (in the proximity of a police station) with redefined functionality, normative predispositions and institutional framework. The new space was designed with the following distinct features:

(i) The new space created was renamed as SAANJH Police Stations (Citizen-Police Partnership Centres). The new label was a departure from the past memory of the police stations being the spaces usually considered to be infested by the criminals and the authoritarian police.

(ii) The SAANJH Kendra will not have a police person at the entrance, a symbol of the police station being a restrictive space. It will be replaced with a transparent building with see-through glass structures.

(iii) The new space has been designed to give a feeling of being accessible, dignified and comfortable. Unlike the police stations, in which the conduct of the functionaries, the layout and the movement inside sends a loud message that you are not welcome.

(iv) The new space will be managed and maintained by the citizens and the police together to build a perception that it is just like a school or a public health centre, etc. In other words, to encourage the community to have a sense of ownership of the space. To reinforce this, these centres are registered as non-government societies.

(v) It has been designed to provide dignified spaces to the community, complainants, and beneficiaries to have access to the services. A marked space is created for the police-community interaction to resolve the disputes, plan activities together for the security and safety of their locality.

(v) Above all, through these spaces, the vulnerable sections can have access to the police services without being stigmatised.

Figure 3.2 A 3D-Imagery of the SAANJH Kendra

SAANJH Kendras are established as the front-end of the police stations to ensure delivery of the police services in a time-bound manner. These centres are also the nodal places for the police-community extension services having provisions for the registration of the public complaints, grievance redressal and victim relief. SAANJH Kendras also provide space to facilitate the victims of the crime in getting legal aid and compensation, and for resolution of the domestic, economic and social disputes.

Institutionalisation of Collaborative Partnership

The main thrust has to be to empower both the community and the police together for crime prevention, for building a safe, secure environment and efficient delivery of justice. There has to be a built-in mechanism of partnership and coordination between the community and the police. It is to be channelised through procedures and protocols rather than voluntary efforts.

There has to be an institutional system of mainstreaming the diversity in terms of representation, participation and decision-making both for the police and the community.

A number of crimes remain invisible due to the normative sanctions attached to them. For instance, the invisibility of the gender-related crimes, especially those occurring within the family, is quite high. Besides, these violations are not reported for lack of perception of injustice. The community, police personnel, change agents, and potentially vulnerable sections have to be sensitised to the existing societal biases and prejudices and accorded priority to build social fencing.

Registered as an NGO: Why NGO?

The SAANJH Kendras have to be autonomous registered societies in partnership with the representatives of the police, the administration and the civil society.

The registered societies have to include statutory provisions to enable the police-community partnership to manage these centres collectively and in a transparent manner.

It has an institutionalised system of taking decision collectively for providing harassment and corruption-free delivery of services, building a safe and secure environment and for the resolution of the societal conflicts. SAANJH Kendras work as a society and charge a facilitation fee for every service, thereby, generating income, which is exempted from income tax. SAANJH Kendras use the revenue for self-maintenance and also contribute fifty per cent of its income in the government treasury. As a registered society, there is a statutory provision to have an annual audit of their accounts.

- **Institutionalised Participatory Process:** The partnership has been institutionalised through a government order. The stakeholders are from among the existing support system, such as the local self-government, education and health departments, social welfare, women and child development departments. The representatives of these departments shall be ex-officio members of the community-policing programme. There shall be representatives from the social welfare organisations, legal experts, social workers, cultural, social and academic personalities and community members engaged in productive pursuits like commerce, industry, trade, etc. These will be co-opted members.

  This will help the integration of the support systems into policing activities. Another level of integration is through the management of the community policing programmes, including disbursement of the resources together with the community representation.
- **Establish Procedures for Working in Partnership:** Integral to governance is the accountability of its institutions and transparency in the process of

delivery of justice. While internal accountability, referring to the hierarchical chain of command, has been part of the traditional authority systems, it is the accountability to the citizens and to the rule of law that is being strengthened. The institutional accountability structures that are democratic in their responsiveness, protective of the rights and sensitive to the varied cultures have to be built. Internal accountability within the institutions needs to be made more transparent and responsive rather than status quo-ist.

The procedures detailing the partnership have to be listed in the government order and rules and regulations described in the registration of the document. This should include internal and external linkages of administration, finances and human resources. There have to be transparent processes of decision-making. The proceedings of the meetings have to be formally recorded. Exhaustive appraisal tools have to be developed to monitor the implementation of the community-policing programmes and the allocation and disbursement of funds.

- **Defining Role and Functions:** The role and functions of the stakeholders need to be clearly defined as also to identify the complementary goals. The sustainability of the programme demands that an integrated plan should be mooted in relation to the activities besides the mainstreaming of the community-policing initiatives.

A standardised service-delivery mechanism needs to be instated. For instance, redressal of the complaints against the policemen, counselling and advocacy for dealing with the crimes against women, free legal aid for the vulnerable and poor, single-window police services for the citizens, etc.

Administrative Structure of SAANJH and Functions

There is a five-tiered vertical administrative structure. Horizontally, each tier has multi-sectoral linkages with the government departments and the community structures. Each sector is woven into the functions of the tier.

Box 3.2 Administrative Structure of Community Policing Programme - SAANJH	
State Police Headquarters	**Community Affairs Division (CAD) at the State Police Headquarters**
Range Offices	**Community Policing Monitoring Units**
District Police Headquarter	**District SAANJH Committee**
	District SAANJH Kendra 1. Grievance Redressal Unit 2. Community Services cum Information Unit (a) NRIs and Foreign Counter (b) Crime Prevention Counter (c) Verification and Permission Counter (d) RTI Counter (e) Traffic Management and Information Counter 3. Legal Aid and Victim Relief Unit 4. Sensitisation and Dispute Resolution Unit (a) Gender Dispute Resolution (b) Economic Dispute Resolution (c) Social and Political Conflict Resolution
Sub-Division Police Office	**Sub-Division SAANJH Committee**
	Sub-Division SAANJH Kendra 1. Community Services-cum-Information Unit 2. NRI and Foreign Counter 3. Gender Dispute Resolution Unit
Police Station	**Police Station SAANJH Committee**
	Police Station SAANJH Kendra 1. Community Services-cum-Information Unit 2. Gender Dispute and Social Conflict Resolution Unit
Police Station Beats	**To provide police services at the doorstep**

I. Community Affairs Division (CAD): Police Headquarters Level

The Community Affairs Division (CAD) is located at the Punjab Police Headquarters to design, develop, implement and monitor programmes in the area of Community Policing. The CAD takes the decision about the various reports as the periodical returns are required to be received from the field units for better monitoring and implementation of the programme. A Nodal Officer of the CAD in the rank of ADGP is responsible for policy formulation, implementation, review and evaluation of the scheme. The Nodal Officer is assisted by IGP/Headquarters, who is redesignated as IGP/Headquarters-cum-Community Affairs. An officer in the rank of DIG is posted in CAD and is designated as DIG Community Affairs. The CAD functions in consultation and conjunction with a State Level Steering Committee and District Committees.

Box 3.3 Functions of Community Affairs Division (CAD)

- To lay down the policy for conceptualising and institutionalising community policing initiatives in the State.
- To issue broad guidelines for the successful running of the District SAANJH Kendras (DSKs), Sub-Division SAANJH Kendras (SDSKs), and Police Station SAANJH Kendras (PSSKs).
- To coordinate and conduct a periodical review of the working of these centres.
- To provide budgetary and financial support.

The community affairs division has a grievance redressal unit which will facilitate the citizens to seek remedy and redressal of their grievances. The dispute resolution unit oversees the performance of the dispute resolution committees at the District, Subdivision and Police Station level and issues appropriate guidelines from time to time.

The economic offence, women cells, non-resident Indian (NRI) units shall also be located to monitor the work within their purview at a different level. The monitoring and coordination unit shall lay down guidelines for the smooth functioning of convergence with the police, civil society, civil administration and information and technology. These units function within boundaries defined by the scope of work allocated to the CAD.

Box 3.4 Units of Community Affairs Division

- Grievance Redressal Unit
- Dispute Resolution Unit
- Economic Offence, Women, NRI Affairs and Delivery of Police Services Units
- Monitoring and Coordination Unit

Functions of CAD

- To lay down the policy for conceptualising and institutionalising community policing initiatives in the State.
- To issue broad guidelines for the successful running of the District SAANJH Kendras (DSKs), Sub-Division SAANJH Kendras (SDSKs), and Police Station SAANJH Kendras (PSSKs).
- To coordinate and conduct a periodical review of the working of these centres.
- To provide budgetary and financial support.

II. Community Policing Monitoring Unit: Range Level

The DIG Ranges shall monitor the community policing SAANJH programme and submit the report to the CAD for perusal after getting the same from the District SAANJH Kendras (DSKs), Sub-Division SAANJH Kendras (SDSKs) and Police Station SAANJH Kendras (PSSKs) within its preview.

III. District SAANJH Kendras: District Level

At the district level, these are District SAANJH Kendras and the District Level SAANJH Committees to ensure the networking of the DSKs with other government departments and administrative structures. It also streamlines the training of the personnel at the district level and coordinates with the fourth and fifth tier, i.e. Sub-Division SAANJH Kendras, and Police Stations SAANJH Kendras.

The district SAANJH Kendras will be nodal for the data management, creation of information pool and allocation of resources to Sub-Division and police station SAANJH Kendras. The SAANJH Kendras located in the districts shall function under the overall supervision of district-level Community Police Committees coordinated by the District Police Chief.

Box 3.5 Units of District SAANJH Kendra

1. Grievance Redressal Unit
2. Community Services cum Information Unit
   (a) NRIs and Foreign Counter
   (b) Crime Prevention Counter
   (c) Verification and Permission Counter
   (d) RTI Counter
   (e) Traffic Management and Information Counter
3. Legal Aid and Victim Relief Unit
4. Sensitisation and Dispute Resolution Unit
   (a) Gender Dispute Resolution
   (b) Economic Dispute Resolution
   (c) Social and Political Conflict Resolution

*Note: For detailed functions of the Units, see Box 3.6

The district-level SAANJH Kendra shall be located in the close proximity of the district police headquarters. The district SAANJH Kendras will be managed by the Chief Community Police Officer (Inspector rank) and assisted by other staff members.

These Kendras have four resource centres that provide services directly to the citizens and also through various SAANJH Kendras located in the police stations and sub-divisional police offices within a district.

The four units are; grievance redressal, dispute resolution, community services-community-information, legal aid and victim relief. These units perform the following functions;

A Traffic Advisory Committee is set up in the District SAANJH Kendra to function as an interface between the traffic police and the commuters. The SAANJH Committee acts as a Traffic Advisory Committee to avoid multiplicity of oversights.

Box 3.6 Functions of Different Units at District, Sub-Division, and Police Station Level SAANJH Kendras

1. Grievance Redressal Unit (GRU)

This unit receives complaints against the police from the whole district and disposes of them after the necessary and time-bound action is taken.

2. Community Services–cum-Information Unit

This unit provides police services and information to the visitor and has the following counters. All these units have dedicated officers for efficient and accountable service delivery. All sorts of permissions and verifications are handled, and service requests are acknowledged properly with receipts.

(a) NRIs and Foreign Counter: This counter provides all the services to NRI and foreign tourists who are visiting the district, state or country. This unit is solely dedicated to the service of foreign visitors to make their stay more safe, secure and comfortable.

(b) Crime Prevention Counter: This counter provides the copies of the First Information Report (FIR), untraced report and progress report on the investigation of the ongoing criminal case if the applicant is unable to get the same from the concerned until the police station.

(c) Verification and Permission Counter: All sorts of

permissions and verifications are handled at this counter for the convenience of the service seeker. All service requests are acknowledged with proper receipts having the expected time to be taken. This counter has a charter of services mentioning documentation required and tentative time to be taken.

(d) RTI Counter: Applications under the Right to Information Act are received here. The information asked for is provided to the applicant from this counter only within the given time frame.

(e) Traffic Management and Information Counter: This is a dedicated counter in all the centres to receive payments of traffic challans. At the DSK level, there is centralised pooling of information on traffic challans, impounded vehicles or documents held for traffic violation anywhere in the district. Traffic rule violator is allowed to make payment of his penalty in these centres and is provided with the payment slip and whereabouts of his impounded vehicle or documents.

3. Legal Aid and Victim Relief Unit

The **Victim Relief Unit** focuses on the victims, their rights, needs and expectations. The dedicated victim relief and legal aid unit shall improve the police response to the victims of sexual and violent crime assisted by trained women officers to avoid insensitive questioning. For easy access, **Victim Helplines** and **Women Helplines** are set up.

4. Sensitisation and Gender Dispute Resolution Unit

(a) Gender Dispute Resolution Cell: This Cell, specifically, deals with the cases of women who are the victims of domestic violence.

(b) Economic Dispute Resolution Cell: This special cell deals with all the economic offences like fraud and embezzlement cases, with the help of a Committee of Experts having representation of financial experts, law professionals, and governance specialists.

(c) Social and Political Conflict Resolution Cell: The conflict resolution cells shall function to resolve caste or communal conflicts—latent or manifest, with the help of arbitration between the conflicting parties

These SAANJH Kendras provide a unique identification

number to facilitate tracking of the complaints, status of FIR, investigation, charge sheeting, etc. The conflict and dispute resolution is achieved with the active engagement of the counsellors, civil society groups and social activists. It will also have dedicated staff to assist the citizens in getting legal aid, relief for the victims and provide facilities to the NRIs for resolution of their local disputes. These centres actively engage community members for taking the decision to smoothly run the SAANJH Kendras and also for pooling human and material resources.

Box 3.7 Types of Disputes / Conflicts

- **Gender Dispute**—Matrimonial and family disputes involving females.
- **Economic Disputes**—Any dispute between two legal entities, between a legal entity and an individual, or between individuals that may arise from the breach of a contract, or from a dispute related to production or business operations.
- **Political Disputes**—Conflict subjected to debate at any of the political levels, even as low as municipal, regional, inter-ethnic, which cannot be resolved by reducing it to a neutral argument.
- **Social Conflict**—When two or more actors oppose each other in social interaction, and each exerts social power to achieve desired goals while preventing the other from attaining their own.

Administration of the Distinct SAANJH Kendra

The main role of the SAANJH Kendras in charge is to coordinate with the Convenor (District Police Chief) and Co-convenor (Citizens Representative), the subdivision and police station SAANJH Kendras within the district, the state-level community affairs division (CAD). He shall review the daily performance of the district SAANJH Kendra, liaise with civil administration, maintain records of the proceedings of the SAANJH Committees and organise various outreach community programmes.

Box 3.8 Structure of the District SAANJH Committee

- Chairperson of the District SAANJH Committee (SP/DSP*)—Convenor
- Community Representative—Co-convenor
- District SAANJH committee members should not exceed 25 members

Box 3.9 Members of the District SAANJH Committee

Official Members (7)	Non-Official Members (12)
• SSP/Commissioner of Police will be the Chairperson of this Committee; • SP/DSP* Community Policing (Nodal Officer) will function as District Community Policing Officer (DCPO) and will function as the Convener of this committee; • In-charge District SAANJH Kendra; • District Health Officer/ Civil Surgeon; • District Education Officer; • District Programme Officer (Department of Social Security and Development of Women and Child); • District Welfare Officer (Department of Welfare of BC and SC); and, • District Red Cross Officer.	• Social workers (state or national awardees); • Academicians; • Principals of Colleges; • Lawyers; • Human Rights Activists; • Disaster Management Professionals; and, • Cyber or Web Experts and Media Persons • (At least four members should be women) **Tenure:** • Non-official members are selected for a tenure of at least two years. Tenure of a member with efficient and active participation may be prolonged with the consensus among non-official members and approval of the Chairperson of the Committee.

*In minor districts, DSPs have been deputed as DCPOs.

IV. Subdivision SAANJH Kendras at the Sub-Division Level

To enhance the police services outreach to the lowest administrative units, Sub-Division SAANJH Kendras are established at the Sub-Division level. These centres have their own Sub-Division SAANJH Committee. These centres have three units with a redefined scope and reach.

Box 3.10 Units of Sub-Division SAANJH Kendra

- Community Services-cum-Information Unit
- NRIs and Foreign Counter
- Gender Dispute Resolution Unit

*Note: For detailed functions of the Units, see Box 3.6

Through these units, the police services shall be delivered with a facility to track the complaints online, status of FIR, investigation and charge sheeting. The main focus of these Kendras would be to resolve disputes through counselling, negotiation and mediation and also actively work to provide for legal aid and implement crime prevention strategies along with the community. To make its service delivery transparent, accountable, and efficient, a receipt with a unique ID number is given to the beneficiary or complainant.

Administration

The role of the SAANJH Kendra (sub-division) in charge is similar to the in charge of the district SAANJH Kendra within their territorial jurisdiction. At the sub-division level, the major focus is to actively engage with the police station outreach centres. These centres are actively engaged in the implementation of dispute resolution functions.

Box 3.11 Structure of the Sub-Division SAANJH Committee

- Deputy Superintendent of Police—Convenor
- Community Representative—Co-convenor
- The number of members of a Sub-Division Level Committee should not exceed 20

Box 3.12 Members of the Sub-Division SAANJH Committee	
Official Members (6) • DSP (Sub-Division) (Convener-cum-Chairperson); • In-charge Sub-Division SAANJH Kendra; • Sub-Divisional Magistrate (SDM) • Senior Medical Officer (SMO); • Child Development Project Officer (CDPO); and, • Block Development and Panchayat Officer (BDPO).	**Non-Official Members (12)** • Social Workers • Heads of Colleges/Schools • Lawyers • Community Representatives • President of Business Associations • Youth Clubs Members • Nehru Yuva Kendra Sangathan (NYKS) Members (At least four members should be women) **Tenure:** • Non-official members are selected for the tenure of at least two years. Tenure of a member with efficient and active participation may be prolonged with the consensus among non-official members and approval of the DSP/ACP.

V. Police Station SAANJH Kendra: Police Station Level

The ultimate goal was to reach out to the grassroots. Hence, every police station has been developed as the Police Station SAANJH Kendra. This is a unique initiative to construct a model of the citizen's engagement in policing from below. The police station is the fulcrum of the five tiers structure discussed above. In other words, the police station SAANJH Kendras act as a foundation for other tiers.

The police station being the nerve centre of policing needed these reforms urgently. It is the first contact point of the citizen to avail the police services. There are two units located in these centres keeping in view the capacity—

human as well as material. These units are the community services-cum-information and gender dispute and conflict resolution. Both these units perform the same functions as are performed by the sub-division SAANJH Kendras, within the close proximity of the residents of the area.

Box 3.13 Units of Police Station SAANJH Kendra

- Community Services-cum-Information Unit
- Gender Dispute and Social Conflict Resolution Unit

*Note: For detailed functions of the Units, see Box 3.6

These centres have the autonomy to add or subtract the services to be provided to the citizens as per the local needs. However, the backbone functions, as described earlier, cannot be changed. The local specific functions and activities can be added with the approval of the SAANJH committees.

For instance, if a Saanjh Kendra is located near the international border, the registration of foreign nationals can be added in the service list.

These SAANJH Kendras function under the overall supervision of the police-citizens committee to ensure transparency, right based citizen-police exchange and holistic response to complex issues. The structure of the police station SAANJH Committee is as under.

Box 3.14 Structure of the Police Station SAANJH Committee

- Station House Officer– **Convenor**
- Community Representative—**Co-convenor**

The number of the members of a District Level Committee should not exceed 15.

These centres are flexible enough to provide space to the individual officer or community leaders to initiate new experiments and, if found viable, can be institutionalised in the system.

Box 3.15 Members of the Police Station SAANJH Committee

Official Members (5)	Non-Official Members (10)
• SHO Police Station (Chairperson-cum-Convener) • In-charge Police Station SAANJH Kendra • Medical Officer of Community Health Centre • Circle Supervisor (Aanganwadi) and • Head of College/School	• Social Workers • Lawyers • Community Representatives • President of Business Associations • Youth Clubs' Members • Nehru Yuva Kendra Sangathan (NYKS) Members (At least three members shall be women) **Tenure** • Non-official members are selected for the tenure of at least two years. Tenure of a member with efficient and active participation may be prolonged with the consensus among non-official members and approval of the SHO Police Station.

All centres located in the police stations, subdivision levels and at the district police headquarters shall perform those functions which are within the capacity, reach and range of each layer of policing. A detailed analysis of the services delivered, disputes resolved, victim relief provided, and complaints registered and grievances redressed shall throw some light on the efficacy of this model.

Service Delivery at SAANJH Kendras: A Review

SAANJH Kendras are the front-end of the police stations. This experiment entails—(a) making police directly accountable to the citizens; (b) institutionalisation of the community-police partnership through establishment of police station outreach centres attached to each police station with the active participation of the citizens in decision-making; (c) activated institutional mechanisms to make police stations responsive to the needs of gender, Dalits, migrants, workers, children, etc.; (d) build the capacities of the police stations commensurate with the citizens' needs.

SAANJH provides the following services:

i. Providing Police Services to the Public
ii. Dispute Resolution
iii. Providing Relief to Victims
iv. Grievance Redressal and Registering Complaints

i. Providing Police Services to the Public

SAANJH police stations have been providing 43 services in the Commissionerates and 27 services in other 24 police districts (for details see Table 3.13, Annexures-II). These services include, verification of passports, arms licenses, service, character, servants/tenants, issuance of various no-objection certificates, registration of complaint, issuance of the copy of FIR, report of the loss of the article, etc. All these services have been timelined under the Punjab Right to Service Act, 2011.

Table 3.9 Services Delivered by SAANJH

S. No.	*Services*
1	Renewal of arms licence
2	Renewal where a licensee has shifted his residence
3	Renewal where an adverse report is received
4	Renewal of arms licence (apply after due date)
5	Addition/Deletion of weapon
6	Entry of weapon on arms license
7	Extension of purchase period of weapon
8	Registration of foreigner (arrival/departure)
9	Extension of residential permit of foreigners
10	Copy of FIR or DDR

11	NOC for the use of loudspeakers
12	NOC for fair/melas/exhibition/sports events
13	Stranger verification
14	Tenant/servant verification (local area)
15	Tenant/servant verification (other district/State)
16	Other verification related service
17	Copy of untraced report in road accident cases
18	Copy of untraced report in case of the stolen vehicle
19	Copy of untraced report in theft cases
20	NOC for pre-owned vehicles
21	Service verification (resident of Punjab)
22	Character verification
23	NOC issuance/renewal of Arms Licence dealer
24	NOC for setting up of cinema hall
25	Passport verification
26	Verification for fresh arms licence
27	Acknowledgement of complaint
28	Information of action taken on the complaint
29	MRG enquiry in case of loss of passport abroad
30	Other services related to passport
31	Countersign of document
32	Issuance of new arms licence
33	Issuance of duplicate arms license
34	NOC for sale of a weapon
35	Application for extension of the jurisdiction (Pb)
36	Cancellation of arms licence on the request
37	Change of address in arms licence
38	Appointment of the retainer of weapon
39	Addition/Deletion of the retainer in arms licence

40	Change of bore
41	Permission for deposit weapon in case death
42	Permission sale/transfer weapon in a death case
43	Permission of addition of cartridges

**Note:* For details, see Table 3.13, Annexures II).

Figure 3.3 Number of Services Delivered by SAANJH

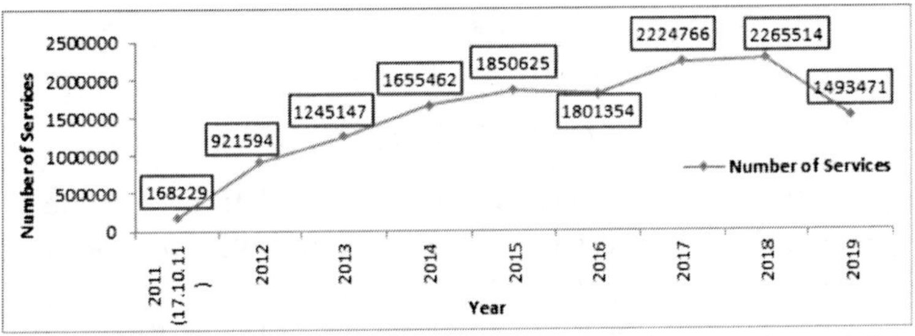

Source: Community Affairs Division, Punjab Police (For details, see Table 3.13, Annexures II).

More than one crore thirty-six lakh (1,36,26,162) different citizen-centric police services have been delivered to the public since its inception. To make the SAANJH experiment self-reliant in its functioning, the police services being provided are charged a certain cost. The facilitation charges are decided by applying a principle of cross-subsidy, whereby services most needed by the poor are nominally priced. Since all these Kendras are registered as NGOs, they have greater autonomy to use these resources to initiate community-oriented projects, upgrade technology, and ensure physical maintenance of these centres. The data clearly show that the services availed by the citizens are multiplying and so is the income. The accounts of each Kendra are audited. This has not only brought efficiency, accountability and transparency but also provided sustainability to these centres.

Figure 3.4 Facilitation Charges Received by SAANJH

Period	Facilitation Charges recieved
Sep, 2012 to March 2013	37,961,084
2013-14	71,839,948
2014-15	90,596,757
2015-16	104,567,794
2016-17	111,306,695
2017-18	148,504,716
2018-19	162,118,781

Source: Community Affairs Division, Punjab Police.

II. Providing Relief to the Victims

SAANJH police stations staff assists the victims of crime in completing the necessary paperwork and other procedural formalities for getting the statutory compensations (compensation to acid attack victims and the victims of the atrocities under the SC/ST Act, National Solatium Fund Scheme, and Accident Compensation) sanctioned from the competent authorities in the following cases.

(a) Untraced Accident Cases,
(b) SC/ST (Prevention of Atrocities) Act, 1989,
(c) Acid Attack Victims,
(d) Victims of General Crimes like Rape, Murder, etc.

Figure 3.5 Victim Compensation Assisted by SAANJH

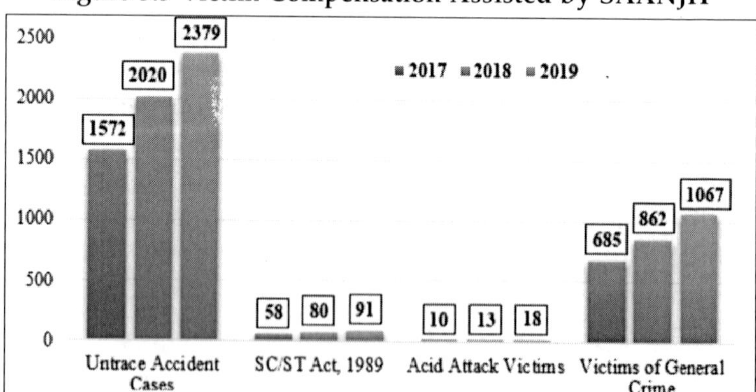

Source: Community Affairs Division, Punjab Police.

Accident Compensation and Interim Compensation of Rs. 50,000 in the event of death, Rs. 25,000 in the event of serious injury. The process begins after receiving the copy of FIR, post-mortem or injury report and a brief report about the accident case. These details are to be sent to the Presiding Officer of Motor Accidents Claims Tribunal (MACT).

III. Dispute Resolution Grievance Redressal and Registering Complaints

SAANJH police stations are staffed with the police personnel who have expertise in dispute resolution and assisted by professionals, and civil society activists have successfully gained the citizens' confidence. More than seventy thousand such disputes have been resolved with the help of the police-citizens committees since the committee was constituted at the SAANJH police stations in 2012.

The SAANJH police stations have also been designated as Complaint Registration Centres for the entire Punjab Police. Besides registration, these SAANJH police stations also handle the complaints marked by the senior officers for dispute resolution, especially those relating to matrimonial and domestic violence disputes. These centres have registered and processed around thirteen lakh complaints till 2017.

Quantification of Outcomes of SAANJH

The model has an inbuilt mechanism to measure the capacity of the SAANJH vis-a-vis human, infrastructural resources and system of management. The capacity of human resources has been assessed in terms of the skills acquired to deliver the services commensurate with the diversity sensitivity, rights of the vulnerable groups and mobilisation of the community. And, infrastructural resources have been mapped to capture built-in systems to overcome spatial disconnect, accessibility to services and pro-people ambience. The system of management is equipped to capture performance, data support, networking procedures and protocols.

The multi-cultural context presupposes that public policy and its operationalisation in terms of representation of diversity, sensitisation of the staff is integral to service delivery in accordance with multicultural needs. It is, therefore, imperative that the SAANJH represents a diverse population and remains responsive to the rights of the vulnerable groups. The efficacy of the model depends on how far the police services and the service provider are able to cater to the special needs of the senior citizens, people on the margins, gender and other victims.

The main challenge is to mainstream the community policing into regular policing, community initiatives and IT application. In other words, it will have to how far the principle of community participation has become operational and the technology integrated into the service delivery application to ensure transparency. The challenge remains, how far the formal institutions of police and informal institutions of community policing have transcended the societal consensus which is impregnated with unequal power.

Therefore, impact evaluation has to be inferential, as well as derivative. The relevant question to be answered is, how far institutionalisation of community policing has contributed to an increase in the confidence of the people in the justice delivery system.

Increased Confidence of the People in the Police

After the introduction of SAANJH in 2011, the 'Third Party Audit Report' mentioned with the help of crime data that the confidence of the people in policing has increased manifold. A proxy variable of the ratio between registration of petty crimes with the heinous crimes shows that an increased number of the people are coming to SAANJH police stations to register their complaints. In 2005, the petty to heinous crime ratio was 1.28, which increased to 2.29 by 2016. This is a remarkable shift.

Table 3.10 Ratio of Petty Crimes Over Heinous Crimes, 2005-16

Year	*Punjab*
2005	1.28
2006	1.30
2007	1.34
2008	1.38
2009	1.34
2010	1.38
2011	1.34
2012	1.37
2013	1.31
2014	1.89
2015	2.07
2016	2.29

Source: Ratio calculated from secondary data on crime incidences provided by Punjab Police Headquarters.

Similarly, the data clearly show that SAANJH centres could overcome the spatial stigma attached to the police stations as evident from the increase in the registration of gender-related crimes and resolution of familial disputes. The ratio of registration of crime against women multiplied from 0.04 in 2005 to 0.09 in 2016. This increase is consistent from 2013 onwards.

Service Delivery: Cost and Benefits

Above all, these functions are police functions which were also performed by the police staff earlier. SAANJH is just a change of the workspace. However, providing services through SAANJH police stations reduced the cost of providing the service from Rs. 494.80 per service to Rs. 412.20 per service. Therefore, SAANJH is financially contributing about Rs. 82.60 per person in providing service and saving the expenditure for the State (For details, see Table 3.14, Annexures II).

Table 3.11 Ratio of Crimes Against Women Over Total Cognisable Crimes, 2005-16

Year	*Crimes Against Women (IPC+SLL)*	*Total Cognisable Crimes (IPC+SLL)*	*Ratio*
2005	1969	53728	0.04
2006	2242	52798	0.04
2007	2694	58406	0.05
2008	2627	55358	0.05
2009	2631	53456	0.05
2010	2853	54986	0.05
2011	2641	51289	0.05
2012	3238	59467	0.05
2013	4994	64283	0.08
2014	5425	64974	0.08
2015	5291	60236	0.09
2016	5105	57739	0.09

Source: *Crime in India*, National Crime Records Bureau (2005-16).
**Note*: Ratio calculated from secondary data on crime incidences.

Financially Viable and Sustainable

These centres are not only self-sustaining but also generate revenue for the police department as well. As in the same financial year, i.e. 2018-19, these centres generated revenue of Rs. 16,21,18,781 through facilitation charges and Rs. 14 crore through passport verification. Since September 2018, 50 per cent of the income of SAANJH police stations, i.e.

Rs. 4,68,90,475 was deposited in the treasury of the Government of Punjab (For details, see Table 3.14, Annexures II).

These centres successfully helped in the image makeover of the police department as indicated by the findings of the recent 'Third Party Audit of SAANJH Kendra'.[2] This report states that 97.4 per cent beneficiaries who availed services from SAANJH police stations accepted that these centres project a better image of the police department and also reduced the scope of corruption. Most of the beneficiaries and the service seekers were satisfied with the working of the SAANJH police stations.

Improved Service Delivery

The services provided by the SAANJH Kendras have improved over the years (For details, see Table 3.13, Annexures-II). As per the Act, these services have to be provided within a time frame defined in the Act, thereby ensuring efficient and accountable service delivery. The citizens from any part of the State can approach the nearest SAANJH Kendra for obtaining information and services from any police station in the State. Hence, the increased outreach of the services.

Reduction of the Burden of the Police Station

A police-citizen committee constituted for each SAANJH Kendra handles multifarious work of these centres, especially, the resolution of disputes. It has also lowered the burden of police stations by taking away certain functions of the police stations like issuance of verification, no objection certificates and police clearance certificates.

1. Nearly 60,000 people belonging to different strata of society are members of these SAANJH Committees and SAANJH Advisory Boards.
2. SAANJH centres have received 2691 e-summons from the High Court till date, which the SAANJH Kendras facilitated.

3. SAANJH police stations have reduced a load of various police units by handling some of the duties that used to be earlier handled by them.

Mitigation of Disputes

SAANJH Kendras are also platforms for the partnership of the community with the police in planning and implementing locally relevant community-oriented projects. SAANJH Committees have co-opted experts, such as lawyers, psychologists and counsellors who are engaged in the panels for resolving disputes pertaining to women, children, senior citizens, and other vulnerable sections. The issues relating to the tenant-landlord disputes, petty traffic offences, public nuisance, etc., which affect the quality of life in the neighbourhood are also being handled by the SAANJH Kendras.

Increased Social Capital and Police-Public Relationship

SAANJH Kendras at the police station level enable every citizen to approach these centres for the delivery of services and aforementioned dispute resolutions. It also provides a platform for the multifaceted interaction between the members of the community and the police where the trained SAANJH staff interacts with the citizens at the front end while the police stations provide services at the back end.

This database is being used for the prevention and detection of crime by the various police units. The SAANJH control room functions round the clock and various field units of Punjab police approach the SAANJH control room for seeking details of crime and criminals as contained in these databases. This provides immediate help to the field units regarding the prevention and detection of crime.

Improved Crime Prevention, Detection and Police Management

- The SAANJH system renders help to the various

police units of Punjab Police in prevention and detection of crime.

- **Checking of Vehicles Lying in Police Station 'Malkhanas'**—Number of vehicles, i.e. stolen, recovered, challaned, etc. are lying in the Malkhanas police station. There is a centralised registry of the stolen vehicles from all over the country with the National Crime Records Bureau, Government of India. A special campaign was launched where the staff of the SAANJH Kendras procured details of the vehicles lying in the various police stations and compared these with the data of the stolen vehicles of the National Crime Record Bureau and data of the vehicles registered with the State Transport Commissioner. More often, it was observed that the vehicles stolen from one police station are recovered as unclaimed vehicles in some other police station and, thus, remain undetected. Now, this possibility has been eliminated by the above-mentioned system developed by SAANJH. The data of the vehicles stolen from Punjab, with effect from, 2011 is also maintained at SAANJH, which is provided to the field units and the police on 'Naka' duties. This again helps the police station staff in the prevention and detection of crime.

Increased Community Orientation of Police

SAANJH Kendras have been deliberately integrated with the local police set up by having local SSPs, sub-divisional police officers and in charge of the police stations as the chairperson of the SAANJH Committees at district, sub-division and police station level respectively. The entire SAANJH staff is on deputation from the police for a fixed period who, after working in SAANJH Kendras, go back to the core police work and new police officials, after proper training, are posted to the SAANJH Kendras. This has been planned so that the majority of the police force should have an orientation in the community policing projects, especially, in running the SAANJH Kendras. This gives a new perspective of policing and orientation to the police force.

To sum up, policing per se involves every facet of human existence. The institutions of the police, courts, and prisons are integrated components of the criminal justice system. The above case study has institutionalised the engagement of the citizens in the delivery of police services and ensured accountability of the police to the citizens. But, there is a need to work out details for quality investigation and an efficient and fair prosecution system. At another level, for deepening of the reforms for justice delivery, three main ideological filters have to be made integral, i.e. to introduce reforms for diversity sensitivity response of the law enforcement agencies; to put in place the private and the public spaces; and also to remove the dichotomy between nationalism and justice.

Case Study II—Meeting Trust Deficits: Rationalisation of Affidavits

Abolition of Affidavits in India*

Historically, governance in the post-colonial societies continued to function within the broad boundary conditions of: (a) Ria-Mai Baap, i.e. dole giver and dole receiver; (b) deficient citizens, i.e. subjects without claims and rights; (c) identity to be granted, but not integral to the citizenship. These boundary conditions contributed to the denial of key values, such as identity and dignity to its citizens leading to an experience of exclusion. This non-

* This case study is being reproduced from the status report of the Governement Reforms Commision of Punjab (2009 to 2017) written by Pramod Kumar, R.N. Gupta and J.R. Kundal.

recognition of personhood across the board made them 'deficient citizens'. To illustrate, even after independence from British colonialism, to prove their name, the citizens have to seek affirmation from a gazetted officer of the government. It can be exemplified in several ways; the most prevalent is the filling of affidavits for almost every interaction with the government. These are affirmations by the applicants in some cases supported by the third parties. Affidavits are symbolic of not only denial but the surrender of the basic rights of the citizens to prove their name and identity to be verified by the government functionaries. These are required for declarations relating to the citizen's profession, income, caste, residence proof, etc. Even to have access to public utilities, such as connections for electricity, sewerage, water supply, house construction, civic services including, birth, death, marriage, income certificates, caste identity and so on, affidavits are to be submitted.

In its preliminary findings, the Punjab Governance Reforms Commission realised that, first, the service delivery is a distinct element in itself and that there is no direct relationship between the economic or other benefits with the delivery of service. It further explained that there might also be other reasons, except affidavits only which could actually cause hurdles in availing the benefits under the public policies. There are many cases where one may not avail the service despite having an affidavit—thus reducing the scope to debate on the essentiality of affidavits any further. Second, the Commission also identified that the affidavits pose their own cost on the citizens—buying stamp paper, locating a deed writer, payment to the notary for attestation and the time and efforts consumed in these processes—thus putting the applicant in pain and harassment and making their belief more firm in the government being distant and indifferent. Third, in a majority of the cases, the affidavits do not have a particular sanctity in law, and the applicant-signatory, in any case, continues to be responsible for the statement made. Fourth, the public agencies get the advantage of imposing penal liability on the applicant for making wrong statements in terms of suspension of service. Fifth, attestations for verifications by the local officials like Municipal Councillors and Sarpanchs, are not custodians of information, especially, pertaining to the residence, and verification by them is not relevant.

Based on these observations, the Commission suggested necessary changes in the processes, procedures, rules, regulations and the policies relating to the affidavits, to the government. The Commission proposed that:

(a) Self-declaration to be accepted in place of affidavits in all cases where the affidavits are not required as per any statutory provisions and that the self-declarations should be a part of the application form.
(b) In cases where the statutory rules provide for an affidavit, the by-laws may be amended.
(c) In cases where the affidavits are required under any Act, the local field officials to be designated by the Deputy Commissioner, accessible at the grassroots level, may be authorised to attest the same;
(d) Format of self-declaration to be provided for the liability of the person making a wrong declaration—the signatory is liable for action under Section 199 (false statement made in declaration which is by law receivable as evidence) and 200 (using as true, such declaration knowing it to be false) of the IPC in case of the wrong declaration.
(e) This decision will cover all the affidavits presently required for the issuance of residence proof, area domicile, caste certificate, income proof, ration (food) card for seeking permission for the new sewerage, water and electricity connections, etc.
(f) The practice of having a photograph of the applicant

> can be continued, even under the revised procedure of self-declaration for freezing the identity of the applicant. It was later proposed that the citizen declarations should be adequate for the third-party verification. This will reduce the number of false attestations as the beneficiary-applicant will remain liable and also reduce the scope of corruption.

The Government of Punjab accepted the Commission's proposal in 2010 to discontinue the affidavits and replace these with self-declaration for all the services in the domain of public utilities; the applicable law was modified, instructions were issued to all the departments and effectively implemented (see Annexure-2.3).

It was further observed that the acceptance of the concept is not enough. What self-certification should mean in concrete terms has to be determined in the context of different services depending on the factors, such as, the risk (of misuse), incentives and transaction costs for the citizens as well as the government.

Self-Declaration: A Valid Alternative

I. Existing Practice

At present, affidavits of the applicants or the guardians are required for the various need-based certificates. In some cases, affidavits are prescribed under some statutory rules and acts. In some cases, Public Notaries are allowed to attest the same, whereas, in the case of others, only the Executive Magistrates are empowered.

An affidavit is a declaration, and, as such, a declaration in itself is adequate for the purposes of the law. Attestation by the officials, thus, does not appear to be necessary. The applicant-signatory continues to be responsible for the statement made. An advantage that the public agencies have is that they can also impose penal liability for making wrong statements in terms of suspension of the services (suspension of ration card facilities, disconnection of power supply, etc.).

Affidavits, therefore, need to be replaced by Self-Declarations for all services in the public utilities and agencies.

There appears to be no legal problem in adopting this practice. The Indian Penal Code contains a number of Sections, such as 177, 193, 197, 198, 199 and 200. These Sections specifically deal with the implications of any false information or evidence or disclosure or declaration made by the deponents, and many such instances have been included to be subjected to the imposition of penalties, fines, registration of criminal cases and even imprisonment. These are reproduced in Annexure I.

In fact, Self-Declaration is nothing but a self-attested affidavit given on a plain piece of paper.

There are cases where the supporting affidavits of the third parties, sarpanch (village head) or other local officials are required as evidence before the issuance of certain certificates, for example, income certificates. In these cases also, declarations should be accepted in place of the affidavits. It has also been proposed that the citizen declarations should be adequate for third party verification. In such cases, the problem of establishing the identity of the third party can be attended to by establishing a third party's Aadhaar Card. This will reduce the number of bogus attestations as the beneficiary-applicant will anyhow remain liable.

II. Self-Attestation of Original Documents

Present position: These documents are required to be attested by the Notary or the Executive Magistrate, and that itself leads to unnecessary delay. In most of the cases, copies are required only for checking the eligibility (for example, for admission in educational institutions) where, in any case, the original documents are checked again finally for the shortlisted candidates.

It was proposed that the self-attestation of documents should be permitted in the case of the documents required for seeking domicile, caste or income certificates or electricity, water connections and similar services for seeking admissions to the educational institutions and for employment.

III. From Government Approvals and Inspections to Self-Certification of Rights and Entitlements

Self-Certification is the third 'S' for citizen empowerment —(the other two are Self-Declaration and Self-Attestation). This is not only ideologically relevant—governments do keep referring to the empowerment of the citizens—but it can be very helpful in reducing substantial transaction costs incurred by the citizens and the government agencies, in the course of delivery of public services.

Acceptance of the concept in principle, however, is not enough. What self-certification should mean in concrete terms has to be determined in the context of different services depending on the factors, such, the as risk (of misuse), incentives and transaction costs for the citizens as well as the government.

The two major areas that need different sets of rules in this regard are:

A. Self-Certification for Need-Based 'Contingent Services'

B. Self-Certification in social and economic regulations

Self-Certification for Need-Based Contingent Services

This covers various documentation services involving the issue of various certificates, such as residence, caste, income, area, birth, senior citizen, etc.

Problems Under the Present System of Official Verification

- **High Transaction Costs:** The verification processes involve the movement of papers from the front desk to the verifying officials and back. In many cases, physical tracking is required to be done by the applicants. This results in substantial transaction costs not only for the citizens, especially in terms of time, but also for the officials. Costs may be much more than in the case of affidavits, in terms of multiple visits and travel to different offices.
- **Uneven Treatment:** Rural applicants are subjected to two sets of verification in most of the cases, involving the revenue department and the PRI officials, whereas, in the urban areas, only the elected officials are entrusted with verification.
- **Verification a Ritual Due to Lack of Information and Incentives:** In the case of elected officials, especially, there is a conflict of interest—they have political interests and may not be able to do independent scrutiny. This makes the reliability of the verification process suspect. In the case of the revenue officials, there is minimal incentive or motivation in the absence of information and dependence on the reports of the elected officials, thus, completing the 'cascade' of ignorance. Therefore, the officials responsible for verification do not have the necessary information and motivation to perform their duty.

Self-Certification Means Self-Incrimination: A self-certifying citizen is a direct beneficiary of certification of the wrong statement or facts. The remarkable thing about self-certification is that it can be evidence for misuse, by itself, wherever detected or investigated.

Low Risk: Most of the basic services do not carry, to use an economic term, high 'consumer surplus'; incentives for misuse are, therefore, low.

For High-Risk Services: Citizen-Friendly Third-Party Certification

The practice of third party citizen certification in place of official verification can be useful for certificates and documents having more risk of misuse, such as, caste, income etc., to be used for getting grants, scholarships, admissions, old age pension, etc., where the consumer utility and the prospects of gain are deemed to be too high to make it prudent to bank upon the beneficiary's self-declaration alone. In such cases, self-certification can be supported by authentication or endorsement by a third party. Needless to say, the third party would need proper identification (e.g. Aadhar). Such kind of third party certification can substitute the process of official verifications and enquiries.

For instance, the known close associates have or claim to have access to authentic information, and they are also aware of the (dis) incentives for certifying false information. Relatively, it is more likely to be reliable than the verification by the unmotivated and least informed officials.

Self-Certification: Economic and Social Regulations

This area provides a different set of problems, but with similar solutions. There are numerous clearances, inspections and thus, a few visits are required for industry, trade, medical facilities, educational institutions for granting approvals or licences to operate and start a business and so on. Prior approvals and clearances are required for environment, local bye-laws for construction, labour (multiple issues of EPF, ESI, Industries Act) and so on. Sometimes multiple visits may be required—first for no objection and, subsequently, for granting the approval.

Why Inspections?

It has been hypothesised that violation of the social and economic regulations is mostly the result of rational and conscious acts, whereas the approvals and licences are based on the compliance of the peripheral conditions, many of which may not have any correlation with the regulatory outcomes. The factories may have the pollution control equipment, but they may rarely be operating the same; fire safety equipment in most of the urban structures may be ascribed as 'dummy'. Inspection under the Electricity Act is an example where the officials do not have the information or the skills and have only limited incentives if at all, to do their jobs. Complex regulations will always be a step ahead of the skill sets of the street level inspectors.

Unproductive Checks and Inspections

Prior inspections and scrutiny pose a number of problems.

- **Laws are Opaque and Complex**: Even a well-meaning Drug Inspector cannot recall all the clauses of the GMP (Good Manufacturing Practices) under the Drugs Control Act; these are difficult, if not impossible to comply. That is why the law does not require compliance in a letter, but it can still provide an excuse for the objections. What we need instead, is the routine clearance unless a limited number of simple requirements are violated—a 'default rule' for approval, rather than refusal.
- **Knowledge Deficit of the Officials:** Production processes and the equipment are sophisticated and maybe beyond the skill and understanding of an average inspector. Enforcement officials dealing with industries, for example, know much less about the boilers or installation of the hazardous machines than the owner or the supplier.
- **Inspections, 'Rents' and Outcomes:** Economic regula-

tions are primarily concerned with socially positive outcomes—unadulterated drugs and food, use of standard weights and measures. Those who violate are punished or penalised, for example, for adulteration of drugs, compensation to the labour for factory accidents. Socially harmful outcomes of the production processes and penalties are, however, rarely a function of compliance with regulations regarding the layout and design of a factory or equipment. These are, without a doubt, important for the economics and profitability of the enterprise but are not a constraint on the production of deficient goods and below-par production quality. A corporate-run drug factory can as easily (or probably even more easily) produce substandard drugs like any other. A biscuit factory has to be geared to produce good biscuits, even though; it may not really do so. Pre-commissioning inspection of the premises would not matter either way. Approvals are mostly a ritual and a function of the speed money (bribes).

Inspection in Informal Trade

The process of the official visits is, especially, damaging to the informal business and trade which, unlike the organised sector, does not have the resources and the wherewithal to negotiate the official procedures and processes—for example licences for rickshaws or street vendors.

Pre-commissioning inspections and visits appear to be unproductive and wasteful and provide, therefore, an opportunity for 'rents'; in any case, any violation noticed later can always lead to the cancellation of the licences, etc.

Inspections in Business and Commerce: Unlike prior pre-commissioning inspections, these may be necessary, but need to be of an advisory nature, except, when conducted in response to complaints/specific information, as almost all the clients may be non-compliant as in the case of most of the labour regulations. Penalties may only lead to the entrepreneurs making obvious, and 'human' choices between the costs of compliance (very high) and the probability of penalty and or punishment (very little); people are known to have an aversion to losses.

In view of these limitations and constraints, it is recommended that the verification and reports from the public officials may be discontinued. Further, in lieu of the affidavits, field reports and verifications, the self-declaration may be accepted.

In case it is considered that the third party verifications are necessary, rather than the public official, declaration of the citizens may be allowed.

In other words, the system of verification and field reports for the issuance of various certificates should be discontinued. The supporting declaration by two citizens (holding Aadhar Card) (including government officials/ elected officials) should be considered sufficient.

As in the case of self-declaration by the applicant, the supporting declaration should be made liable for action under Section 199/200 IPC in case of the wrong declaration; photographs of the supporting witnesses need to be affixed, as in case of self-declaration. The benefit of the change is obvious as per the data reproduced below;

Table 3.12 Reduction in Submission of Affidavit

S. No.	*Year*	*Total No. of Services Disbursed by the Suwidha Centres*	*Total No. of Services Relating to Affidavits in (lacs.)*	*Total Services Relating to Affidavits in (%)*
1.	2009-10	22,68,429	14,88,053	65.60
2.	2012-13	32,70,715	3,20,963	9.81
3.	2013-14	68,70,808	5,78,025	8.41
4.	2014-15	82,35,540	6,72,031	8.16

Source: Reforming Public Service Delivery Systems in India: Rationalisation of Affidavits (February 2016). Punjab Governance Reforms Commission. Chandigarh, p. 11.

The figures clearly show that the abolition of affidavits resulted in the saving of time and money, including, the opportunity cost of loss of productivity and wages. In the case of India, it is estimated that the total number of affidavits filed in a year is more than 200 billion. Assuming that Rs. 400 per affidavit (one-day wage plus stamps, fees, charges and speed money) is the cost, the total expenses incurred by the citizens in India could be approximately Rs. 80 billion.

By abolishing affidavits, the State has achieved its prime objective of trusting the citizens and accepting their self-declarations besides saving the precious time and reducing the material costs to the citizens in relation to the preparation and submission of the affidavits. The abolition of affidavits facilitated the State to change its character from being a 'demand-driven State' to a 'service-oriented State'. It is encouraging that the rationalisation of the affidavits as introduced in Punjab 2010 has been adopted even by the Government of India as well. It has also made the service delivery process more participatory and dignified.

NOTES

1. Not all offences reported are recorded as offences by the police. The amount of resources available to the police and courts is limited and thus subjective and/or administrative decisions are made concerning which crimes to act against (Muncie 2001: 25).
2. The Punjab Police assigned the Third Party Audit of SAANJH Kendras to the Institute for Development and Communication (IDC), Chandigarh. With the aims to evaluate the implementation of objectives, assessment of impact and acclaimed features, verification of the level of uniformity and standardisation in the implementation, structural and spatial designing, financial management, and the present status of IT infrastructure in SAANJH Kendras. Along with appraisal of human resource concerning their strength, orientation and training was also captured alongside. Besides this, cost-benefit analysis, community participation and the level of citizens' satisfaction was also determined.

4

Dalit Identity Architecture: From Selective Adaptation of Cultural Symbols to Nurturing of Exclusive Sites

Introduction

The research on Dalit identity politics has explored themes ranging from deprivations in earning a livelihood, discriminations in political, social and economic domains and atrocities in the public spaces. It has also studied the nature and extent of marginalisation of the Dalits in terms of their access to the economic processes and accommodation of the so-called 'Dalit-interest' in the ongoing economic processes, competitive politics and changing idiom of justice delivery.

All these themes are of immense importance and need to be addressed in each specific regional context. And, also seriously examine the outcome of their interactions with the changing political discourse leading to the blurring of structural realities. The process of globalisation, shift from the command economy to market economy and redefining of the secular space—all this requires an in-depth analysis to capture the Dalit architecture in each regional context.

There has been a qualitative shift in the Dalit architecture in post-colonial societies.

The emergence and evolution of the specific nature of the political and socio-cultural structures in interaction with the primordial institutions have reaffirmed and consolidated the existing reservoirs. In view of the socio-cultural variations at the regional level, the caste-based identity architecture became more complex.

In each regional context, the caste dynamics has been heavily influenced by the local religious and social institutions leading to the varied imposition of behavioural codes of conduct. Further, their interaction with the market and form of government added different dimensions to the specific variation at the regional level. The arguments presented have clearly demonstrated that the regional variations acquired multidimensional articulations ranging from cultural adaptations to evolving parallelism in terms of cultural forms and nurturing of exclusive sites to bargain for equitable representation to resistance against violations of the icons of group honour and use of symbols, language, and rituals to reinforce or question the purity-pollution paradigm. The post-colonial societies have nurtured and appropriated the social institutions of caste and brought about a qualitative shift in the Dalit architecture.

In Punjab, where the Dalit population is one of the highest in India, around thirty-two per cent, the discourse and articulation of the Dalit politics, the social and economic demands raised by the organisations claiming to represent them and the overall social assertion of these social groups has been quite distinct from the issues of the Dalits listed above. This is mainly because of the regional variations in terms of socio-economic, political and, above all, the religio-cultural context, where the Dalit social existence is mediated through the dominant religion of the region.

In Punjab, the introduction of the liberal egalitarian world view by Sikhism, Arya Samaj and other reform movements by the institutionalisation of an alternate mode of sharing space, food and bringing behavioural change by negating the purity-pollution social interactive framework, provided a different flavour to the caste system in the region and well established diaspora across the world. This has initiated the process of redefinition of the socio-cultural and religious positioning of the Dalits in Punjab and at the place of migration which is quite distinct.

Even in mainstream politics, there is no exclusive political formation of the Dalits contrary to the situation in other Indian States and countries. The 'Dalit' politics has been mainstreamed and articulated within the larger regional politics of the State. Even the welfare programmes in Punjab also do not exclusively focus on just the Dalits and their participation in the social sphere is fairly on common lines with the dominant social group (Jats) in the State.

Three Axes: Context

Dalit identity architecture is becoming more complex (see Mendelsohn and Vicziany 2007: 2-10).[1] It is quite visible that it is getting nurtured and is evolving within the given cultural specific variations at the regional level. In Punjab, the given cultural context revolves around three axes. The State and its interaction with the structural conditions muted the articulation of a secular Punjabi identity, distinct religious identities and assertion of the communal groups. All these identities coexist simultaneously. The second axis emerges out of the State's peculiar demographic composition which has provided space for the coexistence of the competing identities. The Hindus struggled with the majority-minority complex, perceiving themselves to be a majority in India and a minority in reorganised Punjab. The Sikhs alternated with a minority-majority complex being the majority in Punjab and minority in India (Kumar 1982: 27-29). Wallace (1986: 363-77) also asserts, 'Sikhs as a "Minority" in a Sikh Majority state in India,' emphasising that all identities in Punjab are minorities. The third axis, relevant to the issue under study, is an interaction of caste, religion and class which provides meaning to the muted assertions—be it caste, religion or communal and acts as a signpost for defining the regional space.

Punjab has evolved as a society in terms of its recognition of the value of liberal and democratic social interactions, notwithstanding the distortions at the level of practice in relation to caste. In Punjab, caste has not been the exclusive social category of political and social organisation. These religions, i.e. Islam, Sikhism and Arya Samaj per se were devoid of caste distinctions, though social divisions did reflect an influence of the caste hierarchies. "The concepts of ritual pollution and *Karmic* retribution are not so strong in the cultures of these religious traditions. Consequently, caste in Punjab does not have the same rigour or force of religious sanction as it has elsewhere" (Juergensmeyer 1988: 6). In fact, Sikhism and the Arya Samaj provided religious space for the liberation of the Dalit population from the stringent behavioural patterns based on purity-pollution (see Ibbetson 1916: 9).[2] For instance, equality in religious gatherings, the establishment of common kitchens and the institution of *langar* were initiated to overcome caste-based superior and inferior relationships. The offering of *Karah Prasaad* by anyone, irrespective of his caste, was a symbolic departure from the notion that forbade food sharing by the upper and the lower castes. According to McLeod, "this ensures that high castes consume food received in effect from the hands of the lower castes or even outcastes and that they do so from a common dish" (McLeod 1975: 87). The behavioural interactive social practices of the upper castes by the lower castes were also adapted in socio-cultural spheres in the background of religious rituals like *langar*, *Sangat* and *Pangat*. Even the holy book of the Sikhs, i.e. *Guru Granth Sahib* contains a selection of compositions of Muslim and Hindu saints, including some from an untouchable background' which demonstrates the liberal characteristics of religious practices in Punjab (Kalsi 1989: 75).

The transnational standards provide centrality to the recognition of difference which is not contextualised in the regional space, which makes it problematic to prioritise as to what difference and whose difference needs to be accorded primacy. These manifest forms have become complexly blurred and negotiated. Located in the variant regional contexts and in interaction with the trinity, i.e. the State, civil society and the market that leads to diverse outcomes. In this, the claims are filtered, entitlements recognised, and the rights are granted within the given political and social structure. The nature of the State is such that the interaction of the citizens (*Awam*) patron-client, Ria-Mai Baap, govern and the governed has to be understood in terms of their recognition of claims, rights and entitlements. The backdrop of those is the colonial constructs as reflected in the functioning of various institutions, administrative norms, rules and procedures leading to a visible disconnect with the people. There is a gap between the societal claims, archaic rules and the political will, despite the constitutional boundaries. The political promise and the constitutional requirements could not transform the spirit of the freedom struggle as imbibed by the activated (*Awam*) nation into a participating civil society, in terms of their recognition of the claims, entitlements and rights unlike some of the countries where the Punjabi immigrants settled over time.

Extractive Colonial Institutions: Context

As mentioned earlier, the post-colonial State continued to rely on the processes and procedures which are 'extractive' in treating the citizens as the colonial subjects and nurtured the social institutions of caste, religion, ethnicity, etc., as exclusive categories. For instance, post-colonial India discontinued the British practice of caste-based enumeration in the census, but religious, ethnicity, and linguistic-based classifications remained in the enumeration (Bhagat 2006).

The perpetuation of these practices made the whole conception of citizenship as 'deficient'.

In many cases, classificatory criteria used by the colonial governmental regimes continued into the postcolonial era, shaping the forms of both political demands and development policy. Thus, caste and religion in India, ethnic groups in Southeast Asia, and the tribes in Africa remained the dominant criteria for identifying the communities among the populations as objects of policy (Chatterjee 2004: 37). In the context of Post-Independent India, the census used the colonial based classification of religious identity, justified on the ground of the strong link between the religious status of a person and categorisation of the Scheduled Castes. And, until the 2001 Census, not only the enumeration process but the ethics of publication were mishandled as only selective demographic data of the religious population (on the growth and size) were published. It challenged the role of religion in terms of population growth and, as a result, also stimulated a communal situation in the country (Bhagat 2006).

In this, populations were treated as targets of 'multiple policies producing heterogeneous constructs of social life'. The classifications and enumerations were used as tools for the purpose of welfare administration to draw legitimacy for the political regimes. This, in a way, to use Michel Foucault's term, 'governmentalisaton of the State' and the policy choices provided continuity to the 'ethnographic state' (Dirks 2001: 43-60) with their excessive reliance on the enumerative technology of the census.

To illustrate, in each regional context, the caste dynamics were heavily influenced by the formation of the distinct institutions in the post-colonial State. For instance, in Pakistan, the classification used in the census was to enumerate the Dalits as Muslim-Dalits, Hindu-Dalits, Christian-Dalits, etc. The administrative fragmentation of the population is not diversity-sensitive, and instead, produces social conflicts along with reinforcing the social-cleavages and results in promoting exclusive sites.

Transition from 'Deficient Citizens' to Full Citizenship

As has been established in the literature, the notion of citizenship and its outreach normative imperatives and characterisation uncover itself in response to emerging fault lines and contexts. Notwithstanding the relational paradigm in which the State relates with the citizens as a subject, the nature of the State, of course, defines the content of citizenship. For instance, freedom, autonomy, claims, entitlements and rights vary from the colonial subjects to the subjects in the democratic and egalitarian societies. In this sense, the articulations and assertions of the diaspora in the identity domain are distinct. For instance, the Punjabi diaspora has shaped the discourse of religion and caste around fundamental and 'pure forms reinforcing cleavages in a glaring manner'. For instance, 'a pub on West End Road, Southall, in the suburbs of London, has come to be known pejoratively as Chamar-Wali pub because of its clientele, and fights between Jat Sikhs and Chamars have broken out in factories and pubs all over industrial England' (Juergensmeyer 1988: 246-47). Similarly, amongst the Sikh diaspora, in the backdrop of the Khalistan Movement, the fundamentalist assertions became more blatant. In 1989, in Montreal, it was reported that a number of Jat Sikhs refused to share food with the Punjabi Hindus as they were considered as traitors of the Sikh Panth. Juergensmeyer (1988: 249) aptly describes, "When Ambedkar became a Buddhist in 1956, the idea did not take hold deeply among the SCs of Punjab; but in England, where tradition had a looser hold, and the concept of voluntary religion was more familiar, the idea appealed to a large number of Chamars". Taylor (2018) also explains how the Dalits followed Ambedkar's Neo-

Buddhist movement that conversion away from Sikhism and Hinduism to Buddhism would enable the development of a more egalitarian society (absence of caste hierarchies and devoid of malpractices like untouchability). They formed their own association, the Indian Republican Group of Great Britain and ran candidates in the British election. The initial impetus for reviving the Ad Dharm Movement came not from India, but from far away. Similarly, in 1968, the Ravidas Temple was built in Wolverhampton. And, it became a symbol of the exclusive identity of the *Ad Dharmi Chamars*, and it placed Guru Ravidas on the same pedestal along with the Sikh Guru, Guru Nanak Dev.

In each context, the dynamic interactions with the social processes and the value-laden public policy interventions are leading to distinct formations of the institutions, behavioural codes of conduct and social capital. These forms are multidimensional articulations ranging from cultural adaptations to evolving parallelism in terms of cultural forms and nurturing of the exclusive sites to bargain for equitable representation to resistance against violations of the icons of the group honour, and use of the symbols, language, rituals to reinforce the purity-pollution paradigm (Kumar and Dagar 2004). Therefore, a study of the identity of the evolution process at the regional level in a global context will help to draw appropriate lessons for the recognition of the individuals as humans, escape from the social abuse, have access to an equitable share in the material resources, participation in the decision-making process and corresponding power, privileges and social status. It would be appropriate if the focus is not merely to capture the cleavages in socially evolving societies, but also to uncover the spheres where moderation and adaptation have moved from particularisms to universalisms.

Cultural Adaptation of Universalism

Sufficient evidence is available to show that the Dalits were selectively appropriating certain traits of the dominant castes. These are mainly in the domain of physical appearance, conduct and lifestyle to have status parity and to seek self-assurance. An intensive field study by Kumar and Dagar (2004: 274-96) fully supported and endorsed the view.

In a narrative, a Dalit woman while describing manliness gave the example of her son and said, "He is tall and well built, and when he goes to the town, everybody thinks that he is a young specimen of a Jat male". Others mentioned that their men were tall and strong like a Jat DSP, and 'one cannot make out the difference from his stride and behaviour that he is any less than a Jat.'

This survey clearly shows that in other spheres also, the Jat standards and symbols are being adopted by the Dalits. For instance, 'honour revenge and levirate marriages are exclusive to peasant groups, where both land and women are to be protected as they reflect the social status of the families (see Manjoo 2012),[3] and instances of these practices are also found among the Dalits. It is not uncommon to find the firing of the guns as a mode of celebrations in the Dalit marriages, again something that was peculiar to the Jat peasantry. In terms of attire also, the Dalits are adopting Jat apparel. In an FGD among the Dalit men, a Dalit male appearance was described as using a small head covering yard of cloth called a 'parna'. But it was mentioned that if a Dalit had to go to his in-laws' house, then he would wear a turban like a Jat so that he appears as a man of influence. Similarly, it was mentioned that white '*kurta-pyjama*' was a dress worn only by the Jat landowners, and dark coloured clothes were the garb of the Dalits. But now, this is decreasing with the *Mazhabi* Sikhs, especially, wearing white '*kurta-*

pyjama' (Kumar and Dagar 2004: 278). In fact, the Dalits are selectively appropriating dominant universal practices to achieve status enhancement. This has added another dimension to the existing debates, whereby universalism of rights, cultures and humanism tend to subsume the differences to a dominant extent.

The study by Kumar and Dagar (2004) concludes that with transnational migration, selective upward mobility and politicisation of the Dalits, their honour, dignity and *rutba* (status) are being shaped in view of the cultural milieu where the women's honour symbolises family and kinship status, values of honour and chastity are beginning to reflect among the Dalits. The value of honour and chastity, for instance, is being invoked by the upwardly mobile Dalits.

Undoubtedly, universalising social norms blurred the boundaries imposed by a ritual and rule hierarchy. It has made the social divide between the Dalits and the dominant castes ambiguous by selectively appropriating symbols and practices of the dominant culture, universalising the earlier pattern of the upper caste exclusivity (see Juergensmeyer 1988: 19).[4] It is important to note that the replication of the rituals, customs and practices of the dominant caste is not a process of Sanskritisation of the Dalits in Punjab (see Srinivas 1966: 6-7).[5] By their very rejection of the assimilation model, they vetoed the acceptance of the 'high born's religio-cultural organisation of society. Instead, they adopted specific cultural practices laying claim to the norms of a distinct status to bring about a 'structural change' rather than only 'positional changes' in the system (see *Punjab Census Report 1911*: 420-21).[6]

The dominant religious tendencies provided space to co-opt the Dalits in their respective folds by the religious moderation of the stringent purity-pollution customs and rituals (see Malhotra 2002: 43).[7] From another perspective, even if it has not fully provided an escape from pollution, it has created sufficient conditions for the Dalits to emerge as a power group to compete politically in a social context, absolved from the hierarchy through a universalised adaptation of cultural norms towards the realisation of full citizenship. As Ram (2004) maintains, caste conflicts in Punjab are the signs of the emerging Dalit assertion. He further states that the demands for a share in the power structure are a manifestation of the emerging Dalit consciousness.

From Cultural Adaptation to Competitive Parallelism

The cultural adaptation to acquire universalistic attributes in the context of institutionalised indifference, denial, discriminations and atrocities provided another dimension to the aggressive assertion to form a common 'Dalit' identity. Judge (2002) also argues as to how a new caste hierarchy emerged among the Sikhs (in the process of the lower caste attempting to occupy the upper caste positions) leading to competing hierarchies despite sharing the same socio-cultural space.

Institutional Indifference and Discrimination

In post-colonial India, institutions like the village panchayats, legislature, police and courts that carry the ethical connotations to provide security and justice remained elusive to the Dalits. The narratives uncover how the people in general, including the Dalits, identify with the State and civil society through the value of identity, dignity and productivity. Non-realisation or occasional realisation contribute to an experience of exclusion. In this sense, they remain 'deficient citizens'. A study conducted by the World Bank and DFID on Dalits (leatherworkers in Nepal) in its report also identified the people living with such a condition of exclusion (on the grounds of caste identity) and termed them as 'Unequal Citizens'.

These are the forms of indignities that are experienced by the Dalits in their everyday interaction. These forms are rooted in the cultural domains in which various institutions have evolved and been nurtured. The indignities range from the denial of 'personhood' to coercive extraction of material wealth. In village Mahansinghwala in District Sangrur, the rural Jat peasant in collusion with the panchayat imposed wage rules and social restrictions on the labourers. The resolution passed had 22 clauses ranging from the fixation of wages to social boycott (Singh 2012; Kamal 2012). The resolution is gender discriminatory in terms of wages, restrictive in terms of labour mobility (cannot seek employment in other villages) abdicative of health hazard consequences (due to exposure to pesticides/insecticides) and follows workplace code of conduct and punitive action against the farmers for violating the prescribed rules of labour engagement.

Bharti (2019) foregrounded such case studies of feudal subjugation. Discriminatory practices like Dalit women and children being the foremost victims of such terror, have been almost normalised. Rape and sexual harassment of the Dalit women, followed by the men being beaten and killed for their debt, and demands for higher wages (as most of the land are under Sardars and Jats) are a few instances to be mentioned. Most of the atrocities are hardly revealed and never reported due to the intensity of terror and intimidation, while the Dalits want to protect the dignity of their womenfolk.

For instance, in Changaliwala village of Sangrur district in Punjab where the notoriety of the feudal lords has been witnessed in its most brutal form, it was the Zameen Prapti Sangharsh Committee, which first raised the issue of Jagmail and refused to cremate his body (The 37-year-old, a Dalit daily wager and father of three was brutally beaten up, 'made to drink urine', left to die in front of the

Gurudwara because he dared to seek his dues. Bharti 2019).

Not only this, but these discriminatory practices are also reflected in the functioning of the various justice-delivery institutions. For instance, it is a socially accepted norm that the upper caste men can have a liaison with the Dalit women, but if a low caste man has a liaison with an upper caste woman, it is considered dangerously violative (see Shah, Thorat et al. 2006: 120).[8] In this case, the severity of the punishment increases as it violates the cultural norms and caste hierarchy.

Consequently, different standards are adopted, for instance, by the panchayats to deal with such cases. For example, in village Mehta, Jandiala, a Majhabi boy had a liaison with a Jat Sikh girl. A case of kidnapping was registered with the police at the behest of the panchayat. Whereas, in Raman Mandi, an upper-caste boy violated the lower caste woman. The matter was reported to the panchayat. In this case, the panchayat intervened to reach a compromise between the two parties rather than reporting the matter to the police. The justification given was that women of the lower caste were 'characterless' and were easily lured by material considerations.

Language of Power, Not Justice

In the socio-cultural sites, it is the language of power which is considered as just. Krishan Gopal (name changed) a Dalit, was feeling aggrieved as his wife was raped by a political leader who was a member of the legislature. During our field survey in the said village, two young activists told us about the increasing atrocities against Dalits and narrated the incident involving the wife of the Krishan Gopal. We inquired if the matter had been reported to the police, village panchayat or to the press? The young activists started persuading Krishan Gopal to lodge the complaint with the police. Krishan Gopal retorted that he did not need our help and told us to leave him alone and mind our own business. He murmured that reporting to the police would further rob his family of their dignity and add to their torture and even risk their survival. And, even the panchayat might alienate him from the village community. The institutions of justice delivery also concede lower status to the Dalits, and they are really meant to serve the dominant hierarchy. The institutions of justice delivery understand with clarity the language of social hierarchy and material wealth rather than to listen to the feeble voices of the dispossessed.

Policy Formulation in Ethnographic State

It is not only in the domain of justice delivery but also giving access to the welfare programmes, based on the demographic profile like caste and religion, within 'restrictive citizenship' has led to the multiplication of social cleavages. In a society where restrictive citizenship is determined by the inferior social placement, and institutional framework requires both social and political transformation. The intimate interactions with the institutions represent different situations. This set includes the whole institutional context for social activity, for it is through institutions of various kinds that values are transmitted into action—that they retain their practical significance (Allen 1975: 213). It will be apt to reproduce an observation from the earlier chapter to elaborate.

> A Dalit in a village, in response to a question about his wish list, replied that his first wish was to have a school; second, to have a health centre, and, lastly, to have bricked lanes for the village. In reply to the related question, would he send his child to the school? He replied in the negative. And, explained that he needs the extra income for survival and, hence, he will send his child to earn a living. In reply to another question, whether he would go to the village dispensary for medical treatment, he again replied in the negative. He clarified that he would prefer to get treatment from a village quack as he would be able to get to work in a short span of time. On

> enquiring whether he owned a bicycle, he said no. Why, then, did he need the bricked lanes in the village? And, the reply is, because everyone else was asking for these.

His foremost need was to be productively engaged to earn a livelihood and, thereafter, he and his family would be able to have access to education, health, physical infrastructure, etc. Paradoxically, it reveals the situation of the blind faith in the communitarian ties as to how someone else's priorities of needs get legitimised as the community's foremost needs.

Pollution as the Marker of Hierarchy

In the religio-caste-based competitive societies, the identity assertions based on caste and religious purity become the boundary demarcations or occupy a superordinate social and political position. For instance, the Khalistani protagonists give their own version of purity and pollution. The followers of Sikhism have to follow the codes of conduct issued by them. For instance, 21 codes of conduct for the women were enforced, and, their violations would make the followers—'Patit' (polluted). They are considered as the vanguard of the identity (Khalsa—the pure). These codes included the covering of the head, banning the dancing on the stage, baptisation of the mothers of the newborn, ban on make-up and the use of 'Hindu' symbols like bangles, 'mehndi', etc. and intergroup marriages. According to the police records, the violators of the societal codes as dictated by the upper castes were punished and, as many as 47 were put to death. The women are seen as the symbols of group identity and boundary markers for purity-pollution discourse.

But, in the caste hierarchy, pollution becomes the norm and is not seen as a violation. In everyday existence, the 'victim' may not be conscious of such normatively accepted violations. These women are targeted by the competing group for symbolic breach of the other group's dignity and its pollution. The normative justification is offered for having a liaison with the Scheduled Caste women. In an interview with a retired Jat army officer, when confronted with a question about an illicit liaison with the Scheduled Caste woman, answered that it is done to improve their progeny.

There is a denial of 'personhood' across the board to the citizens, as the social construct reinforces the demand for what Hannah Arendt (1986: 296-97) termed as 'the right to have rights.' The inferential logic of Arendt's argument is that all rights can be realised if the right to belong to a community is granted and practised. In the Indian caste system, the right to belong to a community is denied to the lower castes, i.e. the Dalits. Globally, the rights are denied to those who have been on the margins or outside the domain of 'community'. The rights are for those who are recognised as members of the community, rather human quo humans. In that context, the Dalits may be de jure right to have rights but de facto they are 'right-less'. To illustrate, Arendt affirms that the human rights can be of meaning if redefined as a right to the human condition (belonging to a human community), and not to be dependent de facto upon some inborn dignity (see Arendt 1986: 295-96).[9]

A study in 2011 by Dagar (2014: 137) of the Punjabi diaspora settled in North America brought out that there is a widespread perception of being looked at derogatively (61 per cent), discrimination against children in schools (43 per cent), and biased response by the police (68 per cent), see Table 4.1. These immigrants are seen as competitors in the job market. As Mitra (2012: 114), in the process of understanding the dynamics of class and race across an immigrant's identity, identifies how the non-white taxi drivers in New York City face inequalities of social class (being at a lower level of occupational hierarchy) and racial (being associated with the identity of a non-white citizen). She further explains how these immigrants are seen as competitors. As one of the respondents said:

> Some do [discriminate]. For example... I've seen that people who are educated and have good jobs don't do anything or say anything even if one makes mistakes. Some who don't have good jobs think that we have taken jobs away from them. That's it. They don't like this job, but they don't let us do it either. That's it.

It is, therefore, hypothesised that the new reality of globalisation might not want racialism, religious fundamentalism and casteism, but needs it and, therefore, need to have representation in politics (45 per cent) (See Table 4.1).

Table 4.1 Perceptions Regarding Cultural Discrimination Among the Punjabi Diaspora Settled in North America

	N = 74	
		%
Discrimination in schools	32	43.2
Element of public ridicule (language, conduct, dress)	45	60.8
Culture as a factor in employment	13	17.5
Police bias against the Punjabi population	50	67.5
Need for representation in politics (as insurance against the law)	33	44.6

Source: 'Decoding Social Capital and the Linkages to Male Child Preference', Field Survey Conducted by the Institute for Development and Communication, 2011. (Dagar 2014: 137).

It is evident that the caste endogamy is strictly maintained amongst the diaspora, and the caste background is used to define the boundaries even amongst the third generation, and caste hierarchy is asserted by the dominant caste and responded with competitive exclusive caste symbols with a sense of pride. It was in search of a separate identity that a large number of the Dalits reported their religion as Ravidasia in the 2011 Census in England (White 2012). Singh (2012: 53-60) further adds that in Britain, the Ravidasia population is estimated to be around 70,000, with 21 places of worship referred to as Mandirs, Temples and Bhavans. And, another route was taken by the transnational migrants, i.e. Chamars to convert to Neo-Buddhism and Christianity; unlike in Punjab, where the association with the Deras help them to escape the caste-based exclusion in certain spheres. This conversion meant denial of the rituals associated with the Sikh religion (Taylor 2014: 224-46). This provides sufficient push to consolidate the group identities based on religion and caste to articulate their legitimate claims. As a derivative, the intra-community tensions between the Scheduled Castes and the Jat Sikhs get reproduced at the place of migration through political assertions at the sites, temples and Deras. This new structural placement of these marginalised groups provides them with sufficient social capital to provide hostile expression to the muted identity expression at the place of origin. The Scheduled Castes, particularly from the Doaba (a region in Punjab), have in their armour narratives of subordination, collective humiliation and discrimination and, coupled with relative prosperity, supporting kinship network, and non-partisan State rebels against the hegemonic institutions, religious and caste groups.

No doubt, there are movements and social mobilisations amongst the Dalits to draw parallels and exclusive sites to restore a sense of dignity and confidence at the place of origin, but it is qualitatively different from the similar trends amongst the diaspora. To illustrate, in Punjabi folk, the parallel is being drawn with a Punjabi folk video '*Putt Jattan De*' (sons of Jats) with '*Putt Chamaran De*' to establish pride in their caste identity (Roy 2011: 91).[10] Likewise, Ravish Kumar (2010) in his NDTV based report titled as 'Ravish ki Report' also emphasises a growing trend of the articulation of pride in Chamar identity by Punjabi singers in Punjabi music videos to promote Chamar pride in response to Jat songs. (Roy 2011: 89-102. For detail, see Judge and Bal 2008: 55).[11]

Interestingly, a group of Dalit activists objected to the use of derogatory language (Chamar) in a book written by Babu Rajab Ali published and reprinted in 2012. The book was banned, and the publisher and printers were arrested. Numerous instances can be cited to show the practice of this dualism. 'Thus, the goal is to form a common Dalit identity, and on the other, the goal is to lose that same identity' (Sikka 2012: 43-60).

This parallelism is in convergence with the exclusive spatial sites being established. Similarly, T-shirts and stickers are being displayed, depicting acquired confidence in their own identity. The narrative makes it explicit that symbols and exclusive sites are used to nurture a collective consciousness. For instance, a group of youngsters on their motorcycles come to pay a visit to Dera Sach Khand, Balan,[12] probably on the occasion of Ravidas Jayanti. What was most distinct about this group was that before entering the Dera, they stopped their vehicles, motorcycles and open jeeps, in front of the gate of the sanctum sanctorum and gave the loud hail—'*Jo bole so nirbhai, Guru Ravidas ki Jai*' three times before parking their vehicles and then obediently entered the sanctum sanctorum of the Dera and paid their obeisance. When the prayers were complete, an elderly man took out stickers with the Dera symbol of 'Har' and pasted the same on the front of motorcycles. Similarly, Sharma (2012) asserts how *Ad Dharmis* developed cultural symbols of pride in the process to develop their identity equivalent to any other religion, such as a flag of *Majith* colour with the symbol of *Har* and *Suhang (Sohum)*, acknowledging the fellow *Ad Dharmis* by '*Jai Gurudev*' (with reference to Guru Ravidas) instead of '*Sat Sri Akal*', etc. The same is the case among the Mazhabhis in Amritsar by publicly (with a symbol of pride) declaring themselves as 'Chuhras of Punjab'.

The parallel is nurturing an exclusive Dalit identity in competition with the Jat Sikh identity. There is a trend of exploration of a number of cultural and institutional choices to put forward to use the phrase, 'imagined narrative of cultural selfhood' which is visible both in Punjab and amongst the diaspora.

To counter the experience of being treated as a second class citizen in the political, social and religious spaces, there is a strong urge to restore the sense of dignity by carving out exclusive sites. As Ram (2013) also states that the growth of the Ravidas Deras in Punjab, in parallel to the Sikh Gurudwaras, created a platform for a distinct Dalit religious sphere. The narratives have further reinforced the Dalit assertion to challenge the spatial disconnect with the social, religious and cultural institutions. This is largely in response to the discriminatory practices that continue to be followed in the social and political institutions. All that has led to the formation of the parallel sites of the Dalits.

Nurturing of Exclusive Sites

The hierarchy of purity among the dominant castes and Dalits in Punjab continued with the acceptance in social exchanges, such as marriages and social celebrations as well. To illustrate, Mahila Mandals were created to uplift the women, and a scheme for income generation through renting out tents and utensils for the social celebrations was launched. However, the assertions for the maintenance of exclusiveness prohibited the Dalits from using these utensils as the non-Dalit castes would not like to reuse the same.[13] Resultantly, separate Mahila Mandals were formed in several villages of Punjab. The formation of separate Mahila Mandals, Deras and Gurudwaras reflected both the intense desire among the Dalits to establish their exclusive identity and to assert their rights based on their emerging political consciousness (see Juergensmeyer 1988: 263).[14]

Historically, Adi movements have nurtured both exclusive Dalit identity, based on the pre-Aryan cultural heritage as well as the inclusive religious-cultural identity represented in the Sikh religious scriptures like, Adi Granth, that contained the Bani (spiritual hymns) of at least six poets belonging to the Sudra castes, who were critical of the claims of the Brahmanical orthodoxy (see Hans 2008: 16).[15] As Chowdhry (1997) also states that in Punjab-Haryana, the Brahmanical model was not so strong, and the concept of caste purity and caste hierarchy lacked the same intensity.

In this context, the institution of the Deras is not a new phenomenon in Punjab as these religious formations have been in existence for a very long time in the landscape of the State (see Ram 2007).[16]

The Deras emerged at different intervals in response to the institutionalised religions, indifferences, denial, discriminations and atrocities. In fact, one of the major factors of one's identity is religion or religion lies nearest to the core of one's identity as other determinants that constitute one's identity do not fully acknowledge or provide an authentic recognition. Religion addresses a complete range of human needs, fears, and concerns in a comprehensive and powerful manner (Seul 1999). Religion plays a shield to fall back when one loses one's other means of identity. For instance, in the present context, the forms of malpractices such a denial, atrocities, and discriminations in the social arena, right-lessness of belonging to any community-created platform for the rise of exclusive religious sites, such as Deras, etc., played a significant role in establishing a more respectable and powerful identity that ought to be is equivalent to the Sikh-Jats of Punjab. As Fox (1987) also highlights that the determinants responsible for the creation of a new social field and cultural pattern are the composite of dominations, subordinations, contradictions, oppositions, and confrontations. He further mentions that such 'social actions are the outcome of an individual or group confrontations, placed within a field of domination and inequality'. They evolve through cultural adaptations of universalistic attributes and simultaneously draw parallels and exclusive sites to provide identity and a sense of dignity to its followers. These are the product of liberal cultural tradition and have been a symbol of the existence of plurality and diversity of religious spectrum. Historically, their evolution has been intermeshed with the evolution of the Sikh religion. The prominent Deras which are the offshoot of the Sikh religion includes Nanak Panthis, Sewa Panthis, Nirmalas, Udasis, etc. The contemporary Deras which have transcended religious, caste and class boundaries include, Radha Soami, Namdhari, Dera Sacha Sauda, Nurmehal, Nirankari, and Dera Sachkhand Ballan. They draw their discourses from multiple traditions like Islam, Sufism, Kabir, Christianity, Sikhism, etc.; and couch them in regional dialects, myths and symbols (Kumar 2017 "Decoding Politics"). However, in recent times, the Deras are at the centre of the public discourse due to multiple incidents of violence involving these sects. The violence has generally erupted from the deep-seated conflict between the Deras and the institutionalised religion, primarily Sikhism. There have been incidents of violence involving the various Dera followers with the sections of the Sikhs, such as Dera Nirankaries in 1978, Dera Bhaniarawala in 2001, Dera Sacha Sauda in 2008-09, Dera Noormahal in 2002 and Dera Sachkhannd Ballan 2009-10. The causes or the immediate provocation for these conflicts are rooted in the various practices and rituals of the Deras, such as, the notion of the living Guru which is strictly opposed to in the institutionalised Sikhism, the imitation of the imagery of the Sikh Gurus by the Dera heads and the replication of the style or context of the Sikh holy book by these sects (Kumar 2017 "Decoding Politics").[17]

The Deras are the "more subaltern poor cousins" of that mainstream Sikhism that they have challenged in numerous ways (see Singh 2012).[18] However, the Deras are also a place that has put the Sikh ethnic claims in a weak and crumbling position by challenging the monolithic claims of Sikhism. Herein lies one of the potential strengths of these Deras as they have not only represented the marginalised sections of the Punjabi society (primarily in terms of caste and class) but at the same time, they have put into question the monolithic projection of Sikhism and, thus, putting the State into a tight spot whereby it has to simultaneously balance the contesting claims of the people voiced through the Deras due to the electoral compulsions with close connections it historically has had with the Sikh clergy in politics, whereby the State and the religio-political institutions of the Sikhs are prominently intermeshed.

The Deras are more of the congregation of the followers—a space that gives a feeling of openness transcending caste, religious and class boundaries and the reverence for the living Guru binds them together. There are variations between the Deras in their representation of religion as faith or religion as an ideology, termed by Ashish Nandy (1988: 177-94). The narrative reproduced reinforces this distinction.

> Ms Dilpreet is living with her children and parents-in-law as her husband, like so many other men in the village, has migrated to Greece. Before her marriage, she used to go to Dera Beas. However, after her marriage, she started going to Sachkhand Ballan as her husband and parents-in-law have taken 'Naam-daan' from Dera Ballan. Since village Raipur is near Dera Ballan, so the Dera Guru has close relations with the villagers as a community. She told that before the murder

of Sant Ramanand, the Dera Guru frequently used to visit the houses of the followers on special occasions. However, after the murder, the Dera is more cautious about such visits of the Guru. Before joining the 'dera', her in-laws' family used to be non-vegetarian, and the men used to indulge in liquor. However, after joining the Dera, they have stopped doing so.

Being a follower of the two Deras at two different junctures of her life, the major difference that she found in both was that there was no casteism in Dera Beas and caste was not a driving force in the dynamics of the Dera. However, in Ballan, one finds 'Chamarvaad', though the people from other castes also visit the Dera. Her husband, being a staunch follower of the Guru, visits the Gurudwara constructed by the Dera in Greece. She feels that after the murder of Sant Ramanand, the anger against caste oppression has increased manifold.

Increased influence of the Deras amongst the lower castes and the lower strata leading to the formation of a distinct identity resulted in a confrontation with the institutionalised religion.

It provided enough provocation to the Ravidasis to set up their own Gurudwaras in 2010 in Punjab.

Satinder Singh is a 68-year-old man who completed his graduation in 1972, unusual for a Dalit to acquire such a high degree during those times in a village in Punjab. He worked in the Army and, later on, in police as a constable before leaving it and getting back to his village to work as a farmer. He laments that despite being a graduate; he did not get a good job and, thus, considered it below his dignity to work as a '*sipahi*'." Aware of the layers of discrimination and humiliation that a Dalit has to face in life, his narrative is tinged with contempt for the upper castes and the prevalence of caste in the society.

There are around 22 houses of Ravidasis in the village. In Satinder's drawing-room, the portraits of the Sufi saints, such as Sheikh Farid, Kabir as well as the modern icons, such as Bhagat Singh are seen. His narrative is spruced with small couplets of Sufi poet Bulleh Shah and medieval

> saint Kabir. While narrating that there is blind faith of the people in their religion, he cites the example of the *bani* of Guru Granth Sahib. According to him, the *bani* of Guru Granth Sahib includes the bani of 'lower caste' saints, except Dhanna Jat.' Jats who practice caste discrimination in their day-to-day lives in the village, bow before the Guru Granth Sahib without any idea of the philosophy of the Sikh holy scripture. He laments that there is no temple of Ravidas in the village. There is conflict in the village between the Balmikis and the Ravidas is over Nishan Sahib. He said that earlier, on the occasion of the *Gurupurab* of Sikh gurus, his family would go to the Gurudwara; however, the *Gurupurab* of Ravidas is not celebrated with equal enthusiasm by the upper castes. Thus, his family has stopped going to the Gurudwara on these occasions, and they just send their share of contribution to these celebrations. He also mentions that during the celebrations or other important occasions in the village Gurudwara, the upper caste Jats, who are at the helm of affairs, would not give much importance to the Dalits when it came to taking the *langar* back home.

In most of the Gurudwaras, Dalits were kept on the margin of management, not encouraged to participate actively in the special functions and discouraged to eat *langar* (food served in Gurudwaras) along with upper-caste Sikhs. They were offered *langar* in separate rows (Jodhka 2004: 62-99). The quest for dignified identity led to the construction of separate Gurudwaras, particularly, by the Dalits who were followers of Guru Ravidas and Maharishi Valmiki. Not only this, but the conglomeration of 142 sants formed Ravidas Sadhu Sant Sampradaya. Besides, building their own Gurudwaras, they established their own religious-'sthal' at Charan Choe Ganga in Khural Garh in Punjab for their congregations and organised celebrations of the birth of Guru Ravidas. Similarly, the Balmiki Samaj also established their own Gurudwaras and Ram Tirath Sthal at Amritsar for their larger congregations. These places have been built with the contributions of the followers, particularly, the Dalit diaspora and, of course, support of the government. These parallel sites were also built in the countries of the migration of the followers. They performed similar religious practices in these exclusive sites. These Gurudwaras continue to coexist without much resistance. Along with the Sikh holy book, the Gurudwaras have pictures of Maharishi Valmiki and Guru Ravidas. The establishment of these exclusive sites was, no doubt, preceded by the tension between the Jat Sikhs and *Ad Dharmis* and other Dalit castes. For instance, in Talhan village in Jalandhar city in 2003, these groups had a fight on the issue of representation of the Dalits in the management of the Gurudwaras (Ram 2004: 171). The simmering tensions transformed into full-scale conflict as became evident on May 24, 2009, when the Guru Ravidas temple in Rudolfsheim, Vienna, was attacked. The victims were Dera Sach Khaand Chief Sant Niranjan Dass and Sant Rama Nand who succumbed to injuries. As a consequence, widespread violence erupted in the districts of Hoshiarpur, Kapurthala, Jalandhar, Ludhiana, Amritsar and Nawanshehr (now SBS Nagar) of Punjab.

There were two groups amongst the Ravidasias, one in favour of keeping Shri Guru Granth Sahib in all the Gurudwaras of Shri Guru Ravidasji and the other one demanding the replacement of Shri Guru Granth Sahib[19] with Shri Guru Amritbani of Shri Ravidas. And, attempts were made to install Shri Guru Amritbani in 18 Gurudwaras at Jalandhar in 2010 leading to violent conflicts. On the State's intervention, new spaces were allocated for installing Shri Guru Amritbani, thus, moving away from the intertextuality to separate text. The intertextuality which incorporates a 'diversity of linguistic expressions, myths, metaphors, symbols and folk genres and the core of which has been the refutation of the claims of Brahmanical orthodox. As Sharma (2012) also affirms the rise of the Scheduled Castes assertion in Punjab in the form of large scale construction of separate Gurudwaras. Judge and Bal (2008) cite Webster (2007) that there are 10,000 Dalit Gurudwaras in Punjab. Sharma (2012) defines such sites of exclusiveness as vacuum, created by the political forces-led Dalits to construct separate Gurudwaras join various Deras, advocating the *bani* of their gurus (representative of their identity, in order to seek a respectable social identity equivalent to that of the upper caste), and matching their economic status, etc. are the new instruments to articulate their grievances.

The movement from the Dera to a separate Gurudwara signifies consolidation of the schism between an institutionalised Sikh religion and the emerging sects.

Along with the socio-cultural determinants, the nature of the economy in the villages has played a dual role in nurturing such exclusive sites. A dual role is meant as favourable economic or employment opportunities are helping to distance them from the downtrodden identity of the Dalit (getting rid of being dependent on the upper castes for socio-cultural and material-based resources), and on the other hand, after securing basic material conditions of subsistence, working as a helping hand for the strata, which is doubly deprived of the caste and poverty as Jodhka (2002) maintains that such alternatives (employment opportunities) are not easily available to everyone. He also explains further that such distancing can only be possible if alternative sources of employment become available to the Dalits. Therefore, the out-turns like emerging political consciousness (Juergensmeyer 1988), emerging Dalit assertion (Ram 2004), attempts to establish pride (Roy 2011), and to achieve a sense of dignity and power to bargain (Jodhka 2002), etc., depicting the results of the same, i.e. non-dependence on the upper castes for the means of subsistence. The duality in play is of the economic power being an agent of creating exclusive site (by distancing from the discriminatory practices through non-dependence on the upper castes) and also an agent to nurture these exclusive sites (providing resources to build separate institutions like Gurudwaras, community centres, organising langars, etc.).

Competing in Social Spaces and Bargaining in Politics

The meaning of citizenship in the post-colonial caste-ridden societies remains ambivalent or extremely vague. However, there are certain 'practical values' associated with the idea of citizenship. In this sense, there are two sets of values through which the people connect as the citizens with the State, i.e. the value of welfare as reflected in the dole-giver and dole-receiver interaction and, second is the value of political power and material wealth. The value of power, position and possession of material wealth enables them to realise their claims. The value of hierarchical power, position and material wealth builds a collaborative arrangement between those who govern and those who are governed that has been rightly phrased by Korten, as 'coalition of indifference' (Korten 1983: 32). The intense explorations of the Dalits with the State have uncovered certain commonalities in their experience, but it could not dismantle the main attributes of the caste system (see Thorat and Deshpande 2001: 50-51).[20]

From cultural adaptation to the formation of exclusive socio-religious sites, politics in Punjab continues to provide the bargaining space to the Dalits. Jodhka (2002) mentions the practices of exclusivity in political spaces in rural Punjab, such as the panchayat buildings seen as the upper caste community centres, where the entry of the Dalits in such political institutions as a member is not welcomed nor is the equal treatment meted out to Dalit panchayat members. There is also discrimination in the seating arrangements in the panchayats, etc. As a result, in many villages, the

Dalits have built separate community centres. Regarding such situations, Jodhka (2002) further explains that so far untouchability is not practised in the election process as the importance of the Dalit votes or having the Dalits as an ally in the factional politics of the village has given opportunities to the Dalits to be elected as a sarpanch / panchayat member. The reserved seats for the Dalits in the panchayats have provided them with the space to be a part of the system but have really failed to blur the caste boundaries as even the selected Sarpanches do not get the dignity and recognition due to them (in the context of no patronage given by the dominant caste to the selected sarpanch). However, such democratisation of these local political institutions such as panchayats, has certainly made a difference by giving the Dalits a sense of dignity and power to bargain (Jodhka 2002). The articulation of the power of the numerical strength by the Scheduled Castes found expression much earlier in 1925 and later in 1931 during the enumeration in the census as *Ad Dharmis* and not as Hindus or Sikhs. This was a political statement made for claiming a dignified existence. The Census of India recorded the opposition of the Scheduled Castes to carve out an exclusive space. To quote, 'a tug of war started in some districts, and the Ad Dharmis were required by the Sikhs and the Hindus as the Sikh landowners employed all sorts of measures, not infrequently bordering on terrorism, to secure the return of Chuhras and Chamars as Sikhs (*Census of India 1931*). This was significant as these classifications formed the basis of the welfare policy formulations for the groups and collectivities. As a consequence, defining the group boundaries became central to the competing factions within the collectivities to seek State recognition and patronage.

Similarly, in the background of the Punjabi Suba Movement, the Scheduled Castes gave their mother tongue as Hindi and not Punjabi in the 1951 Census. They feared that the formation of the Punjab Suba might further lead to the empowerment of the Jat Sikhs and political marginalisation of the Scheduled Castes. This can be substantiated by the speech made by a number of the Scheduled Castes in the Punjab State Legislative Assembly in 1956. To quote, 'We intentionally asked for Hindi. We got this done with a vengeance. It was done only on the threats of the population living in the villages of these areas...we wanted to remove the yoke of domination of one community over the other' ("Punjab Vidhan Sabha Debates" 1956).

However, caste codification and numbers could not emerge as a significant factor for the formation of exclusive political formation, but it emerged as a competing identity in the electoral politics. The effort was not to escape pollution but to emerge as a power group with the universalised adoption of social norms. The slogans like *Garv se Kaho hum Chamar hain* are raised to overlook the traditional polluting attributions.

For instance, the Deras, including Sacha Saudha and Sachkhaand Ballan could not carve out an exclusive space for its lower caste followers to emerge as the dominant factor in the electoral politics. In the 2007 Assembly Elections, Dera Sacha Sauda actively participated in defeating the regional party, Shiromani Akali Dal (SAD) (which controls front organisations of the Sikh religion). Out of 117 assembly constituencies, the Dera has significant influence in 37 constituencies. The SAD could win only in 11 constituencies from these 37 constituencies in the 2007 Assembly elections. However, in the 2012 elections, the SAD could win in 20 constituencies out of 37 Dera dominated constituencies. This was mainly because the Dalit population was targeted with liberal doles, and the Jats got consolidated to dismantle the emerging political clout of the Dera followers.

Further, the composite religio-cultural tradition lends

a distinct flavour to the otherwise divisive politics. In the lower rung in the caste hierarchy, the Dalits do not constitute a captive vote bank. No doubt, they have experienced socio-economic neglect, but they are not hounded like prey in the manner that their counterparts are targeted elsewhere in the country. As Sharma (2012) also affirms the separation of the Dalits from the major political formations and also the social groups they belong to. To illustrate, there is a historical experience and the present political context moderates the emerging extremities. In 2012, one of the Granthis in Kapurthala gave a public speech and used derogatory words about Sant Valmikiji quoting a short story published on Sant Valmiki's life in the Sikh religious book *Bara Mah Maanjh Steek* written by Giani Mohan Singh. The leaders of the Balmiki community and President of the Rangreta Dal Punjab protested and registered a case against the author, publisher and Granthi Gurnam Singh. It was also alleged that Giani Joginder Singh Vedanti, Jathedar of the Shri Akal Takht, had made derogatory comments based on this short story. The leaders of the Balmiki community along with the President of the Rangreta Dal Punjab lodged a complaint with the Kapurthala Police. A criminal case was registered. They approached the senior leaders of the Shiromani Akali Dal and gave a protest call on the eve of Independence Day. The Akal Takht Jathedar issued a press statement that he had a great regard for Sant Valmikiji, and his statement had been distorted. He was deeply hurt and much grieved over this development. There are a built-in socio-cultural capital and political necessity that create situations of moderation. On the contrary, 'the Jat Sikhs do not hesitate, to remind the 'Chamars' that they are still 'Chamars', even in England.' To escape this labelling, the 'Chamars' organised Ravidas Sabhas in Birmingham and Wolverhampton in 1956. And many followed Dr. Ambedkar in the same year to become Buddhists. Not only this, but they also formed their political group, i.e. Indian Republican Group of Great Britain, but also fought the elections (Juergensmeyer 1988: 249).

Interestingly, of the 1,248 MLAs in the State from 1967 to 2012, the Dalits were 25.16 per cent, OBCs 8.97 per cent and the urban traders (Khatris) 22.12 per cent. But, a majority of the MLAs, i.e. 43.74 per cent came from the rural Jat peasantry. Notwithstanding this disproportionate representation of the rural Jat peasantry, the Dalits have been adequately represented in the State's electoral politics.

A detailed analysis of the Dalit factor in Punjab politics can help us to understand the larger issue of caste dynamics in electoral politics. The 'uncertain religious allegiance' of the Dalits, and the absence of caste as a defining parameter for social position, yet the Dalits found representation in all the political parties in the State. It is interesting to note that even the Jat dominated Shiromani Akali Dal gave substantial representation to the Dalits. For instance, in 1969, of the 25 Scheduled Caste elected legislators, a majority of 44 per cent was in the Akali Dal. Not only this, in 1977 (48 per cent), 1985 (62 per cent), 1997 (77 per cent), 2007 (55 per cent) and 2012 (62 per cent), a majority of the Scheduled Caste legislators were from the Akali Dal. Similarly, in 1967 (52 per cent), 1972 (61 per cent), 1980 (45 per cent), 1992 (63 per cent) and 2002 (48 per cent) a majority of the elected Scheduled Caste legislators were from the Congress. Even the Bharatiya Janata Party gave representation to the Dalits. For instance, in 1997, 13 per cent of the Scheduled Caste members belonged to the BJP. Interestingly, the Dalit legislators have been elected from the political parties other than the BSP and the Communist parties (Kumar 2017).

In fact, the Dalits could not emerge as a vote bank for the BSP in Punjab. For instance, the Bahujan Samaj Party (BSP) could find a positive response in Uttar Pradesh (UP), whereas, in Punjab, which has the highest percentage of the Dalit population in the country, it could find only a nominal response. To illustrate, the BSP vote share in Uttar Pradesh increased from 11 per cent in 1993 to 23 per cent in 2002. Both in Punjab and Uttar Pradesh, the initial response of the Dalits was to identify themselves with the BSP as there was a low degree of representation of the Scheduled Castes. But in Punjab, there is a trend to move away from the BSP. For instance, in 1992 it secured 16 per cent votes, which declined to 6 per cent, 4 per cent and 4.29 per cent in 2002, 2007 and 2012 respectively. It could register a win only in 9 constituencies in three assembly elections since 1992. However, the BSP could only act as a spoiler mainly for the Congress in 14 and 11 constituencies in 1997 and 2002 elections, respectively. Interestingly, a two per cent increase in the vote share of the BSP can cost the Congress five to 10 seats. To illustrate, between 1997 and 2002 elections, the BSP votes decreased from 7.4 per cent to 5.6 per cent, and the Congress Party gained in nine constituencies.

Why Could the BSP Not Make Electoral Inroads in the State?

Punjab has been known for its liberal religious practices in relation to caste. Both Sikhism and the Arya Samaj liberated the Dalits to a significant extent from the stringent purity-pollution based behavioural patterns. Furthermore, the political content of the BSP has been unable to capture the regional, cultural and economic specificities of Punjab. The purity-pollution and *Manuwad* that are the BSP's main ideological planks do not find expression in Punjab in view of the role of Sikhism and the Arya Samaj.

The disturbing aspect is that the socio-economic index of the Dalit population (50 per cent of the total poor in Punjab) continues to be dismal as compared to other castes (Table 4.2, Annexures II). The unemployment rate is also higher in the case of Dalits. It is 5.9 amongst the Dalits as compared to 4.9 among others (Table 4.3, Annexures II). The education and health status is also not very favourable for the Dalits. The gross enrolment ratio in higher education (18-22 years) is 21.4 per cent as compared to 30.3 per cent for others (Table 4.4, Annexures II). And, the child mortality rate, under-five mortality rate, infant mortality are quite high amongst Dalits. These factors do not find adequate emphasis in sensitising and creation of accessible facilities for the Dalits. (Table 4.5, Annexures II).

The allocation for the development and welfare schemes is multiplying every year. But, it is making no significant difference to the socio-economic status of the Dalits. The resource allocation, access to jobs, services, health and education facilities must reach the socially deprived sections, failing which the Dalits may emerge as an exclusive vote-bank and disturb the political arithmetic of the State.

To conclude, the emerging Dalit identity architecture is operational in multiple cultural spaces and is in the process of evolving a master narrative. The crucial elements of this identity formation process are a selective adaptation of the dominant cultural standards to blur the exclusivity and thereby restore a sense of pride in the community and shift the site of subjugation and abuse from the public domain (Kumar 2017). Along with this, parallel cultural status markers are being constructed to question the hegemonic subordination of the dominant castes. In redefining the inter-group relations, exclusive sites and spaces are being nurtured to put in place control-oriented mechanisms within the group. These multiple spatial activities within regional and transnational context entail the negation of the polluting aspects and forging positive identity to restore a sense of dignity are also coexisting. Particularly, at the regional level in the context of the historical experience of mistreatment moderated by the various religious reform movements, including Sikhism and Arya Samaj, in which religion and not caste is the defining marker of political participation. But, attribution of 'restrictive citizenship' thereby circumscribed the operationalisation of the core values of identity, dignity and productivity, and the politics continue to function on religio-caste lines engaging the citizens with a number of cultural possibilities and choices. And, at the transnational level, the societal dynamism has thwarted the processes to cultivate caste as a core basis of social and political interactions. However, providing space to the caste-based divisive events have impacted the Dalit architecture at the regional level.

NOTES

1. 'The nomenclature to identify the untouchables has also evolved historically. The two leading terms used are "Harijan" and "Dalit". The prefix "Adi" or "original" was used to assert that they were subordinated by the Aryan immigrants to India. So the terms "Adi-Dravida", "Adi-Karnataka" and "Adi-Andhra" are still used in South India. The "Harijan" term adopted by Gandhiji in 1932 was seen as patronising and is out of circulation. The term Dalit is drawn from the Marathi language. It means "broken" or "reduced to pieces generally" or "ground".' (For details see, Mendelsohn and Vicziany 2007: 2-10).
2. The whole theory of society is that occupation and caste are hereditary, and the presumption that caste passes unchanged to the descendants is exceedingly strong. But the presumption is one which can be defeated, and has already been and is now in the process of being defeated in numberless instances...This friction and inertia are largely due to a set of artificial rules which have been grafted on to the social prejudices common to all communities by the peculiar form which caste has taken in the Brahmanical teachings. But there is every sign that these rules are gradually relaxing. Sikhism did much to weaken them in the centre of the Punjab. (See Ibbetson 1916: 9).
3. As a UN report on 'Special Rapporteur on Violence Against Women, its Causes and Consequences' (Manjoo: 2012) mentions that in India, physical violence is sometimes employed against Dalit women as a mechanism to take possession of their family lands and/or to keep them under economic subjugation, sexual exploitation, gender domination and control.

4. Scholars have noted differences in the customs of Dalits and upper castes in Punjab in matters pertaining to social mores, family patterns and eating habits. (See Juergensmeyer 1988: 19).
5. Srinivas has explained Sanskritisation as the adoption of rituals, customs and ideology by a low caste to that of the dominant caste. If conceded, the resultant mobility leads to positional but not structural changes in an essentially stable hierarchical order. (See Srinivas 1966: 6-7).
6. Assimilation within the dominant folds but with hierarchy instated. The subordination of Dalits in the realm of everyday power play can be captured from the bias that panchayats show in their functioning towards the Jats and the Dalits. Even the 1911 Census of India registered this fact. (see *Punjab Census Report 1911*: 420-21).
7. "This ambiguity on the question of caste persisted despite the Sabhas' encouragement to institutions like the initiation ceremony (Pahul) and communal eating (*langar*) with their apparent disregard for caste distinctions. The Singh sabhas reflected a vision of a hierarchically organised society, with some groups within it more privileged than the others, even though a Sikh identity hinged upon declaring everyone in its fold as equal". (see Malhotra 2002: 43).
8. As a well-off Dalit from a village in the prosperous Doaba region of Punjab asserted: "As long as we remain dependent on the Jats for collecting fodder for our cattle, and our women keep going to their fields, there is no way that we can uphold our dignity." (See Shah, Thorat et al., 2006: 120).
9. The calamity of the rightless is not that they are deprived of life, liberty, and the pursuit of happiness, or of equality before the law and freedom of opinion—formulas which were designed to solve problems within given communities—but that they no longer belong to any community whatsoever. Their plight is not that they are not equal before the law, but that no law exists for them. (see Arendt 1986: 295-96).
10. The emergence of a Jat consciousness has been visible since the 1970s with the Jat synchronically serving as signifier not only of Sikhs but also of Punjabi identity (Roy 2011: 91).
11. The most popular graffiti is 'putt jattan de' (sons of Jats).No other caste group would find such mention. Recently a similar trend could be found among the Chamars of Punjab, as is evident from the following graffiti: 'putt Chamaran de' (sons of Chamars),

then "Chamar power". However the following graffiti behind a truck is notable for its identity assertion: 'Awen bharam ne mutiaran de, marhi neet rakhade munde Chamaran de' (Young women are mistaken in thinking that the Chamar boys have evil intentions). (see Judge and Bal 2008: 55).

12. Dera Sach Khand was set up 70 years before by Sant Pipal Singh in Ballan village near Jalandhar. The sect follows the ideals of Sant Ravidas, a late fifteenth century preacher.
13. A scheme was launched in the mid-1980s to provide a grant of Rs. 60,000 to each Mahila Mandal to buy utensils and the income earned to be used for the girl child's education.
14. These demands have been raised in the 1971 conference. Ad Dharmi representative to be included in the new Scheduled Caste Corporation; land distributions to move at a faster pace; poverty line to be raised from 3,600 to 6,000 and for Dalits to register themselves as *Ad Dharmi* in the Census. (see Juergensmeyer 1988: 263).
15. Finding solutions within the religious paradigm, one course that was tried with great success was the *Ad Dharam* movement in the 1920s. Asserting that Dalits and Adivasis were the original inhabitants of the subcontinent, it drew its inspiration from Sant Valmiki, Ravidas, Kabir and Namdev. Its founder, Mangoo Ram Mugowalia's appeal that Dalits were the real inhabitants of this land made an enormous psychological impact on the untouchables of Punjab. It laid stress on distinct Dalit identity independent that of Hindus, Sikhs, Muslims and Christians. Within a short time, it became a Dalit mass struggle for their separate Dalit identity. In the 1931 Census, 4,18,789 Dalits recorded themselves as *Ad Dharmis*. (see Hans 2008: 16).
16. However, the phenomenon of Deras is not new to Punjab. Rather it was as old as the very process of the evolution of the Sikh faith. Bidhi Chand, the dissenter, made first such an attempt during the Guru-period (1552-74) of third Guru, Amar Dass. He formed the Handalis sect, instituted the worship of Niranjan, 'the bright God' and declared himself as the Prophet or Handal...During the fifth Guru-period of Arjan Dev (1581-1606), Dhirmaliye and Mine sects were organised in opposition to the main religious Sikh body, and they established their Deras along the Sutlej River...The descendants of Ram Rai, son of the Guru Har Rai (1644-61), also organised a sect known as Ramraiyas during the Gurus-period... Some of the more prominent among them were Nanakpanthis,

Udasis, Sewapanthis, Nirmalas and the Nihangs also known as Akalis or Shahids. What distinguished the contemporary Deras from their counterparts during the Guruship period of the ten Masters is that in the case of the former their founders were/are not related to the Gurus of the mainstream Sikh body nor do they claim Guruship over and above the ten Masters. (see Ram 2007).

17. In the 1980s, the Nirankari guru was presented as Guru Nanak Devji which led to a violent confrontation between institutionalised religion and the Dera. Similarly, in an advertisement issued by Dera Sacha Sauda in which the Guru was attired similarly to Guru Gobind Singh led to violent clashes in the state.
18. Remembering the lovelorn Bulleh Shah who had this to say on the prevailing state of affairs in the religious institutions, "Dharamsaal vich dharvi rahinde, thakur dware thug. Wich maseet kusatti rahinde, aashiq rahin alag." And we must be wary in attributing these expedient followers who dared to challenge the status quo as fools, especially when they number in lakhs and were previously part of the same faith on whose pedestal the apologists have based their counter-argument...The time is ripe for the Sikh clergy to shed its hegemonic and dogmatic traits: the society is clamouring for a "Protestant Reformation". (see Singh 2012).
19. In Ravidasia Gurudwaras, the Amritbani of Guru Ravidasji was to be recited. Amritbani Granth was installed on January 30, 2011 in Seer Govardhanpur Varanasi. On its title page, appear the symbol of Hari Nishaan photo of Guru Ravidasji and picture of Shri Guru Ravidas Janam Asthan Mandir at Seer Govardhanpur, Varanasi. It contains 240 hymns of Guru Ravidasji.
20. The attributes of the caste system are as described by Ambedkar and summarised by Thorat and Deshpande. Fixation of occupation by caste and its continuity ensured by heredity. Unequal distribution of economic rights regarding ownership of property, employment, wage, education, etc., among the caste groups and the operation of the principle of graded inequality afflicting the economic field as well. Occupations were not only fixed and unequal, but some of them were considered lower or higher depending upon the social stigma attached to them. The Hindu religious order recognised slavery and the principle of graded inequality were also applicable to slavery. The Hindu social order punished socially and economically those who infringed the caste-based economic order. (see Thorat and Deshpande 2001: 50-51).

Concluding Remarks

The idea of new India has taken shape as an alternative to the Nehruvian nation-building project of secular nationalism, mixed economy and non-aligned foreign relations. The idea of new India is a transformation from the secular nationalism to cultural nationalism, from a mixed economy to market economy, and from the non-aligned foreign policy to the interest-based global alignments. The process of change of the State-led capitalism to neoliberal market reforms initiated in 1994 was claimed as a main achievement of the Congress Party. And subsequently, the other parties supported these neoliberal economic reforms, and a sort of consensus emerged amongst the competing political parties. However, there is transitional instability and disagreement around the cultural nationalism. It has been termed as an ideology of the Hindu majoritarianism around which identity politics and contemporary nationalism have been woven.

In this sense, nationalism is an abstract concept and cultural, secular, religious, developmental, communal and theocratic nationalisms are its various forms. These forms provide an understanding and interpretation of the phenomena of nationalism, having a basis in a specific context rather than providing causal explanations. These are descriptive categories and hence provide visibility to practise as a static discourse. For instance, the label of 'cultural nationalism' overlooks the internal conflict of interest involved in appropriation of cultural capital and external spectrum of the interactive process between globalisation, nature of the state, the path of development. To take form as an analytical category is to remain within the boundaries of practices as captured through a labelled category is to be tautological. For instance, the political assertions in Kashmir are labelled as Pan-Islamic or communal secessionism as the Kashmiri Muslims are seen as homogeneous and different from other Kashmiris, thereby proving the assumption built into the label itself.

The descriptive categories of the cultural and development nationalism, undoubtedly, have made the phenomenon of nationalism intelligible in terms of purposes, beliefs, values and intentions of the interests groups. The interpretive understanding has provided elucidation of the norms, rules and mechanisms, which underlined the growth of institutions and movements. For instance, under the Nehruvian leadership, it was assumed that since communalism was a pre-capitalist notion and was caused by colonialism, it would get eroded after independence and with the development of capitalism.

Therefore, it is submitted that the various forms of nationalism are related to each other, having their basis in similar structural conditions and are interlinked in terms of explanations of reasons rather than causes. To illustrate, communalism is seen as a cause rather than as a reason for the weak secular or developmental nationalism thereby, providing invisibility to the phenomenon like globalisation which has empowered the market and made developmental nationalism redundant. These descriptive categories are inadequate. In other words, descriptive category is—static in nature, reductionist in interpretation, and problem-centred in their approach (For instance, communalism and nationalism versus colonialism).

Nationalism as a concept is a derivative of the interaction between the nature of the State, path and pace of development and cultural reservoir and has shown its capacity to transcend its empirical context.

Therefore, in this discussion, an attempt should be made to understand the phenomenon of nationalism in multicultural reality in the context of the specificities of historical experiences, the nature of socio-economic, political, cultural and religious formations by not taking precedent as an essence. This theoretical modification in no way overlooks the relevance of the experiences of other societies. For the post-colonial South Asian region, if the mid-twentieth century was a period of the consolidation of nationalism into nation-States, the last decade of this century witnessed the assertion of sub-national identities. Today, it seems that the bone and flesh of a self-determined nation-State is either being substituted by the redefined (not organic) subnationalities on the part of the people or by an aggressive state-controlled nation.

These assertions have been accentuated by the so-called globalisation syndrome. This syndrome represents a kind of dualism, i.e. on the one hand, there is the globalisation of capital and, on the other, localisation of the human capital (labour), their aspirations, culture, history, language, etc. This phenomenon has provided the impetus to the 'sons of the soil' movements throughout the world. This is visible within and even among the countries. For instance, the movements like Punjab for Punjabis (Sikhs), Kashmir for Kashmiris (Muslims), Maharashtra for Marathas (Hindus), etc., have acquired structural logic because of the resource crunch and intense competition for the jobs due to the process of liberalisation and globalisation within the country. These negative factors are also quite visible in the advanced countries. For instance, in Canada, the East Indians are usually considered derogatively, along with other South East Asians, and are called 'Pakis'. Many of them are new immigrants. These ethnic groups are perceived as more threatening in the job market because of their higher educational attainment. It is, therefore, hypothesised that the new reality of capitalism does not *want* racialism and religious fundamentalism but *needs* it.

These redefined and reformulated sub-nationality identities are also acquiring fundamentalist overtones. These fundamentalist assertions reinforce the 'traditional purity of culture' and project the perceived dominant culture as a threat. In a multicultural society, extremisms survive and even thrive on the reservoir or on the state of mind of a group arising out of a feeling that a threat, real or imaginary, exists to their faith which should be combated by collective action.

In this context, the multicultural character of the societies in India could not find the corresponding expression in the practice of politics and the State structure. This adversely affected the State's claim to the allegiance of its members and the members' claim to some conception of shared purpose or sense of shared benefits with others belonging to different cultural groups. In other words, the denial of access to the members to their own language, culture and other resources due to the nature of the interactive relationship between the structural conditions of violence and the State apparatus alienated a large section from the State, their cultural, lingual and their own physical and material resource base. In these societies, the areas governed by the caste or religious beliefs and dominant politics are increasingly becoming consistent. This is providing sufficient space to the politics to distort and use caste and religious belief systems and blur the real issues.

These distortions are persisting mainly due to the centralisation of the powers, the co-option of the retrogressive aspirations through preferential policies, excessive reliance on the repressive State apparatus and unequal distribution of the resources between the regions and within the regions amongst groups.

The need is to reverse this process. There are no middle paths available either. In other words, if there is discrimination, the answer should not be found in preference; if there is centralisation, the answer is not to be found in decentralisation. The effort should be made to evolve parameters of alternate political solutions to provide well-being to the people.

Therefore, in a multicultural society like India, mechanisms should be evolved to negate those aspects which vitiate the ethos of cultural pluralism. This, perhaps, is happening because the process of historic development and the human explosion of knowledge is transforming the undifferentiated cultures into differentiated cultural groups. These explorations are aimed at identifying the differences in a setting where greater emphasis is laid to produce a canopy culture, and colourless homogeneity leads to ethnic explosions. It is in this context that there is a need to institutionalise the framework of cultural federalism within the broad design of politico-economic federalism.

It has been argued that the interactive relationship between structural reality, the State and the path of development have shaped the nationality assertion in India. The question arises: are the economic, social, and cultural dimensions mutually reinforcing to promote equity and distributive justice? Since politics has a primacy, harmonisation of these dimensions with equity and distributive justice will largely depend on the ideological and political persuasions of the people who govern. It is also well established that the dynamics of market and growth processes on their own cannot moderate the widening disparities. Similarly, fiscal management policy interventions on their own are not fully equipped to make the development inclusive, governance citizen-centric and the population more productive.

The alternatives to contemporary policies, have to

relook at the neoliberal path of development with its excessive focus on globalisation, which is leading to the exclusion of a large section of the population. And, the policies being implemented are accentuating inequalities and deprivation. For example, the new land legislation is leading to the accumulation of capital by the dispossession of the land of the poor farmers. Labour reforms are basically about bringing casualisation of the workers; reduction in their real wages and without any social safety nets. The unchallenged hegemony of the market and simultaneous weakening of the capacity of the State to provide resources for human development and social security.

A fragmented labour market is an essential component of this global commodity chain of production and exchange. The expansion of the markets into supermarkets and the spread of the commodity chains to newer areas have undoubtedly created new work opportunities and expanded the labour market, and at the same time created new aspirations among the people in the new locations. The need is to revisit the phenomenon of migration and human trafficking with a rights-based perspective.

As has been argued, the globalisation does not create a 'common national culture', it only breaks down the local culture of separate nationalities and replaces them with a cosmopolitan culture of separate nationalities accessible in very different ways to the different classes. Further, the cultural process has provided legitimacy to these inequalities through the filter of communalism, racism and casteism.

It has impacted the human existence, manufactured the language of politics, intermingled with the social and cultural interactions, cascaded into cultural discourse and ultimately administer and monitor the thought processes of its inhabitants. These processes have nurtured restricted social relations, demarcated human self-expression and developed particular interests giving rise to exclusion.

In view of the neoliberal reforms, the State has reinvented itself to co-opt the excluded groups. For instance, all political parties have shared the wealth with the marginal sections as a dole without engaging them in the productive processes. During the Congress regime, some schemes like MGNREGA, debt waiver for the farmers, etc., were introduced. The BJP and the AAP followed them with more doles like free electricity, water, local travel, etc.

The objectives of these initiatives are political; their interpretation is partisan and non-secular. Its classification is erroneous. In a nutshell, it has nothing to do with providing equal or little less than equal access to justice. It is solely concerned with the strategy of co-option by multiplying the cleavages and to achieve the balance of interests. Therefore, it contains within itself the logic for its rejection by the downtrodden and underprivileged sections of the society.

There exists a vast space for politics to reinvent itself. Rather than merely negating and partially adopting the dominant right-wing majoritarianism, and start competing within it. It would be prudent to come out with superior alternatives to the politics of convergence of the market with religions and caste cleavages of the Hindu civilisational cultural nationalism. It has to move beyond the boundaries demarcated by the State. And, it involves revealing the contradictions which provide sustenance to the retrogressive interests. In other words, politics has to redefine the dominant ideas of the existing politico-economic structures to create a society free from hunger, inequalities, deprivation, and discrimination on the basis of gender, caste, religion, and ethnicity and, also refrain from the environmental exploitation leading to widespread and irreparable devastations.

For instance, during the Nehruvian times, the State and the government were inward-looking with a focus on the development of the public sector and trade protections. And to become self-reliant, the focus was on basic industries like steel, iron, etc., and products like food and water. While the society was outward-looking along with the trained youth venturing out and many more people striving to settle in their dreamlands, generally across the seas. Notwithstanding the fact that the mixed economy model produced distortions in governance like Inspector Raj, corruption, and inefficiency instead of fixing these, we moved away from the core of development perspective, i.e. self-reliance. And in turn, the state transformed itself to become a regulatory, an advanced version of Inspector Raj. The corruption continued to rock, and inefficiency engulfed even the private sector.

What is the message? The first and foremost message is that for the existential crisis, it is the State which can help. Perhaps, for the first time during COVID-19 phase, the State has made an effort to deliver, 'what is essential' for the human existence, be it food, vegetables, medical services, medicines, transport, shelter, hygiene and sanitation. All this has been done efficiently by the public sector institutions. There is a thought that it would be worthwhile to institutionalize these and other related initiatives into the planning process. But, if the State has been rendered weak and becomes subservient to the market, including outsourcing of its basic functions to the private players, then the basics for human existence are compromised.

The signal is quite clear to strengthen the welfare functions of the State and not outsource the same to the private interests.

Another message that is loud and clear is that in order to have a decent living, only fewer of the consumption goods are essential, and the rest are non-essentials. And the State in its wisdom has defined 'what is essential and non-essential for the human existence. In the non-essentials, the State included places of worship like, temples, Gurudwaras, and masjids. It was evident that there was glut of non-essential services while essentials were in short supply.

All these years, the political establishments worked overtime to disinvest the public sector from the essential goods and services and outsourced the same to the private sector. And today, the COVID-19 challenge to the human existence is being fought by the ill-equipped medical fraternity, police and other do-gooders. The existential challenge has once again given us the opportunity to make the right kind of choices, for instance, employment can be generated by producing automobiles and armaments, but it can also be done by producing essentials like ventilators, sanitisers, etc. The choice has to be exercised, keeping the focus on social purpose. Is the purpose of allowing the plundering of the environment without considering the ecological needs and wasteful consumption or fulfil the community's existential needs adequately?

The State has to reposition itself as a welfare State rather than surrender to the market. In other words, it has to redefine its role in relation to the market, particularly in education, health, food security, public health and housing sectors.

There is also a need to incentivise revenue-generating industries like hospitality, tourism, etc. The governments may formulate policies for encouraging and incentivising supply and production chains having social well-being as a core value.

In education and health, the policies may simultaneously strengthen the public sector medical services, support missionary and NGOs-run educational institutions and hospitals and facilitate private sector initiatives. Simultaneously, skill development policies may be formulated not merely having interface with the industry, but also keeping the social, national and civilizational purpose in mind. For instance, the skill of an astronaut, philosopher, social researchers, and others could also be developed.

Further, it is evident that technology alone cannot answer the basic needs of human existence. It is, of course, a great facilitator, but not a panacea. The pandemic has reiterated the need for human passion, compassion and empathy. For instance, it is not possible to download food, medicines and other essentials from the internet directly without the delivery persons. And, the capital on its own cannot manufacture, for instance, ventilators, masks or other essentials without the workers. Further, the patients cannot be treated through telemedicine alone without hospitalisation. The cities and the villages cannot be sanitised or put under lockdown without human labour. And, the households cannot be run with technology-driven gadgets as one needs the people to take care of the elderly or do babysitting, etc. This is the time to revisit the direction we want to give to our social existence.

The investment in research and development is a must. The knowledge industry and institutions have become victims of the governmentality. The skill of a professional is subordinate to the non-professional administrator. Can you pay a medical doctor less remuneration than a civil servant and then expect the nation to be healthy? And, also to go back to the basics, as has been said *'Jaan hai to Jahaan Hai'*. The Welfare State has to reclaim its place by liberating itself from its subservient position to the market. As to how far will market shall allow the State do the right things and not mess up the environment, and nature will have to be seen.

Annexures

ANNEXURE, CHAPTER 1

Annexure 1.1

The massive electoral mandate on its own was not sufficient to match the resistance to these economic reforms and outcomes of pursuits of cultural nationalism. The Supreme Court verdict on the Ram Janambhoomi-Babri-Masjid dispute legitimised the BJP's promise.

Ram Janmabhoomi-Babri Masjid Land Dispute Milestones

1885: One Mahant Raghubar Das files a suit seeking permission to construct a Ram temple at the disputed site. A trial court rejects the petition fearing such a permission would lead to riots. Appeals are also rejected.

1934: A mob damages parts of the disputed structure. The British repair it. Muslims continue to offer prayers at the mosque and Hindus worship at Ram-Chabutra and Kaushalya Rasoi.

1949-59: Lord Ram's idols are planted inside the central dome of Babri masjid. Both sides file court cases; the site is locked. Ten years after that, Nirmohi Akhara files a suit seeking possession of the site and claims to be the custodian of the disputed land.

December 18, 1961: The Sunni Central Board of Waqf files a suit claiming ownership of the site 1984: Vishwa Hindu Parishad (VHP) launches a campaign for the construction of a Ram temple at what it claims to be the birthplace

(Janmabhoomi) of Lord Ram. Two years after, the Faizabad district court orders that gates of the mosque be opened and Hindus be allowed to worship there. Muslims protest the move and form the Babri Masjid Action Committee.

November 9, 1989: VHP lays the foundation of a Ram temple on the land next to the Babri Masjid after receiving permission to do so from the Rajiv Gandhi government of the day.

September 25, 1990: Then BJP President L.K. Advani launches a Rath Yatra from Somnath in Gujarat to Ayodhya, demanding the construction of a Ram temple. However, he is arrested in Bihar's Samastipur in November.

December 6, 1992: The Babri Masjid is razed to the ground by hundreds of kar sevaks. **April 2002:** A three-judge Bench of the Allahabad High Court begins hearing to determine the ownership of the disputed land in Ayodhya. The HC orders the Archaeological Survey of India (ASI) to excavate the site and determine if it was a temple earlier.

2003: ASI finds evidence of the presence of a temple under the mosque. Muslim organisations dispute these findings.

September 30, 2010: The HC rules that the disputed land should be divided into three parts—a third should go to Ram Lalla Virajman, represented by the Akhil Bharatiya Hindu Mahasabha; one-third to the Sunni Waqf Board; and the remaining to the Nirmohi Akhara. In December, the parties move to the Supreme Court.

May 2011: The Supreme Court stays the Allahabad HC order.

March 2017: The Supreme Court says charges against Advani and other leaders in the Babri Masjid demolition case cannot be dropped. The apex court adds that the matter is sensitive and must be settled out of court

May 30, 2017: L.K. Advani, Murli Manohar Joshi, Uma Bharati and Vinay Katiyar are charged with criminal conspiracy in the Babri Masjid demolition case.

December 5, 2017: The SC says it will hear the civil appeals filed by various parties challenging the 2010 Allahabad High Court verdict on February 8.

September 2018: The Supreme Court rejects the plea for a review of the 1994 Farooqui judgment but then clarifies that this would have no bearing on pending title suits.

October 2018: The Supreme Court decides that the land dispute case will only be listed before an "appropriate Bench" in January 2019. A Bench consisting of Chief Justice Ranjan Gogoi and Justices S.K. Kaul and K.M. Joseph says: "The appropriate Bench will fix the schedule with regard to the hearing of appeals in the case."

January 8, 2019: The Supreme Court sets up a five-judge constitution Bench to hear the land dispute case.

January 10, 2019: A five-judge Constitution Bench of the Supreme Court hears the Ayodhya land title dispute case, sets January 29 as the next date for hearing in the case

March 8, 2019: The SC refers the Ayodhya land dispute case for mediation, asks the panel to complete proceedings within 8 weeks.

August 1, 2019: The mediation panel submits its report to the apex court. The SC says the mediation panel failed to find a solution.

August 6, 2019: The top court begins day-to-day hearing in the case.

October 16, 2019: After a marathon 40-day daily hearing, the SC concludes hearing in the case. It says that a verdict will be delivered by CJI Gogoi before his retirement on November 17, 2019.

November 9, 2019: In a unanimous verdict, the Supreme Court Bench led by Chief Justice Ranjan Gogoi orders that the disputed land in Ayodhya should be given to Ram Janmabhoomi Nyas for construction of a temple, and the Muslim side should be compensated with five acres of land at a prominent place in Ayodhya for a mosque. The court also orders the central government to formulate a scheme within three months to implement the order.

Source (Reproduced): The Ayodhya case timeline: Events leading up to the historic judgment. January 08, 2020. *Business Standard*. New Delhi (Retrieved from https://www.business-standard.com/article/current-affairs/the-ayodhya-case-timeline-events-leading-up-to-the-historic-judgment-119111000010_1.html).

Annexure 1.2

Article 370 and 35A of the Constitution of India was scrapped on August 5, 2019, and deprived the state of Jammu & Kashmir of its autonomous status. Gopalaswami Ayyangar drafted the article (with temporary nature initially, and accordingly included it in Temporary and Transitional Provisions in Part XXI) quoting that 'Jammu and Kashmir State which is now a part of India will continue to be a part of India, will be a unit of the future Federal Republic of India and the Union Legislature will get jurisdiction to enact laws on matters specified either in the Instrument of Accession or by later addition with the concurrence of the Government of the State' (*EPW* Engage 2019).

Annexure 1.3

There are three types of Talaq (Divorce) in Islam. First Talaq-e-Ahsan, second Talaq-e-Hasan (both are revocable), and the third Talaq-e-Biddat (the instant or triple-talaq). Talaq-e-Biddat is considered a sinful (but permissible) practice in Islamic law. Talaq-e-Biddat provides a right for particular Muslim men to divorce their wives in the irrevocable and instantaneous manner and for the ban of the same practice, Shayara Bano filed the litigation (PIL) in the apex court in response to his abruptly ended marriage in 2015 as being the victim of the same practice by her husband. Though, the

All India Muslim Personal Law Board (AIMPLB) opposed the bill by claiming the practice as 'essential' under Islamic religion.

In response to the central government's report on "Women and the Law: An Assessment of Family Laws Relating to Marriage, Divorce, Custody, Inheritance and Succession," Supreme Court forms five-judges bench to discuss the matter of triple talaq and in August 2017 decares the practice of triple talaq illegal and further orders Centre to frame a law. Muslim Women (Protection of Rights on Marriage) Bill, 2017 was passed in Lok Sabha. In Sepetember 2018 the bill clears ordinance and on July 30, 2019 Rajya Sabha passed the bill and practicing Triple Talaq becomes punishable offence with a three year jail term.

ANNEXURE 2.1

PUNJAB GOVERNMENT GAZETT (EXTRA.),
APRIL 26, 2011
(VYSK 06, 1933, SAKA)

PART I

Department of Legal and Legislative Affairs, Punjab
Notification

The April 26, 2011

No.19-Leg./2011. The following Act of the Legislature of the State of Punjab received the assent of the Governor of Punjab on April 20, 2011, and is hereby published for general information :-

THE PUNJAB LAND REVENUE (AMENDMENT) ACT, 2011

(Punjab Act No. 15 of 2011)

AN

ACT

further to amend the Punjab Land Revenue Act, 1887.

BE it enacted by the Legislature of the State of Punjab in the Sixty-Second Year of the Republic of India as follows:-

1. *(1)* This Act may be called the Punjab Land Revenue (Amendment) Act, 2011. (Short title and commencement)

(2) It shall come into force at once.

2. In the Punjab Land Revenue Act, 1887 (hereinafter referred to as the principal Act), in Section 13, in clause *(c)*, in item *(ii)*, at the end, for the sign ",", the sign "," shall be substituted and thereafter, the following items shall be added, namely:- (Amendment in Section 13 of Punjab Act XVII of 1887)

(iii) No authority, except the first appellate authority, shall remand the case to the lower authority to decide the case afresh; and

(iv) No appeal shall lie against any interim order passed by a Revenue Officer under this Act.

Note:-The provisions of items *(iii)* and *(iv)* shall not be applicable to the authorities mentioned under Section 16 of this Act".

3. In the principal Act, for Section 16, the following section shall be substituted, namely:-

"16. *(1)* A Commissioner may call for the record of any case pending before, or disposed of by any Revenue Officer under his control and such orders, as he thinks fit. (Submission of Section 16 of the Punjab Act XVII of 1887)

(2) A Collector may also call for the record of any case pending before, or disposed of by any Revenue Officer under his control, and if he is of the opinion that the proceedings taken or order made, should be modified or reversed, he shall report the case with his opinion thereon for the orders of the Commissioner whose decision shall be final:

Provided that he shall not pass an order reversing or modifying any proceeding or order of a subordinate Revenue Officer and affecting any question of right between private persons without giving them an opportunity of being heard."

4. In the principal Act, in Section 20, after sub-section *(5)*, the following sub-section shall be added, namely:- (Amendment in Section 20 of Punjab Act XVII of 1887)

"6. If is is not possible to serve summons in accordance with any of the modes, as provided in sub-sections (1), (2), (3), (4) and (5), then:

(a) Summons may be sent by the Revenue Office by whom it is issued whether within or out of the State by post or by courier service, as approved by the High Court of Punjab and Haryana or by fax message or by Electronic Mail Service or by any other means, as may be provided in the rules made by the High Court.

(b) where the person is confined in prison, the summons may be delivered by post or may be sent by courier service, as approved by the High Court or by fax message or by Electronic Mail Service or by any other means, as may be provided in the rules made by the High Court to the officer-in charge of the prison for service to the person.

(c) Where the person resides out of India and has no agent in India, empowered to accept service, the summons may be addressed to the person at the place, where he is residing or may be sent to him by post or by courier service, as approved by the High Court or by fax message or by Electronic Mail Service or by any other means, as may be provided in the rules made by the High Court, if there is postal communication between such place and the place, where the Court is situated; and

(d) Where the Central Government, by notification in the Official Gazette, has declared in respect of any foreign country that summons should be served on the persons actually and voluntarily residing or carrying business or personally working for gain in that foreign country through an office of the Government of foreign country, as specified by the Central Government, the summons may be sent to such officer, through the Ministry of Government of India dealing with foreign affairs or in such other manner as may be specified by the central government, and if such officer returns any such summons with an endorsement purporting to have been made by him that the summons have been served on the persons, such service shall be deemed as evidence of service".

5. In the principal Act, for Section 111, the following section shall be substituted, namely:- (Substitution of Section 111 of Punjab Act XVII of 1887)

"111. Any joint owner of land, or any joint tenant of a tenancy in (Application for partition) which a right of occupancy subsists, may apply to a Revenue Officer for partition of his share in the land of tenancy, as the case may be, with the proposed plan of partition indicating the quality and location of the land in question along with the reasons for partition and copy of the latest jamabandi, if,-

(a) On the date of application, the share is recorded under Chapter IV as belonging to him; or

(b) His right to the share has been established by a decree which is still subsisting at that date; or

(c) A written acknowledgement of that right has been executed by all persons interested in the admission or denial thereof."

6. In the principal Act, in Section 113, for clauses *(a)* and *(b)* the following clauses shall be substituted, namely:- (Amendment in Section 113 of Punjab Act XVII of 1887)

(a) Cause notice of the application and of the day so fixed to be served on such of the recorded co-shares, as have not joined in the application to submit their replies and plans of partition with cogent reasons, and, if the share for which partition is applied for, is a share in a tenancy, on the landlord also, and

(b) If he thinks fit, cause the notice to be served on any other person whom he may deem to be directly or indirectly interested in the application to submit their replies and plans of partition with cogent reasons."

7. In the principal Act, section 114, for shall be omitted (Omission of Section 114 of Punjab Act XVII of 1887)

8. In the principal Act, for Section 115, the following sections shall be substituted, namely:- (Substitution of Section 115 of Punjab Act XVII of 1887)

"115. After examining such of the co-sharers and other persons, as (Absolute disallowance of partition) may be present on that day, the Revenue Officer may, disallow the partition in those cases only where application is made for the partition of common path, common water-course or such like place, used for common purposes.

"115-A. *(1)*Where it appears to the Revenue Officer that a settlement (Settlement of disputes by conciliation) may be acceptable to both the parties to the partition, he shall formulate the terms of settlement and submit the same to the parties for their suggestions. After receiving their objections or suggestions, the Revenue Officer, shall re-formulate the terms of settlement possible in the prevailing situation, and refer the same for conciliation with the intervention of the elders where the property is situated; and if the settlement is agreed upon by both the parties through a written deed, the Revenue Officer shall pass an order in accordance with such deed. The orders so made by the Revenue Officer shall be final, and a partition deed shall be issued accordingly.

(2) If no settlement is reached under sub-section *(1)*, the Revenue Officer shall within a period of four months after the date of making reference for conciliation, but not later than six months from the date of initiation of conciliatory

proceedings, pass such order on merits, as he may deem appropriate in the circumstances of the case after hearing the parties."

9. In the principal Act, for Section 118, for the following Section shall be substituted, namely:- (Substitution of Section 118 of Punjab Act XVII of 1887)

"118. *(1)*When there is a question as to the property to be divided, (Disposal of other questions) or the mode of making a partition, the Revenue Officer shall, after such inquiry, as he deems necessary, record an order stating his decision on the question and the reasons for the decision.

(2) No appeal shall lie against the decision referred to in sub-section *(1)*."

GOBINDER SINGH,
Secretary to Government of Punjab,
Department of Legal and Legislative Affairs.

ANNEXURE 2.2

PUNJAB GOVERNMENT GAZETT (EXTRA),
JANUARY 28, 2013
27
(MAGHA 08, 1934, SAKA)

PART I

DEPARTMENT OF LEGAL AND LEGISLATIVE AFFAIRS, PUNJAB

NOTIFICATION

January 28, 2013

No.5-Leg./2013.- The following Act of the Legislature of State of Punjab received the assent of the Governor of Punjab on the January 23, 2013, is hereby published for general information :-

THE PUNJAB LAND REVENUE (AMENDMENT) ACT, 2012
(Punjab Act No. 5 of 2013)

AN

ACT

further to amend the Punjab Land Revenue Act, 1887.

BE it enacted by the Legislature of the State of Punjab in the Sixty-third Year of the Republic of India as follows:-

1. *(1)* This Act may be called the Punjab Land Revenue (Amendment) Act, 2012. (Short title and commencement)

(2) It shall come into force on and with effect from the date its publication in the Official Gazette.

2. In the Punjab Land Revenue Act, 1887, for Section 16, the following section shall be substituted, namely:- (Substitution of Section 16 of Punjab Act XVII of 1887)

"16. *(1)* Except a case pertaining to question of division of property of the mode of making a partition under Section 118,- (Power to call for examine and revise proceedings of Revenue Officers)

(i) The Financial Commissioner may, it any time, call for the record of any case pending before or disposed of by any Revenue Officer subordinate to him; and

(ii) A Commissioner or collector may call for the record of any case pending before or disposed of by any Revenue Officer under his control.

(2) If any case in which a Collector has called for a record and he is of the opinion that the proceedings taken or order made should be modified or reversed, he shall report the case with him opinion thereon for the orders of the Commissioner whose decision shall be final.

(3) The Financial Commissioner or Commissioner may, in any case called for by himself under sub-section *(1)* or under sub-section *(2)*, as the case may be, pass such orders as he thinks fit:

Provided that he shall not under this section pass an

order reversing or modifying any proceeding or order of a subordinate Revenue Officer and affecting any question of right between private persons without giving those persons an opportunity of being heard.

(4) Notwithstanding anything contained in this section, the cases called for by the commissioner or Collector, as the case may be, under sub-section *(1)* and *(2)* as it existed prior to the commencement of the Punjab Land Revenue (Amendment) Act, 2012 shall be decided by them as heretofore."

H.P.S. MAHAL,
Secretary to Government of Punjab,
Department of Legal and Legislative Affairs.

0141/1-2013/Pb. Government Press, S.A.S. Nagar

ANNEXURE 2.3

GOVERNMENT OF PUNJAB
DEPARTMENT OF PERSONNEL
(TRAINING BRANCH)

To

All Heads of Departments,
Commissioners of Divisions,
Registrar, High Court of Punjab and Haryana,
Deputy Commissioners and Subdivisional Officers (Civil).

Memo No. 3/7/2010-Trg. (3)/1007
Dated Chandigarh March 10, 2010.

Subject: Implementation of the recommendations of the Punjab Governance Reforms Commission, regarding;

Punjab Governance Reforms Commission was set up on January 8, 2009 under the Government orders. The Commission has already submitted two Reports to the Government. The proposed recommendations of the

Commission were considered carefully by the Government and it was decided that the recommendations will be considered by the Empowered Committee under the Chairmanship of Chief Secretary and, thereafter, the Department of Personnel, in consultation with the concerned Secretaries, will be responsible for getting the Government decisions implemented regarding the recommendations of the Commission.

The recommendations of the Commission were carefully considered. The following orders were issued regarding the specific recommendations related to affidavits and attestations.

All concerned are requested to immediately act in accordance with the revised procedures within the defined time frame.

1. Attestation System Related to Need-Based Services

1.1 Presently, the applicants/guardians have to submit affidavits to get various need based certificates such as Residence//Kandi Area/SC/BC etc. In some cases, affidavits are required due to some rules, sub rules etc. under the authority of some specific law. For such cases, these are attested by Public Notary while in other cases, attestation rests with the Executive Magistrates.

1.2 The view of the Government is that by asking for affidavits, the citizens are put to unnecessary harassment and as such, attestation should be replaced by self-declaration in majority of the cases because there is a provision for stern action under the law for making a wrong declaration. Therefore, it has been decided that no Government Department or organisation will ask for affidavits from the applicants except in those cases where affidavits are required under law. In place of having affidavits, self-declaration has been accepted and this system will be implemented with effect from April 1, 2010 onwards. It will be ensured by the Deputy Commissioners of the State that the self-declaration forms will be available at all the Suwidha Kendras to the citizens. Though, the self-declaration will carry a photo of the applicant.

1.3 All the Secretaries of the Departments, especially, Education, Health, Technical Education, Irrigation and Power etc. and others where affidavits are required for seeking admission or employment, will ensure that all organisations/agencies will replace the existing system of submission of affidavits with self-declaration and implement the changed system within the time frame.

1.4 All the Departments will submit a list of affidavits which have been replaced by self-declaration to the PGR Cell of the Department of Personnel and another list of the subjects where affidavits are required to continue due to legal formalities or on account of any other reasons. This list should be submitted by April 30, 2010.

2. Attestation of Documents

2.1 Presently, the applicants seeking admission in educational institutions and employment in Government Departments, are required to prove their eligibility to submit the attested copies of certificates. In some cases, the applicants are required to have the particulars mentioned in the applications duly attested by the Executive Magistrates.

2.2 The Government has decided that the applicants while submitting documents for admission in educational institutions and for seeking employment will be permitted to submit self-attestation with effect from April 1, 2010 onwards.

2.3 For admission to educational institutions and for providing employment, the concerned agencies should accept the self-attested copies from the applicants and the original certificates should be called only from finally selected candidates.

3. Action to be Taken by the Authorities

3.1 The Administrative Secretaries of the Departments of Education, Higher Education, Medical Education and Research and Technical Education are requested to ensure the implementation of the government decision in all the educational institutions. The format of the application form is, thus, required to be revised properly before seeking applications for admission by the applicants during the Academic Session of 2010-11.

3.2 Chairmen of the Punjab Public Service Commission and Subordinate Services Selection Board are requested to ensure the implementation of the decision while making recruitments. The recruitments which are not covered by the above two authorities, the Administrative Secretaries and Heads of Departments concerned are required to take appropriate steps in the Departmental Selection Committees.

3.3 The Deputy Commissioners of the State are required to ensure that the decision will be disseminated through the District Suwidha Centres by publicizing the same widely and prominently. While doing so, due attention may also be drawn to the relevant provisions of The Indian Penal Code for wilfully filing wrong declaration (Annexure-1).

3.4 Self-declaration format will also be properly included in the applications for employment being provided by various organisations under the control of the State Government (Annexure-2).

S. C. Agrawal.
Chief Secretary, Government of Punjab.

Endst. No.3/7/2010-Trg.(3)/1008 Dated Chandigarh March 10, 2010.

Copy is forwarded to Shri Satish Chandra, IAS, Principal Secretary, Health & Family Welfare, Planning and ex-officio Member Secretary, Punjab Governance Reforms Commission & Chairman, Core Implementation Committee for information and necessary action.

Sd/-

Under Secretary Personnel

Endst. No. 3/7/2010-Trg.(3)/1009 Dated Chandigarh March 10, 2010.

Copy is forwarded to the following for ensuring early follow up action:-

1. Chairman, Punjab Public Service Commission
2. Chairman, Subordinate Services Selection Board, Punjab
3. Vice-Chancellor, Guru Nanak Dev University, Amritsar;
4. Vice-Chancellor, Punjabi University, Patiala
5. Vice-Chancellor, Baba Farid Medical University of Health Sciences, Faridkot
6. Vice-Chancellor, Punjab Technical University, Jalandhar
7. Vice-Chancellor, Central University, Punjab, Bathinda
8. Vice-Chancellor, Guru Angad Dev Veterinary and Animal Science University, Ludhiana
9. Vice-Chancellor, Rajiv Gandhi National University of Law, Patiala and
10. Vice-Chancellor, Punjab Agriculture University, Ludhiana

Sd/-

Under Secretary Personnel

ANNEXURE 2.4

Birth Certificates

For Birth and Death Registration and Certificates, the Act provides for the appointment of Local Registrars and Sub-Registrars to assist the District Registrar. Section 8 {(1) (a)} declares it to be the duty of the household to give intimation, but Section 8 (2) also authorises the government to notify any other agent to provide information. Section 12 provides that extracts of the entries be given immediately on registration. Section 13 provides for a simple process of registration within 21 days, registration by the Local Registrar within 21-30 days provided a notarised affidavit is given and with the written permission of the prescribed authority. After one year, orders of the Executive Magistrate are required, and the Magistrate is expected to verify the correctness of the event. Thus, up to one year, the process is simple, whereas, after one year, a number of formalities (not found certificate, evidence of knowledgeable persons, etc.) are required to be completed to the satisfaction of the competent authority (Kumar 2009, From 'Introduction' to the Report).

'Different States have notified authorities, such as Panchayat, Health, Revenue Officials for local registration purposes and for delayed registration. In Andhra Pradesh, the Mandal Revenue Officer is competent for delayed registration up to one year. The custody of the records remains with the Local Registrar up to one year (counted from the end of a relevant calendar year) and, after that, these are transferred to the Executive Officer in case of the Municipal Committees and the concerned Registrar in case of the Panchayats. In Maharashtra, records after 1996 have been digitised. One can search the registration record, and CFCs (Citizen Facilitation Centres) run through PPP mode, are authorised to issue certificates. The BDO in the rural areas is authorized to make late registration (30 days to one year), whereas the authority for entry in the records beyond that period, is the SDM. In Delhi, the authorities for registration are the Health Centres in the rural and urban areas; proof of birth/ residence and affidavit regarding place, time/date of birth is required in the case of delayed registration' (Kumar 2009, From 'Introduction' to the Report).

The registration of births was not compulsory in Punjab till 1989. The chowkidar in the village used to be the 'notifier' in the rural areas and SHO was the local registrar, but from January 1, 2004, the head of the family was made notifier and Panchayat Secretary, the local registrar. The registrations are forwarded for a calendar year to the Chief Medical Officer of the district who is the District Registrar and is responsible for the maintenance of the records. In urban areas, in case of births which are at the health institutions, the responsibility for the reporting is of the health institutions concerned. The family is responsible for reporting in other cases.

Another issue is of the entry of the names. This can only be done within one month of the event, but due to ignorance or lack of anticipation, the people do not come forward to have the entry made and, only realise its significance, when the need arises, which may be much later. The problem is that generally in the Indian traditions, the naming ceremony is held sometime after birth and, therefore, the process of entry of the name is generally detached from the event of birth. The rules need to take account of this cultural tradition.

In the given structure of the local governance in the rural areas, it may not be appropriate to continue with the Panchayat Secretary as the Local Registrar. The village Panchayats will continue to be being reconstituted; Panchayat Secretaries are also frequently transferred and not handing over the record (unlike Himachal Pradesh where a gram karmi—village assistant is provided to Panchayat Secretary, no such help is available in Punjab). It may be appropriate to streamline the system and to give the authority to the health department personnel for proper coordination (Kumar 2009, From 'Introduction' to the Report).

ANM's jurisdiction for the revenue villages can be defined if required at the local level, and she can be declared the local registrars; (C) The birth and death registers can be collected by the PHC in charge and sent to the District Registrar—CMO after one year as per law. This will improve registrations within time and ANM's being under Health Department control, proper upkeep and timely transfer of the records to the CMOs will be ensured (Kumar 2009, From 'Introduction' to the Report). As and when the administrative infrastructure in the village panchayats is adequate, the status quo ante can be restored.

An incentive-compatible procedural amendment is to make the 'ASHA' worker the Notifier, instead of the family and Auxiliary Nurse Midwife (ANM) be made the local registrar and authorised to issue the birth certificates.

ANNEXURE 2.5

Sanjay Kothari,
SECRETARY

GOVERNMENT OF INDIA,
MINSTRY OF PERSONNEL, PUBLIC GRIEVANCES & PENSIONS
DEPARTMENT OF ADMINISTRATIVE REFORMS, PG& PENSIONS
SARDAR PATEL BHAVAN, SANSAD MARG,
NEW DELHI—110001

D.O. No. 11022/67/2012-AR Dated June 17, 2013.

Dear Shri Rakesh Singh,

I compliment you on the efforts made by the Punjab Government to do away with affidavits as a citizen friendly governance reform. It would be a worthwhile effort to extend this successful policy to other State Governments as well as Central Government. In this context, I would request you to forward us a concept paper so as to have it successfully replicated.

With warms regards,

Yours sincerely,
Sd/-
(Sanjay Kothari)

Shri Rakesh Singh,
Chief Secretary,
Government of Punjab,
Chandigarh.

Copy to: Dr. Pramod Kumar, Chairman, Punjab Governance Reform Commission, Chandigarh.

ANNEXURES II (TABLES)

Chapter 1

Unfolding Challenges of Democracy in India: 2019 Electoral Verdict

Table 1.3 Party-wise Seats Won and Votes Polled, Lok Sabha Election, 1951-2019

1951			
PARTY	Won	Seats %	VOTES %
BJS	3	0.61	3.06%
BPI	0	0.00	0.02%
CPI	16	3.27	3.29%
FBL(MG)	1	0.20	0.91%
FBL(RG)	0	0.00	0.13%
HMS	4	0.82	0.95%
INC	364	74.44	44.99%
KLP	1	0.20	1.41%
KMPP	9	1.84	5.79%
RCPI	0	0.00	0.06%
RRP	3	0.61	1.97%
RSP	3	0.61	0.44%
SCF	2	0.41	2.38%
SP	12	2.45	10.59%
NATIONAL PARTIES	418	85.48	76.00%
OTHER STATE PARTIES	34	6.95	8.10%
REGISTERED Unrecognised) PARTIES		0.00	

INDEPENDENTS	37	7.57	15.90%
Total	**489**	100.00	
1957			
PARTY	*Won*	*Seats %*	*VOTES %*
BJS	4	0.81	5.97%
CPI	27	5.47	8.92%
INC	371	75.10	47.78%
PSP	19	3.85	10.41%
NATIONAL PARTIES	421	85.22	73.08%
OTHER STATE PARTIES	31	6.28	7.60%
REGISTERED Unrecognised) PARTIES		0.00	
INDEPENDENTS	42	8.50	19.32%
Total	494	100.00	
1962			
PARTY	*Won*	*Seats %*	*VOTES %*
CPI	29	5.87	9.94%
INC	361	73.08	44.72%
JS	14	2.83	6.44%
PSP	12	2.43	6.81%
SOC	6	1.21	2.69%
SWA	18	3.64	7.89%
NATIONAL PARTIES	440	89.07	78.50%
OTHER STATE PARTIES	28	5.67	9.28%
REGISTERED Unrecognised) PARTIES	6	1.21	1.17%
INDEPENDENTS	20	4.05	11.05%
Total	494	100.00	
1967			
PARTY	Won	Seats %	VOTES %
BJS	35	6.73	9.31%

CPI	23	4.42	5.11%
CPM	19	3.65	4.28%
INC	283	54.42	40.78%
PSP	13	2.50	3.06%
SSP	23	4.42	4.92%
SWA	44	8.46	8.67%
NATIONAL PARTIES	440	84.62	76.13%
OTHER STATE PARTIES	43	8.27	9.69%
REGISTERED (Unrecognised) PARTIES	2	0.38	0.39%
INDEPENDENTS	35	6.73	13.78%
Total	520	100.00	
1971			
PARTY	*Won*	*Seats %*	*VOTES %*
BJS	22	4.25	7.35%
CPI	23	4.44	4.73%
CPM	25	4.83	5.12%
INC	352	67.95	43.68%
NCO	16	3.09	10.43%
PSP	2	0.39	1.04%
SSP	3	0.58	2.43%
SWA	8	1.54	3.07%
NATIONAL PARTIES	451	87.07	77.84%
OTHER STATE PARTIES	40	7.72	10.17%
REGISTERED Unrecognised) PARTIES	13	2.51	3.62%
INDEPENDENTS	14	2.70	8.38%
Total	518	100.00	
1977			
PARTY	*Won*	*Seats %*	*VOTES %*
BLD	295	54.43	41.32%

CPI	7	1.29	2.82%
CPM	22	4.06	4.29%
INC	154	28.41	34.52%
NCO	3	0.55	1.72%
NATIONAL PARTIES	481	88.75	84.67%
OTHER STATE PARTIES	49	9.04	8.80%
REGISTERED (Unrecognised) PARTIES	3	0.55	1.03%
INDEPENDENTS	9	1.66	5.50%
Total	542	100.00	
1980			
PARTY	*Won*	*Seats %*	*VOTES %*
CPI	10	1.89	2.49%
CPM	37	6.99	6.24%
INC(I)	353	66.73	42.69%
INC(U)	13	2.46	5.28%
JNP	31	5.86	18.97%
JNP(S)	41	7.75	9.39%
NATIONAL PARTIES	485	91.68	85.07%
OTHER STATE PARTIES	34	6.43	7.69%
REGISTERED (Unrecognised) PARTIES	1	0.19	0.81%
INDEPENDENTS	9	1.70	6.43%
Total	529	100.00	
1984			
PARTY	*Won*	*Seats %*	*VOTES %*
BJP	2	0.39	7.74%
CPI	6	1.17	2.71%
CPM	22	4.28	5.87%
ICS	4	0.78	1.52%
INC	404	78.60	49.10%

JNP	10	1.95	6.89%
LKD	3	0.58	5.97%
NATIONAL PARTIES	451	87.74	79.80%
OTHER STATE PARTIES	58	11.28	11.56%
REGISTERED (Unrecognised) PARTIES	0	0.00	0.72%
INDEPENDENTS	5	0.97	7.92%
Total	514	100.00	
1989			
PARTY	*Won*	*Seats %*	*VOTES %*
BJP	85	16.07	11.36%
CPI	12	2.27	2.57%
CPM	33	6.24	6.55%
ICS(SCS)	1	0.19	0.33%
INC	197	37.24	0.3953
JD	143	27.03	0.1779
JNP (JP)	0	0.00	1.01%
LKD (B)	0	0.00	0.20%
NATIONAL PARTIES	471	89.04	79.33%
OTHER STATE PARTIES	27	5.10	9.28%
REGISTERED (Unrecognised) PARTIES	19	3.59	6.13%
INDEPENDENTS	12	2.27	5.25%
Total	529	100.00	
1991			
PARTY	*Won*	*Seats %*	*VOTES %*
BJP	120	23.03	0.2011
CPI	14	2.69	2.49%
CPM	35	6.72	6.16%
ICS(SCS)	1	0.19	0.36%
INC	232	44.53	0.3626

JD	59	11.32	11.84%
JD(S)	0	0.00	0.00%
JP	5	0.96	3.37%
LKD	0	0.00	0.06%
NATIONAL PARTIES	466	89.44	80.65%
OTHER STATE PARTIES	50	9.60	12.98%
REGISTERED (Unrecognised) PARTIES	4	0.77	2.21%
INDEPENDENTS	1	0.19	4.16%
Total	521	100.00	
1996			
PARTY	Won	Seats %	VOTES %
AIIC(T)	4	0.74	1.46%
BJP	161	29.65	0.2029
CPI	12	2.21	1.97%
CPM	32	5.89	6.12%
INC	140	25.78	0.288
JD	46	8.47	8.08%
JP	0	0.00	0.19%
SAP	8	1.47	2.17%
NATIONAL PARTIES	403	74.22	69.08%
OTHER STATE PARTIES	129	23.76	22.43%
REGISTERED (Unrecognised) PARTIES	2	0.37	2.20%
INDEPENDENTS	9	1.66	6.28%
Total	543	100.00	
1998			
PARTY	Won	Seats %	VOTES %
BJP	182	33.52	0.2559
BSP	5	0.92	4.67%
CPI	9	1.66	1.75%

CPM	32	5.89	5.16%
INC	141	25.97	25.82%
JD	6	1.10	3.24%
SAP	12	2.21	1.76%
NATIONAL PARTIES	387	71.27	67.98%
OTHER STATE PARTIES	101	18.60	18.79%
REGISTERED (Unrecognised) PARTIES	49	9.02	10.87%
INDEPENDENTS	6	1.10	2.37%
Total	543	100.00	
1999			
PARTY	Won	Seats %	VOTES %
BJP	182	33.52	0.2375
BSP	14	2.58	4.16%
CPI	4	0.74	1.48%
CPM	33	6.08	5.40%
INC	114	20.99	28.30%
JD(S)	1	0.18	0.91%
JD(U)	21	3.87	3.10%
NATIONAL PARTIES	369	67.96	67.11%
OTHER STATE PARTIES	158	29.10	26.93%
REGISTERED (Unrecognised) PARTIES	10	1.84	3.22%
INDEPENDENTS	6	1.10	2.74%
Total	543	100.00	
2004			
PARTY	Won	Seats %	VOTES %
BJP	138	25.41	0.2216
BSP	19	3.50	5.33%
CPI	10	1.84	1.41%
CPM	43	7.92	5.66%

INC	145	26.70	0.2653
NCP	9	1.66	1.80%
NATIONAL PARTIES	364	67.03	62.89%
OTHER STATE PARTIES	159	29.28	28.90%
REGISTERED (Unrecognised) PARTIES	15	2.76	3.96%
INDEPENDENTS	5	0.92	4.25%
Total	543	100.00	
2009			
PARTY	Won	Seats %	VOTES %
Bahujan Samaj Party	21	3.87	6.17
Bharatiya Janata Party	116	21.36	18.8
Communist Party of India	4	0.74	1.43
Communist Party of India (Marxist)	16	2.95	5.33
Indian National Congress	206	37.94	28.55
Nationalist Congress Party	9	1.66	2.04
Rashtriya Janata Dal	4	0.74	1.27
NATIONAL PARTIES	376	69.24	63.58
OTHER STATE PARTIES	146	26.89	23.6
REGISTERED (Unrecognised) PARTIES	12	2.21	
INDEPENDENTS	9	1.66	
Total	543	100.00	
2014			
PARTY	Won	Seats %	VOTES %
Bharatiya Janata Party	282	52.51	31.34
Bahujan Samaj Party	0	0.00	4.19
Communist Party of India	1	0.19	0.79
Communist Party of India (Marxist)	9	1.68	3.28
Indian National Congress	44	8.19	19.52

Nationalist Congress Party	6	1.12	1.58
NATIONAL PARTIES	342	63.69	60.7
OTHER STATE PARTIES	176	32.77	27.74
REGISTERED (Unrecognised) PARTIES	16	2.98	
INDEPENDENTS	3	0.56	
Total	537	100.00	
2019			
PARTY	Won	Seats %	VOTES %
All India Trinamool Congress	22	4.06	4.07
Bahujan Samaj Party	10	1.85	3.63
Bharatiya Janata Party	303	55.90	37.38
Communist Party of India	2	0.37	0.58
Communist Party of India (Marxist)	3	0.55	1.75
Indian National Congress	52	9.59	19.49
Nationalist Congress Party	5	0.92	1.39
NATIONAL PARTIES	397	73.25	68.27
OTHER STATE PARTIES	137	25.28	23.15
REGISTERED (Unrecognised) PARTIES	8	1.48	8.34
Total	542	100.00	

Source: *Statistical Reports of General Election to Lok Sabha, 1951-2019.* Election Commission of India (1951-2019).

Table 1.5 State-wise Number of Seats Won by Political Parties (National, State and Other) in Lok Sabha Elections, 1951, 1989, 2009, 2014, and 2019

State-wise Number of Seats Won by Political Parties (National, State and Other) in Lok Sabha Elections									
N = National Party		*S = State Party*		*U = Registered (Unrecognised) Party*			*Z = Independent*		
1951		*1989*		*2009*		*2014*		*2019*	
State	*Seats Won*	*State*	*Seats Won*	*State*	*Seats Won*	*State*	*Seats Won*	*State*	*Seats Won*
Ajmer	2	A & N Island	1	A & N Island	1	A & N Island	1	A & N Island	1
N	2	N	1	N	1	N	1	N	1
Assam	12	Andhra Pradesh	42	Andhra Pradesh	42	Andhra Pradesh	42	Andhra Pradesh	25
N	12	N	39	N	33	N	5	S	25
Bhopal	2	S	2	S	8	S	27	Arunachal Pradesh	2
N	2	U	1	U	1	U	10	N	2
Bihar	55	Arunachal Pradesh	2	Arunachal Pradesh	2	Arunachal Pradesh	2	Assam	14
N	48	N	2	N	2	N	2	N	12
S	6	Bihar	54	Assam	14	Assam	14	S	1
Z	1	N	49	N	11	N	10	Z	1

State-wise Number of Seats Won by Political Parties (National, State and Other) in Lok Sabha Elections									
N = National Party		*S = State Party*		*U = Registered (Unrecognised) Party*			*Z = Independent*		
1951		*1989*		*2009*		*2014*		*2019*	
State	*Seats Won*	*State*	*Seats Won*	*State*	*Seats Won*	*State*	*Seats Won*	*State*	*Seats Won*
Bilaspur	1	U	5	S	2	S	3	Bihar	40
Z	1	Chandigarh	1	U	1	Z	1	N	18
Bombay	42	N	1	Bihar	40	Bihar	40	S	22
N	41	D & N Haveli	1	N	18	N	25	Chandigarh	1
S	1	Z	1	S	20	S	12	N	1
Delhi	4	Daman & Diu	1	Z	2	U	3	Chhattisgarh	11
N	4	Z	1	Chandigarh	1	Chandigarh	1	N	11
Himachal Pradesh	3	Goa	2	N	1	N	1	D & N Haveli	1
N	3	N	1	Chhattisgarh	11	Chhattisgarh	11	Z	1
Hyderabad	25	S	1	N	11	N	11	Daman & Diu	1
N	16	Gujarat	26	D & N Haveli	1	D & N Haveli	1	N	1
S	8	N	26	N	1	N	1	Goa	2
Z	1	Haryana	10	Daman & Diu	1	Daman & Diu	1	N	2

State-wise Number of Seats Won by Political Parties (National, State and Other) in Lok Sabha Elections									
N = National Party		*S = State Party*		*U = Registered (Unrecognised) Party*				*Z = Independent*	
1951		*1989*		*2009*		*2014*		*2019*	
State	*Seats Won*	*State*	*Seats Won*	*State*	*Seats Won*	*State*	*Seats Won*	*State*	*Seats Won*
Kutch	2	N	10	N	1	N	1	Gujarat	26
N	2	Himachal Pradesh	4	Goa	2	Goa	2	N	26
Madhya Bharat	11	N	4	N	2	N	2	Haryana	10
N	11	Jammu & Kashmir	6	Gujarat	26	Gujarat	26	N	10
Madhya Pradesh	29	N	2	N	26	N	26	Himachal Pradesh	4
N	27	S	3	Haryana	10	Haryana	10	N	4
Z	2	Z	1	N	9	N	8	Jammu & Kashmir	6
Madras	75	Karnataka	28	U	1	S	2	N	3
N	52	N	28	Himachal Pradesh	4	Himachal Pradesh	4	S	3

State-wise Number of Seats Won by Political Parties (National, State and Other) in Lok Sabha Elections									
N = National Party		*S = State Party*		*U = Registered (Unrecognised) Party*				*Z = Independent*	
1951		*1989*		*2009*		*2014*		*2019*	
State	*Seats Won*	*State*	*Seats Won*	*State*	*Seats Won*	*State*	*Seats Won*	*State*	*Seats Won*
S	8	Kerala	20	N	4	N	4	Jharkhand	14
Z	15	N	17	Jammu & Kashmir	6	Jammu & Kashmir	6	N	12
Manipur	2	S	2	N	2	N	3	S	2
N	2	U	1	S	3	S	3	Karnataka	28
Mysore	11	Lakshadweep	1	Z	1	Jharkhand	14	N	26
N	11	N	1	Jharkhand	14	N	12	S	1
Orissa	20	Madhya Pradesh	40	N	9	S	2	Z	1
N	13	N	39	S	2	Karnataka	28	Kerala	20
S	6	Z	1	U	1	N	26	N	16
Z	1	Maharashtra	48	Z	2	S	2	S	4
PEPSU*	5	N	44	Karnataka	28	Kerala	19	Lakshadweep	1
N	2	U	1	N	25	N	14	N	1
S	2	Z	3	S	3	S	3	Madhya Pradesh	29

State-wise Number of Seats Won by Political Parties (National, State and Other) in Lok Sabha Elections									
N = National Party		*S = State Party*		*U = Registered (Unrecognised) Party*			*Z = Independent*		
1951		*1989*		*2009*		*2014*		*2019*	
State	*Seats Won*	*State*	*Seats Won*	*State*	*Seats Won*	*State*	*Seats Won*	*State*	*Seats Won*
Z	1	Manipur	2	Kerala	20	Z	2	N	29
Punjab	18	N	2	N	17	Lakshadweep	1	Maharashtra	48
N	16	Meghalaya	2	S	3	N	1	N	28
S	2	N	2	Lakshadweep	1	Madhya Pradesh	29	S	19
Rajasthan	20	Mizoram	1	N	1	N	29	Z	1
N	14	N	1	Madhya Pradesh	29	Maharashtra	48	Manipur	2
Z	6	Nagaland	1	N	29	N	29	N	1
Saurashtra	6	N	1	Maharashtra	48	S	18	S	1
N	6	NCR (Delhi)**	7	N	34	U	1	Meghalaya	2
Travancore Cochin	12	N	7	S	11	Manipur	2	N	1
N	7	Orissa	21	U	2	N	2	S	1
S	1	N	21	Z	1	Meghalaya	2	Mizoram	1
Z	4	Pondicherry	1	Manipur	2	N	1	S	1

State-wise Number of Seats Won by Political Parties (National, State and Other) in Lok Sabha Elections

N = National Party | *S = State Party* | *U = Registered (Unrecognised) Party* | *Z = Independent*

1951		*1989*		*2009*		*2014*		*2019*	
State	*Seats Won*	*State*	*Seats Won*	*State*	*Seats Won*	*State*	*Seats Won*	*State*	*Seats Won*
Tripura	2	N	1	N	2	S	1	Nagaland	1
N	2	Punjab	13	Meghalaya	2	Mizoram	1	S	1
Uttar Pradesh	86	N	3	N	2	N	1	NCR (Delhi)**	7
N	84	U	7	Mizoram	1	Nagaland	1	N	7
Z	2	Z	3	N	1	S	1	Odisha	21
Vindhya Pradesh	6	Rajasthan	25	Nagaland	1	NCR (Delhi)**	7	N	9
N	6	N	25	S	1	N	7	S	12
West Bengal	34	Sikkim	1	NCR (Delhi)**	7	Odisha	21	Puducherry	1
N	34	S	1	N	7	N	1	N	1
Grand Total	485/ 489	Tamil Nadu	39	Odisha	21	S	20	Punjab	13
		N	28	N	7	Puducherry	1	N	10
		S	11	S	14	S	1	S	3
		Tripura	2	Puducherry	1	Punjab	9	Rajasthan	25

State-wise Number of Seats Won by Political Parties (National, State and Other) in Lok Sabha Elections									
N = National Party		*S = State Party*		*U = Registered (Unrecognised) Party*			*Z = Independent*		
1951		*1989*		*2009*		*2014*		*2019*	
State	*Seats Won*	*State*	*Seats Won*	*State*	*Seats Won*	*State*	*Seats Won*	*State*	*Seats Won*
		N	2	N	1	N	5	N	24
		Uttar Pradesh	85	Punjab	13	S	4	U	1
		N	80	N	9	Rajasthan	25	Sikkim	1
		U	3	S	4	N	25	S	1
		Z	2	Rajasthan	25	Sikkim	1	Tamil Nadu	38
		West Bengal	42	N	24	S	1	N	12
		N	34	Z	1	Tamil Nadu	38	S	25
		S	7	Sikkim	1	N	1	U	1
		U	1	S	1	S	37	Telangana	17
		Grand Total	529/ 529	Tamil Nadu	39	Tripura	2	N	7
				N	10	N	2	S	10
				S	28	Uttar Pradesh	80	Tripura	2
				U	1	N	73	N	2
				Tripura	2	S	5	Uttar Pradesh	80
				N	2	U	2	N	73

State-wise Number of Seats Won by Political Parties (National, State and Other) in Lok Sabha Elections									
N = National Party		*S = State Party*		*U = Registered (Unrecognised) Party*				*Z = Independent*	
1951		*1989*		*2009*		*2014*		*2019*	
State	*Seats Won*	*State*	*Seats Won*	*State*	*Seats Won*	*State*	*Seats Won*	*State*	*Seats Won*
				Uttar Pradesh	80	Uttarakhand	5	S	5
				N	51	N	5	U	2
				S	23	West Bengal	42	Uttarakhand	5
				U	5	N	8	N	5
				Z	1	S	34	West Bengal	42
				Uttarakhand	5	Grand Total	537/ 543	N	42
				N	5			Grand Total	542/ 543
				West Bengal	42				
				N	18				
				S	23				
				Z	1				
				Grand Total	543/ 543				

PEPSU*; Patiala and East Punjab States Union
NCR (Delhi)**; National Capital Region of Delhi
Source: Statistical Reports of General Election to Lok Sabha, 1951, 1989, 2009, 2014, and 2019.

Table 1.6 Performance of Top Ten State Parties in the Lok Sabha Elections, 1996-2019

Ranks/Year/Votes Polled %	*1*	*2*	*3*	*4*	*5*	*6*	*State Parties in Total*
1996	BSP	SP	TDP	TMC(M)	DMK	SHS	22.4
Percentage of Votes Polled	4.02%	3.28%	2.97%	2.19%	2.14%	1.49%	
1998	SP	TDP	ADMK	SHS	DMK	TMC(M)	18.8
Percentage of Votes Polled	4.93%	2.77%	1.83%	1.77%	1.44%	1.40%	
1999	SP	TDP	RJD	AITC	NCP	ADMK	26.9
Percentage of Votes Polled	3.76%	3.65%	2.79%	2.57%	2.27%	1.93%	
2004	SP	TDP	RJD	JD(U)	ADMK	AITC	28.9
Percentage of Votes Polled	4.32%	3.04%	2.41%	2.35%	2.19%	2.07%	
2009	SP	AITC	TDP	DMK	ADMK	BJD	23.6
Percentage of Votes Polled	3.23	3.19	2.51	1.83	1.67	1.59	
2014	AITC	ADMK	SP	TDP	SHS	DMK	27.7
Percentage of Votes Polled	3.72	3.31	3.28	2.57	1.83	1.76	
2019	YSRCP	SP	DMK	SHS	TDP	BJD	23.2
Percentage of Votes Polled	2.56	2.56	2.29	2.08	2.06	1.68	

*Ranks are assigned on the basis of most votes secured by a political party.

**Data is for major parties only, therefore sum of all not equal to total.

Source: *Statistical Reports of General Election to Lok Sabha and State Assembly, 2018, 2019, and 2020*. Election Commission of India.

Table 1.7 Votes Polled in States by Parties in Lok Sabha Elections, 1951, 1989, 2009, 2014, and 2019

Votes Polled in States by Parties in Lok Sabha Elections														
N = National Party			S = State Party				U = Registered (Unrecognised) Party				Z = Independent			
1951			1989			2009			2014			2019		
States	Party Type	% of Votes	States	Party Type	% of Votes	States	Party Type	% of Votes	States	Party Type	% of Votes	States	Party Type	% of Votes
Ajmer	Z	6.0	Andaman & Nicobar Island	N	94.66	Andaman & Nicobar Island	N	44.21	Andaman & Nicobar Islands	N	94.39	Andaman & Nicobar Islands	N	92.47
	N	88.0		Z	5.34	Andhra Pradesh	N	38.95		U	0.23		Z	4.54
	S	6.0	Andhra Pradesh	N	59.94		S	31.07		Z	1.86		S	2.30
Assam	Z	13.7		S	34.45		U	0.73	Andhra Pradesh	N	21.70		NOTA	0.68
	N	78.6		U	2.97	Arunachal Pradesh	N	51.11		S	43.39	Andhra Pradesh	N	2.73
	S	7.7		Z	2.65	Assam	N	51.10		U	0.73		Z	0.78
Bhopal	Z	14.9	Arunachal Pradesh	N	49.99		S	30.70		Z	1.98		S	95.00
	N	79.9		S	35.21		U	5.41	Arunachal Pradesh	N	89.31		NOTA	1.48
	S	5.2		Z	14.79	Bihar	N	43.50		S	9.51	Arunachal Pradesh	N	78.91
Bihar	Z	13.1	Bihar	N	88.3		S	24.04		U	0.17		Z	2.06
	N	73.4		U	7.4		Z	12.12		Z	0.40		S	17.88
	S	13.6		Z	4.3	Chandigarh	N	46.87	Assam	N	67.38		NOTA	1.14
Bilaspur	Z	0.0	Chandigarh	N	95.21	Chattisgarh	N	82.34		S	21.06	Assam	N	71.95
Bombay	Z	12.0		U	1.54	Dadra & Nagar Haveli	N	46.43		U	0.16		Z	4.25
	N	79.9		Z	3.26	Daman & Diu	N	65.49		Z	9.62		S	22.80
	S	8.2	Dadra & Nagar Haveli	N	39.39	Goa	N	67.38	Bihar	N	43.28		NOTA	0.99
Coorg	Z	40.4		U	1.36	Gujarat	N	89.90		S	43.00	Bihar	N	35.13
	N	59.7		Z	59.25	Haryana	N	41.77		U	0.12		Z	5.46
Delhi	Z	12.7	Daman & Diu	N	56.21		U	10.01		Z	4.34		S	57.41
	N	87.3		Z	43.79	Himachal Pradesh	N	95.19	Chandigarh	N	73.06		NOTA	2.00
Himachal Pradesh	Z	8.6	Goa	N	67.67	Jammu & Kashmir	N	24.67		U	0.21	Chandigarh	N	92.60
	N	91.5		S	27.87		S	19.11		Z	1.89		Z	1.03
Hyderabad	Z	8.0		U	1.29		Z	6.28	Chhattisgarh	N	91.79		S	5.41
	S	3.8		Z	3.18	Jharkhand	N	42.55		U	0.14		NOTA	0.95
Kutch	Z	29.1	Gujarat	N	95.6		S	11.70		Z	4.29	Chhattisgarh	N	94.21
	N	70.9		U	1.5		U	10.48	Dadra & Nagar Haveli	N	97.30		Z	1.91
Madhya Bharat	I	15.7		Z	2.9		Z	11.12		U	0.21		S	2.44
	N	182.4	Haryana	N	94.36	Karnataka	N	79.28		Z	1.72		NOTA	1.44
	S	1.9		U	2.04		S	13.57	Daman & Diu	N	99.15	Dadra & Nagar Haveli	N	45.72
Madras	Z	23.2		Z	3.59	Kerala	N	70.61	Goa	N	92.39		Z	48.98
	N	69.8	Himachal Pradesh	N	96.45		S	7.60		U	0.16		S	3.82
	S	7.0		U	2.82	Lakshadweep	N	51.88		Z	2.13		NOTA	1.48

Votes Polled in States by Parties in Lok Sabha Elections

N = National Party | S = State Party | U = Registered (Unrecognised) Party | Z = Independent

1951			1989			2009			2014			2019		
States	Party Type	% of Votes	States	Party Type	% of Votes	States	Party Type	% of Votes	States	Party Type	% of Votes	States	Party Type	% of Votes
Manipur	Z	9.0		Z	0.73	Madhya Pradesh	N	89.44	Gujarat	N	95.63	Daman & Diu	N	75.51
	N	51.7	Jammu & Kashmir	N	77.21	Maharashtra	N	57.06		U	0.02		Z	22.79
	S	39.3		S	8.97		S	17.00		Z	2.14		NOTA	1.70
Mysore	Z	10.4		U	4.22		U	1.90	Haryana	N	62.80	Goa	N	94.09
	N	89.7		Z	9.6		Z	8.06		S	30.57		Z	0.90
Orissa	Z	8.7	Karnataka	N	91.2	Manipur	N	42.96		U	0.02		S	3.54
	N	65.1		S	0.27	Meghalaya	N	63.62		Z	1.67		NOTA	1.46
	S	26.2		U	4.09	Mizoram	N	65.58	Himachal Pradesh	N	96.50	Gujarat	N	95.28
PEPSU*	Z	21.1		Z	4.43	Nagaland	S	69.96		U	0.04		Z	2.15
	N	46.5	Kerala	N	79.88	NCR (Delhi)**	N	57.11		Z	0.93		S	1.18
	S	32.4		S	8.1	Orissa	N	35.32	Jammu & Kashmir	N	57.25		NOTA	1.38
Punjab	N	63.9		U	2.51		S	37.23		S	33.17	Haryana	N	90.21
	S	17.5		Z	9.49	Puducherry	N	49.41		U	0.29		Z	1.07
Rajasthan	N	70.7	Lakshadweep	N	52.27	Punjab	N	55.29		Z	6.32		S	8.40
	S	0.2		Z	47.73		S	33.85	Jharkhand	N	56.43		NOTA	0.33
Saurashtra	Z	7.7	Madhya Pradesh	N	86.57	Rajasthan	N	83.76		S	27.10	Himachal Pradesh	N	97.64
	N	88.5		S	0.09		Z	9.31		U	0.35		Z	0.93
	S	3.9		U	5.77	Sikkim	S	63.30		Z	3.33		S	0.57
Travancore Cochin	Z	36.2		Z	7.57	Tamil Nadu	N	20.08	Karnataka	N	85.73		NOTA	0.86
	N	54.6	Maharashtra	N	84.01		S	51.63		S	11.07	Jammu & Kashmir	N	83.90
	S	9.2		S	2.31		U	2.41		U	0.03		Z	6.21
Tripura	Z	7.0		U	5.45	Tripura	N	61.69		Z	1.57		S	8.73
	N	93.0		Z	8.23	Uttar Pradesh	N	63.17	Kerala	N	71.84		NOTA	1.16
Uttar Pradesh	Z	11.3	Manipur	N	58.1		S	23.26		S	8.69	Jharkhand	N	68.90
	N	87.3		S	29.64		U	3.27		U	0.37		Z	4.15
	S	1.4		U	0.08		Z	4.52		Z	11.50		S	25.68
Vindhya Pradesh	Z	13.5		Z	12.19	Uttarakhand	N	43.14	Lakshadweep	N	98.87		NOTA	1.27
	N	86.6	Meghalaya	N	60.17	West Bengal	N	56.29	Madhya Pradesh	N	94.35	Karnataka	N	84.54
West Bengal	Z	18.5		Z	39.83		S	37.78		U	0.04		Z	3.90
	N	81.5	Mizoram	N	48.45		Z	3.08		Z	1.88		S	10.85
				S	31.28				Maharashtra	N	65.10		NOTA	0.71
				U	19.31					S	22.29	Kerala	N	82.33
				Z	0.95					U	0.14		Z	4.01
			Nagaland	N	60.29					Z	3.27		S	13.15
				S	39.71				Manipur	N	72.33		NOTA	0.51
			NCR (Delhi)**	N	86.16					S	23.76	Lakshadweep	N	96.93
				S	0.2					U	0.12		S	2.85
				U	4.25					Z	3.06		NOTA	0.21
				Z	9.38				Meghalaya	N	48.89	Madhya Pradesh	N	95.15
			Odisha	N	96.99					S	33.03		Z	1.89
				U	0.92					Z	17.24		S	2.03
				Z	2.09				Mizoram	N	49.33		NOTA	0.92
			Puducherry	N	50.73					Z	47.89	Maharashtra	N	60.50

Votes Polled in States by Parties in Lok Sabha Elections

N = National Party | S = State Party | U = Registered (Unrecognised) Party | Z = Independent

1951 States	1951 Party Type	1951 % of Votes	1989 States	1989 Party Type	1989 % of Votes	2009 States	2009 Party Type	2009 % of Votes	2014 States	2014 Party Type	2014 % of Votes	2019 States	2019 Party Type	2019 % of Votes
				S	41.65				Nagaland	N	30.22		Z	3.69
				U	6.88					S	68.84		S	34.91
				Z	0.75					U	0.94		NOTA	0.90
			Punjab	N	42.29				NCR (Delhi)**	N	63.13	Manipur	N	67.28
				S	6.65					S	33.08		Z	5.29
				U	38.35					U	0.01		S	27.10
				Z	12.72					Z	3.18		NOTA	0.33
			Rajasthan	N	94.94				Odisha	N	49.77	Meghalaya	N	56.21
				S	0.07					S	44.77		Z	1.18
				U	1.45					U	0.14		S	41.82
				Z	3.53					Z	1.57		NOTA	0.80
			Sikkim	N	21.56				Puducherry	N	29.22	Mizoram	N	5.75
				S	68.52					S	65.73		Z	46.19
				U	9.62					U	0.06		S	47.56
				Z	0.31					Z	3.73		NOTA	0.50
			Tamil Nadu	N	47.35				Punjab	N	44.42	Nagaland	N	48.11
				S	43.78					S	26.37		Z	0.46
				U	6.62					U	0.04		S	51.23
				Z	2.27					Z	3.61		NOTA	0.21
			Tripura	N	97.8				Rajasthan	N	89.31	NCR (Delhi)**	N	80.15
				U	1.09					U	0.05		Z	0.35
				Z	1.1					Z	6.75		S	18.97
			Uttar Pradesh	N	79.14				Sikkim	N	4.75		NOTA	0.53
				S	0.03					S	53.74	Odisha	N	53.42
				U	12.47					U	40.03		Z	0.67
				Z	8.37				Tamil Nadu	N	11.42		S	44.60
			West Bengal	N	85.93					S	74.02		NOTA	1.31
				S	9.06					U	0.22	Puducherry	N	56.73
				U	2.88					Z	2.16		Z	1.98
				Z	2.12				Tripura	N	85.92		S	39.75
										U	0.49		NOTA	1.54
										Z	0.89	Punjab	N	53.74
									Uttar Pradesh	N	70.13		Z	1.71
										S	23.21		S	43.43
										U	0.02		NOTA	1.12
										Z	1.76	Rajasthan	N	94.13
									Uttarakhand	N	95.41		Z	1.07
										U	0.05		S	3.79
										Z	1.75		NOTA	1.01
									West Bengal	N	52.52	Sikkim	N	5.85
										S	44.42		Z	0.74
										U	0.06		S	92.77
										Z	0.93		NOTA	0.65

Votes Polled in States by Parties in Lok Sabha Elections														
N = National Party			S = State Party				U = Registered (Unrecognised) Party				Z = Independent			
1951			1989			2009			2014			2019		
States	Party Type	% of Votes	States	Party Type	% of Votes	States	Party Type	% of Votes	States	Party Type	% of Votes	States	Party Type	% of Votes
												Tamil Nadu	N	21.65
													Z	7.30
													S	69.77
													NOTA	1.28
												Telangana	N	50.02
													Z	3.15
													S	45.81
													NOTA	1.02
												Tripura	N	91.68
													Z	1.59
													S	5.65
													NOTA	1.08
												Uttar Pradesh	N	75.49
													Z	0.98
													S	22.69
													NOTA	0.84
												Uttarakhand	N	97.14
													Z	0.99
													S	0.82
													NOTA	1.05
												West Bengal	N	53.33
													Z	1.01
													S	44.71
													NOTA	0.95

PEPSU*; Patiala and East Punjab States Union
NCR (Delhi)**; National Capital Region of Delhi
Source: Statistical Reports of General Election to Lok Sabha, 1951, 1989, 2009, 2014, and 2019.

Table 3.13 Services Delivered by SAANJH from 2011 to 2019

Sr. No.	*Name of Service*	*2011 (17.10.11)*	*2012*	*2013*	*2014*	*2015*	*2016*	*2017*	*2018*	*2019*	*Total*
1	Renewal of arms licence	8770	49244	75215	73511	61088	56762	76715	77075	58559	536939
2	Renewal where licensee has shifted his residence	0	0	0	0	85	105	42	51	20	303
3	Renewal where adverse report is received	0	0	0	0	124	148	310	156	83	821
4	Renewal of arms licence (Apply after due date)	0	0	0	0	0	23	342	171	159	695
5	Addition/Deletion of weapon	0	0	0	0	7153	5944	3070	2595	1443	20205
6	Entry of weapon on arms license	0	0	0	0	1178	1444	998	524	291	4435
7	Extension of purchase period of weapon	0	0	0	0	148	1272	200	69	38	1727
8	Registration of foreigner (Arrival/Departure)	1751	8984	10125	8679	9382	9518	8648	7705	312	65104
9	Extension of residential permit of foreigners	326	3920	3307	3482	5047	5027	5133	4737	1974	32953
10	Copy of FIR or DDR	44781	270561	447094	509059	518253	521705	486280	402103	263996	3463832
11	NOC for use of loud speakers	297	2100	3016	3704	3795	3919	3776	4754	2397	27758

Sr. No.	*Name of Service*	*2011 (17.10.11)*	*2012*	*2013*	*2014*	*2015*	*2016*	*2017*	*2018*	*2019*	*Total*
12	NOC for fair/melas/exhibition/sports events	442	2640	2457	2895	3144	3144	2705	2990	2101	22518
13	Stranger verification	48	290	294	66	207	7187	25090	42064	17833	93079
14	Tenant/servant verification (local area)	519	2405	10406	7142	22495	23106	19465	23506	32233	141277
15	Tenant/servant verification (other district/State)	1361	6168	1555	1534	5179	7309	16702	20145	24084	84037
16	Other verification related service	1860	10580	15379	17411	22033	23296	36258	37508	23549	187874
17	Copy of untraced report in road accident cases	15	65	0	32	130	169	36	19	35	501
18	Copy of untraced report in case stolen vehicle	44	222	120	197	379	193	135	54	18	1362
19	Copy of untraced report in theft cases	27	129	29	45	185	220	66	72	4	777
20	NOC for pre-owned vehicles	17069	87500	70363	54523	50606	41953	39032	25664	23905	410615
21	Service verification (Resident of Punjab)	5207	28029	35236	32599	30905	30778	40587	34400	27535	265276
22	Character verification	9670	57294	68665	87513	110487	122173	165632	201091	121558	944083
23	NOC issuance/renewal of arms licence dealer	2470	10710	649	364	1240	165	217	93	90	15998

Sr. No.	*Name of Service*	*2011 (17.10.11)*	*2012*	*2013*	*2014*	*2015*	*2016*	*2017*	*2018*	*2019*	*Total*
24	NOC for setting up of Cinema hall	101	463	167	149	266	171	118	1274	371	3080
25	Passport verification	67940	352818	411541	488527	594832	604164	971542	1058527	701214	5251105
26	Verification for fresh arms licence	5531	24726	21175	19840	20867	28779	4720	8166	5186	138990
27	Acknowledgement of complaint	0	0	24886	160020	181725	135737	139148	132729	83301	857546
28	Information of action taken on complaint	0	0	15794	148456	159960	132135	137186	132877	72674	799082
29	MRG enquiry in case of loss of passport abroad	0	131	3281	2109	1875	2059	2250	2114	1231	15050
30	Other services related to passport	0	570	11602	16986	18625	18669	22870	24702	15658	129682
31	Counter sign of document	0	1847	6159	8630	16295	7007	9699	10891	7631	68159
32	Issuance of new arms licence	0	0	0	0	0	306	703	686	248	1943
33	Issuance of duplicate arms license	0	0	0	0	306	252	287	112	93	1050
34	NOC for sale of weapon	0	0	0	0	834	1744	2231	3451	2295	10555
35	Application for extension of jurisdiction (Pb)	0	0	0	0	73	669	376	349	144	1611

Sr. No.	*Name of Service*	*2011 (17.10.11)*	*2012*	*2013*	*2014*	*2015*	*2016*	*2017*	*2018*	*2019*	*Total*
36	Cancellation of arms licence on request	0	0	0	0	160	219	284	364	212	1239
37	Change of address in arms licence	0	0	0	0	255	367	537	698	440	2297
38	Appointment of retainer of weapon	0	9	225	462	773	147	182	159	67	2024
39	Addition/Deletion of retainer in arms licence	0	189	6407	7527	214	506	418	543	265	16069
40	Change of bore	0	0	0	0	60	82	33	31	12	218
41	Permission for deposit of weapon in case of death	0	0	0	0	14	13	17	29	28	101
42	Permission sale/transfer of weapon in case of death	0	0	0	0	131	738	684	249	169	1971
43	Permission of addition of cartridges	0	0	0	0	117	2030	42	17	15	2221
Total		168229	921594	1245147	1655462	1850625	1801354	2224766	2265514	1493471	13626162

Source: Community Affairs Division, Punjab Police

Table 3.14 Cost-Benefit Analysis, 2018-19

Row Number	*Head*	*Amount in Rupees*
A	Money received from Passport Offices [Rs. 14 crores]	140000000
B	Money deposited by SAANJH police stations in Government Treasury [Rs. Four Crore Sixty-Eight Lakh Ninety Thousand Four Hundred Seventy-Five]	46890475
C	Annual salary of the 1646 SAANJH Personnel [Rs. One Billion Eleven Crore Ninety Five Lakhs Fifty-Two Thousand]	1119552000
D	Total State Expenditure [C-B-A]	932661525
E	Number of beneficiaries	2262628
	Cost per beneficiary providing services without SAANJH [C/E]	494.80
	Expenditure per beneficiary providing services through SAANJH [D/E]	412.20
	SAANJH Contribution per beneficiary	82.60

Source: Calculated from data provided by Community Affairs Division, Punjab Police.

Chapter 4

Dalit Identity Architecture: From Selective Adaptation of Cultural Symbols to Nurturing of Exclusive Sites

Table 4.2 Poverty Ratio by Tendulkar Method in Punjab, 2011-12

Type	*SC*	*OBC + Others*	*Total*
Rural			
Self-employed in agriculture	7.6	0.0	0.5
Self-employed in non-agriculture	6.5	3.2	4.4
Regular wage earning	9.0	0.8	5.3
Casual labour in agriculture	17.9	13.1	17.2
Casual labour in non-agriculture	21.7	3.6	16.1
Casual labour in others	3.3	1.8	2.4
Wage earner household	17.0	3.4	12.9
Total	14.7	1.7	7.7
Urban			
Self-employed	26.5	4.7	9.0
Regular wage-earning	9.7	5.9	6.9
Casual labour	25.0	23.5	24.5
Others	4.9	2.6	2.9
Total	18.3	6.1	9.2
Rural + Urban	**15.6**	**3.6**	**8.2**

Source: NSS 68th Round. Level and Pattern of Consumer Expenditure, 2011-12.

Table 4.3 Unemployment Rate by Current Daily Status in Punjab in 2011-12

Household Type	*SC*	*OBC*	*Others*	*Total*
Rural				
Self-employed in agriculture	3.3	2.2	1.4	1.7
Self-employed in non-agriculture	8.7	2.4	3.7	5.4
Regular wage earning	3.3	1.1	5.5	3.6
Casual labour in agriculture	4.7	42.8	15.8	8.3
Casual labour in non-agriculture	8.8	14.0	5.5	9.2
Casual labour in others	32.7	0.0	50.5	31.1
Total	6.2	7.8	3.2	5.2
Urban				
Self-employed	3.9	4.4	4.1	4.1
Regular wage earning	2.7	2.4	2.7	2.6
Casual labour	12.5	5.8	7.0	8.9
Others	75.9		76.4	76.3
Total	4.8	3.7	4.4	4.3
Rural + Urban	**5.9**	**6.0**	**3.7**	4.9

Source: NSS 68th Round. Employment and Unemployment Situation in India, 2011-12.

Table 4.4 Gross Enrolment Ratio (GER %) in Higher Education (Age Group 18-22 years) by Gender and Social Group in Punjab in 2018-19

Gender/Social Category	*All Categories*	*SC*
Male	27.6	19.4
Female	33.6	23.8
Total	30.3	21.4

Source: All India Survey on Higher Education (AISHE), 2018-19. Ministry of Human Resource Development, Govt. of India.

Table 4.5 Some Health Indicators in Punjab in 2015-16 (NFHS-IV)

	SC	*OBC*	*Others*	*Total*
Percent of underweight children (below 3 years)	24.1	22.7	18.3	22
Infant mortality rate	39.6	25.5	22.4	29
Child mortality rate	6.5	3.3	1.9	4.1
Under-five mortality rate	45.9	23.7	24.2	33
Women's Body Mass Index (BMI) below 18.5	14.2	11.8	9.4	11.7

Source: *The National Family Health Survey (NFHS)-IV, 2015-16.*

Bibliography

Introduction

Allen, V.L. 1975. *Social Analysis: A Marxist Critique and Alternative.* London and New York: Longman.

Althusser, L. 2006. Ideology and Ideological State Apparatus (Notes Towards an Investigation). In *Lenin and Philosophy and Other Essays*. Delhi: Aakar Books, pp. 127-186.

Bharatiya Janata Party. 2004. 'Summary,' In *Vision Document: Election Manifesto 2004*. Lok Sabha Election.

Camus, A. 1943, July. "Letters to a German Friend." Retrieved from: https://boards.fool.com/words-from-camus-15743674.aspx?sort=postdate.

Carr, E.H. 1961. *What is History*? New York: Vintage.

Chandra, B. 1984. *Communalism in Modern India*. Delhi: Vikas Publishing House.

Crosthwaite, P. 2011. "The Accident of Finance. In J. Armitage." *Virilio Now: Current Perspectives in Virilio Studies.* Cambridge, UK: Polity Press, pp. 177-199.

Desai, A.R. 1985. *Caste and Communal Violence in Independent India.* CGSMT.

Gandhi, M. 1919. *Young India: A Weekly Journal, 1919-1931*. 14 Vols. Ahmedabad: Navajivan Publishing House. September 19, p. 305.

Gopal, S. 1976. *Jawaharlal Nehru: A Biography*. Volume One, 1889-1947. Calcutta: Oxford University Press.

Gopal, S. J. 1975. 'Presidential Address at the Lucknow Congress, 1936, April 12.' In *Selected Works of Jawaharlal Nehru*. Vol. 7, New Delhi: Orient Longman.

Government of India, Ministry of Human Resource Development. 2019. "Quality Universities and Colleges: A New and Forward - Looking Vision for India's Higher Education System." In *National Education Policy 2019, Draft*, pp. 202-203.

Indian National Congress. 2004. *Lok Sabha Elections 2004: Manifesto of the Indian National Congress*, p. 8.

Lee, R. July 27, 2016. A Study Claims that Cow Urine Contains Gold. *Agilent Technologies Blog*. Retrieved fromhttps://blog.agilent.com July 27, 2016 a-study-claims-that-cow-urine-contains-gold.

Mashable News Staff. 2019. BJP Leader Ranjit Bahadur Srivastava Just Invented 'Love-Jihad' Theory For Cows. *Mashable India*. Retrieved from https://in.mashable.com/culture/5300/bjp-leader-ranjit-bahadur-srivastava-just-invented-love-jihad-theory-for-cows.

Mohanty, M. 2017. *Selected Writings of Randhir Singh*. Delhi: Aakar Books.

Myrdal, G. 1960. *Beyond the Welfare State: Economic Planning and Its International Implications*. London: Yale University Press.

Mythology, Science and BJP. June 4, 2018 *Sirf News*. Retrieved from: https://www.sirfnews.com/mythology-science-and-bjp.

Peterson, V.S. 1990. Whose Rights? A Critique of the "Givens" in Human Rights Discourse. *Alternatives XV*, pp. 303-344.

Samayam Malayalam. January 13, 2020. The Cow Love of Political Leaders in India. Malyalam News. Retrieved fromhttps://malayalam.samayam.com/latest-news/india-news/bizarre-statements-by-indian-political-leaders-on-cow/articleshow/73231177.cms.

Savarkar, V.D. 1969. *Hindutva: Who is a 'Hindu?'* Savarkar Sadan, Bombay: Veer Savarkar Prakashan.

Sen, A., Fitoussi, J.P. and Stiglitz, J. 2011. *Mismeasuring Our Lives: Why GDP Doesn't Add Up*. New York, USA: The New Press. p. 15.

Shukl, S.L. 1968. *Raag Darbaari*. Delhi: Rajkamal Prakashan Private Limited.

Singh, R. 2006. *Crisis of Socialism: Notes in Defence of a Commitment*. Delhi: Ajanta Books International.

Singh, R. 2007. "Introduction to Man Against Myth." In D. Barrows. *Man Against Myth*. New Delhi: National Book Trust, India.

Singh, R. 2008. *Marxism, Socialism, India Politics: A view from the Left*. Delhi: Aakar Books.

Stern, R.W. 2003. *Changing India: Bourgeois Revolution on the Subcontinent*. Cambridge: Cambridge University Press.

Technology of Spirituality - A talk by Khurshed Batliwala (Video File). May 24, 2015. *YouTube*. Retrieved from: https://www.youtube.com/watch?v=LN6Kx4ybqsU.

Titmuss, R. 1964. The Limits of Welfare State. *New Left Review*, No. 27, September-October, p. 34.

Yoga Integral Part of Our Culture, Says PM Modi. June 21, 2019. *The Economic Times*.

How Pak's Hindu Population Dropped Sharply. February 13, 2020. *The Times of India*.

Chapter 1

After Yogi, Mayawati, EC Bans Azam, Maneka from Campaigning. April 15, 2019. *The Economic Times*. New Delhi. Lucknow.

Akhilesh Yadav 'Sexist' Remark: Mayawati Takes So Much Space, Even Her Party Symbol is that of an Elephant. January 29, 2017. *The Times of India*.

Constituent Assembly Debates, 1948. Volume VII. Speech by Dr. B.R. Ambedkar, November 15. Sixth Reprint, 2014. New Delhi: Jainco Art India.

Anandan, S. February 25, 2009. Abuse is Modi's Best Defence. *Hindustan Times*.

Anderson, W. and Damle, S.D. 2018. *Messengers of Hindu Nationalism: How the RSS Reshaped India*. London: Hurst & Company.

Arjun Modhwadia Gets EC Notice for 'Modi is Monkey' Jibe. November 23, 2012. *The Times of India*. Ahmedabad.

Arun Jaitley Again Sues Arvind Kejriwal for Rs. 10 Crore After Delhi CM's Lawyer Ram Jethmalani Calls Him a 'Crook'. May 22, 2017. *India Today*. New Delhi.

Azam Khan calls Narendra Modi an Elder Brother of a Dog's Pup. April 3, 2014. *News 18*. Press Trust of India.

Babu, R. December 23, 2019. CAA Extraordinary Solution as Problems Created by Partition were Extraordinary: Kerala Governor Arif Mohammed Khan. *Hindustan Times*. Kerala.

Balakot Strike Not Political, Can't Think About it in Terms of Votes: Harsh Vardhan. May 1, 2019. *The Economic Times*.

Bharatiya Janata Party. 2009. *Good Governance. Development. Security. Manifesto Lok Sabha Election 2009*.

Bharatiya Janata Party. 2014. *Ek Bharat Shreshtha Bharat. Sabka Saath Sabka Vikas. Election Manifesto 2014*.

Bharatiya Janata Party. 2019. *Sankalpit Bharat Sashakt Bharat. Sankalp Patra*. Lok Sabha 2019.

BJP Leader Kailash Vijayvargiya Compares Opposition Unity to 'Pack of Dogs'. February 6, 2017. *The Economic Times*. Kolkata.

BJP Scrambling Like Panic-Stricken Rats: Priyanka Gandhi April 28, 2014. Business Insider. *The Times of India*. Rae Bareli.

Chandra, B., Mukherjee, A. and Mukherjee, M. 1999. *India after Independence 1947-2000*. New Delhi: Penguin Books. p. 48.

Chronology of Ayodhya Case. November 10, 2019. *The Hindu*. The Hindu Net Desk.

Dikshit, S. February 2, 2020. Deep Cuts Will Benefit Middle Class. *The Tribune*.

D'Souza, S.M. December 26, 2014. Rashtriya Janata Dal. *Encyclopædia Britannica*. Encyclopædia Britannica, Inc.

D'Souza, S.M. September 14, 2014. Janata Dal (United). *Encyclopædia Britannica*. Encyclopædia Britannica, Inc.

D'Souza, S.M. March 17, 2016. Bahujan Samaj Party. *Encyclopædia Britannica*. Encyclopædia Britannica, Inc.

EPW Engage. August 6, 2019. Article 370: A Short History of Kashmir's Accession to India. *Economic and Political Weekly*.

Ghadyalpatil, A. April 13, 2018. Maharashtra: Aggressive Fadnavis Takes the Battle to the Opposition Camp. *Livemint*. Mumbai.

Gupta, D. 2019. Caste and Electoral Outcomes: Misreading Hierarchy and the Illusion of Numbers. *Economic and Political Weekly*. Vol. 54, Issue No. 25, pp. 24-28.

Hansen, T.B. 1993. RSS and the Popularisation of Hindutva. *Economic and Political Weekly*. Vol. 28, Issue No. 42, pp. 2270-2272.

Human Development Report. 2000. New York: Oxford University Press.

Huntington, S.P. 1996. *The Clash of Civilisations and the Remaking of World Order*. New York: Simon and Schuster.

India Today Web Desk. August 5, 2019. Arvind Kejriwal, Who Wants Full Statehood for Delhi, Supports J&K Becoming two UTs. *India Today*. New Delhi.

India Today Web Desk. August 6, 2019. Congress's Jyotiraditya Scindia Backs Modi Government Move on Article 370, J&K Bifurcation. *India Today*. New Delhi.

India Today Web Desk. August 18, 2019. Congress Has Lost its Way: Bhupinder Hooda Slams Party, Backs Scrapping of Article 370. *India Today*. New Delhi.

Jaffrelot, C. 2016. Quota for Patels? The Neo-Middle-Class Syndrome and the (Partial) Return of Caste Politics in Gujarat. *Studies in Indian Politics*. Sage, Vol. 4, Issue No. 2, pp. 218-232.

Jawaharlal Nehru Speeches. 1958. Volume III, March 1953—August 1957. New Delhi: Publication Division, Ministry of Information and Broadcasting, Governement of India.

Jayaram, N. 2019. Protection of Workers' Wages in India: An Analysis of the Labour Code on Wages, 2019. Engage, *Economic and Political Weekly*, Vol. 54, Issue No. 49.

Kronstadt, K.A. August 16, 2019. Kashmir: Background, Recent Developments, and US Policy. CRS Report. *Congressional Research Service*.

Kumar, N. April 10, 2019. 'I-T Raids Should be Ruthless But Without Bias': CEC Sunil Arora Explains Rationale Behind EC Advisory. *News 18*.

Kumar, P. 2017. Crafting Electoral Politics in Gujarat. *The Tribune*. December 7.

Kumar, P. 2018. Simultaneous Elections: Feasibility Conditional and Desirability Debatable? *The Tribune*. March 10.

Kumar, P. 2019. Dehumanising Language: A New Low in Politics. *The Hindustan Times*. April 18.

Lok Sabha Elections 2019: A Look at Sexist Remarks Made Against Female Politicians. April 15, 2019. *The Indian Express*. New Delhi.

Mandal, B.P. 1980. *Report of the Backward Classes Commission*, Government of India, Vol. I.

Mills, C.W. 1963. 'The New Left', in I.L. Horowitz (ed.), *Power, Politics, and People; The Collected Essays of C. Wright Mills*, pp. 249-251. New York: Oxford University Press.

Mukherjee, A. 2019. *The Absent Dialogue: Politicians, Bureaucrats, and the Military in India*. New York: Oxford University Press.

Mukhopadhyay, N. 2019. *The RSS: Icons of the Indian Right*. Chennai: Tranquebar, Westland Publications Private Limited.

Nair, P. 2009. Religious Political Parties and Their Welfare Work: Relations Between the RSS, The Bharatiya Janata Party and The Vidya Bharati Schools in India. *Religions and Development Research Programme*. Working Paper 37. DFID.

Narendra Modi is Like a Virus: Congress. June 8, 2013. *Business Standard*. New Delhi.

Narendra Modi Text Speech. February 7, 2020. Bodo Accord Will Bring Progress and Prosperity for the Community and Assam: PM. Retrieved from https://www.narendramodi.in/text-of-prime-minister-narendra-modi-s-address-at-kokrajhar-in-assam-548326

Narendra Modi Text Speeches. 2014 (onwards). Retrieved from https://www.narendramodi.in/category/text-speeches

Nehru, J. 1946. *Discovery of India*. New Delhi: Jawaharlal Nehru Memorial Fund.

No Relation Between RSS and BJP, Says Mohan Bhagawat. *Rediff.com*. October, 2012.

Opposition United Like Cats, Dogs, Snakes and Mongoose after PM Modi's Political Flood: BJP Chief Amit Shah. April 6, 2018. *The New Indian Express*. Mumbai.

Peer, G. and Rahman, J. 2012. An Unpleasant Autonomy. Revisiting the Special Status for Jammu and Kashmir. *Economic and Political Weekly*, Vol. 47 Issue No. 23, pp. 72-75.

Politics Meaningless without Religion: J.P. Nadda. January 3, 2020. *India Today*.

Pradhan, S.D. December 10, 2018. Understanding the Politicisation of Surgical Strike. *The Times of India*.

Press Information Bureau. 2014 (onwards). *Text of PM's Speech*. Government of India. Retrieved from https://pib.gov.in/newsite/pmreleases.aspx?mincode=3

Press Information Bureau. July 30, 2019. *Parliament Passes the Muslim Women (Protection of Rights on Marriage) Bill 2019*. Ministry of Home Affairs. Government of India.

Publications Division. 2019. Sabka Saath Sabka Vikas. *Prime Minister Narendra Modi Speaks 2018-2019*, Vol. 5. Publications Division Ministry of Information & Broadcasting. New Delhi, Government of India.

Quraishi, S.Y. 2019. 'Participation Revolution with Voter Education', in S.Y. Quraishi (ed.), *The Great March of Democracy: Seven Decades of India's Elections*. Gurgaon: Penguin Random House, pp. 111-121.

Rai, G., Burman, R.D. and Chopra, Y. 1975. *Deewar* (Universal). India: Trimurti Films Pvt. Ltd.

Rajeevan, R. and Balakrishnan, D. March 28, 2019. 'From Today, Real Politics Will Start': JD(S), Congress Grab Chance to Turn I-T Raids into Poll Ploy. *News18*. Bengaluru.

Rajya Sabha. December 11, 2019. *Supplement to Synopsis Debate*. Proceedings Other Than Questions and Answers. Government Bill. The Citizenship Amendment (Bill), 2019

Ramesh, J. 2015. *To the Brink and Back: India's 1991 Story*. New Delhi: Rupa Publications.

Rej, A. and Sagar, R. 2019. 'The BJP and Indian Grand Strategy', in M. Vaishnav (ed.), *The BJP in Power: Indian Democracy and Religious Nationalism*. Washington, DC: Carnegie Endowment for International Peace. Publications Department, pp. 73-82.

Routray, B.P. September 9, 2014. Samajwadi Party. *Encyclopædia Britannica*. Encyclopædia Britannica, Inc.

Routray, B.P. September 22, 2015. Telugu Desam Party. *Encyclopædia Britannica*. Encyclopædia Britannica, Inc.

Roy, A. 2010. *Mapping Citizenship in India*. New Delhi: Oxford University Press.

RSS Economic Wing Passes a Resolution, Slam Government's PSU Disinvestment Move. December 2, 2019. *Hindustan Times*.

Rukmini, S. 2019. 'The BJP's Electoral Arithmetic', in M. Vaishnav (ed.), *The BJP in Power: Indian Democracy and Religious Nationalism*. Washington, DC: Carnegie Endowment for International Peace. Publications Department, pp. 37-50.

Sampal, R. December 11, 2019. RSS Has a New Global Hindutva Mascot- Nobel Laureate Sir V.S. Naipaul. The Print. New Delhi.

Sawant, G.C. October 22, 2012. Delhi CM Sheila Dikshit Sues Arvind Kejriwal Over Derogatory Remarks. *India Today*. New Delhi.

Saxena, N.C. 2019. *What Ails the IAS and Why it Fails to Deliver. An Insider's View*. New Delhi: Sage Publications.

Selected Works of Jawaharlal Nehru. 1985. Second Series, Vol. 3. New Delhi: Jawaharlal Nehru Memorial Fund.

Selected Works of Jawaharlal Nehru. 2005. From the 'Editorial Note.' Second Series, Vol. 34. 21 June–31 August 1956. New Delhi: Jawaharlal Nehru Memorial Fund.

Selected Works of Jawaharlal Nehru. 2006. Vol. 37. New Delhi: Jawaharlal Nehru Memorial Fund.

Sen, R. 2019. From Chaiwala to Chowkidar: Modi's Election Campaigns Online and Offline. *Engage, Economic and Political Weekly*, Vol. 54, Issue No. 51.

Smriti Irani Mocks Rahul Gandhi with 'Chhota Bheem' Jibe Over 'Data Theft' Row. March 26, 2018. *The Statesman*. New Delhi.

Sood, A. and Nath, P. 2020. Labour Law Changes: Innocuous Mistakes or Sleight of Hand? *Economic and Political Weekly*, Vol. 55, Issue No. 22, pp. 33-37.

"Supreme Court to Hear Case Against Withdrawal of Drug Price Cap." October 10, 2014. *The Economic Times*. New Delhi.

Supreme Court Serves Rahul Gandhi Notice, Says, 'We Never Said Anything About Modi.' April 16, 2019. *The Times of India*. New Delhi.

The Citizenship (Amendment) Act, 2019. No. 47 of 2019. Ministry of Law and Justice. Government of India.

The Constitution (Fifty-Second Amendment) Act, 1985 (Anti-Defection Act). Ministry of Law and Justice. Government of India.

The Gazette of India. July 31, 2019. *The Muslim Women (Protection of Rights on Marriage Act, 2019)*. Extraordinary, Part II, Section 1, Ministry of Law and Justice (Legislative Department). New Delhi.

Trivedi, S. September 23, 2014. MP Agrees to Amend 20 Labour Laws. *Business Standard*, Bhopal.

Trivedi, V. April 7, 2019. Income Tax Officers Raid Properties of Kamal Nath's Nephew and Close Aides in MP and Delhi. *News 18*. New Delhi, Bhopal.

Wallace, P. 2015. *India's 2014 Elections: A Modi-Led BJP Sweep*. New Delhi: Sage Publications.

Weiner, M. 1989. *The Indian Paradox: Essays in Indian Politics*. Delhi: Sage Publications.

Chapter 2

Anderson, B. 1998. *The Spectre of Comparisons: Nationalism, Southeast Asia and the World*. London: Verso.

Arendt, H. 1986. *The Origins of Totalitarianism*. London: André Deutsch.

Burke, J. September 12, 2012. "Indian Cartoonist Aseem Trivedi Jailed After Arrest on Sedition Charges." *The Guardian*.

Chatterjee, P. 2004. *The Politics of the Governed: Reflections on Popular Politics in Most of the World*. New York: Columbia University Press.

Dagar, R. 2014. *Gender Identity and Violence: Female Deselection in India*. New Delhi: Routledge.

Deaton, A. and Cartwright, N. 2018. "Understanding and Misunderstanding Randomized Controlled Trials." *Social Science & Medicine*. Vol. 210, pp. 2-21.

Desai, M. October 21, 2019. "Out of my Mind: Hail Macaulay for Our Outdated Laws." *The Indian Express*.

Dirks, N.B. 2001. *Castes of Mind: Colonialism and the Makings of Modern India*. Princeton University Press. Delhi: Permanent Black.

Drèze, J. October 15, 2019. "Some Questions Around the Use of 'Evidence-Based' Policy." *The Wire.*

Foucault, M. 1991. "Governmentality." In B. Burchell (eds.), *The Foucault Effect Studies in Governmentality. Studies in Governmentality.* Chicago: The University of Chicago Press, pp. 87-104.

Gupta, D. 1999. "Survivors or Survivals: Reconciling Citizenship and Cultural Particularisms." *Economic and Political Weekly*, Vol. 34, Issue No. 33, pp. 2313-2323.

Hasan, Z. 2006. "Constitutional Equality and the Politics of Representation in India." *Sage.* Vol 53, Issue 4, pp. 54-68.

"Howdy, Modi! Event: PM Modi Says India's GDP Growth Unprecedented with 5-Year Average of 7.5%." September 23, 2019. *Business Today.* New Delhi.

"Concept of Governance." *International Bureau of Education.* UNESCO. Retrieved from http://www.ibe.unesco.org/en/geqaf/technical-notes/concept-governance

Janardhanan, A. September 12, 2016. "8,856 'Enemies of State': An Entire Village in Tamil Nadu Lives Under Shadow of Sedition." *The Indian Express.*

Khan, M.A. 2005. "Engaged Governance: A Strategy for Mainstreaming of Citizens into the Public Policy Process." *Economic and Social Affairs, United Nations.*

Khera, R. October 17, 2015. "A Nobel for the Idea of Well-Being." *The Hindu.*

Kumar, 2011. "Correcting Distortions in Governance." *Kayedakanoonandactivism.*

Kumar, P. 2009. "Recommendations of the Punjab Governance Reforms Commission: Second Status Report (From Introduction)." Punjab Governance Reforms Commission (PGRC).

Kumar, P. 2009. "Status Report on Delivery of Citizen Services." Punjab Governance Reforms Commission (PGRC), Government of Punjab.

Kumar, P. 2010. "Recommendations of the Punjab Governance Reforms Commission: Third Status Report (From Introduction)." Punjab Governance Reforms Commission (PGRC).

Kumar, P. 2011. "Recommendations of the Punjab Governance Reforms Commission: Fifth Status Report (From Introduction)." Punjab Governance Reforms Commission (PGRC).

Kumar, P. 2011. "Coalition Politics: Withering of National-Regional Ideological Positions?" In P. Wallace and R. Roy (eds.), *India's*

2009 Elections: Coalition Politics, Party Competition and Congress Continuity. New Delhi: Sage Publications, pp. 42-63.

Kumar, P. 2013. "Reforming Public Service Delivery Systems in India. Rationalisation of Affidavits." Punjab Governance Reforms Commission (PGRC), Government of Punjab.

Kumar, P. 2015. *Punjab Electoral Spectrum: Unfolding Challenges for Democracy*. Chandigarh, India: Institute for Development and Communication (IDC).

Kumar, P. 2016. "Reforming Public Service Delivery Systems In India: Rationalisation of Affidavits (From Introduction)." Punjab Governance Reforms Commission (PGRC).

Kumar, P. and Dagar, R. 2004. "Gender and Dalit Identity Construction in Punjab." In Harish K. Puri (eds.), *Dalits in Regional Context*, Jaipur: Rawat Publications.

Laclau, E. 1977. *Politics and Ideology in Marxist Theory*. London: Vesro.

Muncie, J. 2001. "The Construction and Deconstruction of Crime." In E. Mclaughlin and J. Muncie (eds.), *The Problem of Crime*. London: Sage Publications, pp. 7-69.

Pandey, A.K. October 5, 2019. "Sedition FIR Against 49 Celebs for Letter to Modi on Lynching." *The Times of India*.

"Prohibition and Drugs: Press Down, Pop Up." May 24, 2014. *The Economist*.

Roy, A. 2010. *Mapping Citizenship in India*. New Delhi: Oxford University Press.

Sharma, A. 2008. *Logics of Empowerment: Development, Gender, and Governance in Neoliberal India*. Minneapolis: University of Minnesota Press.

Sood, A. 2016. "Majoritarian Rationale and Common Goals. Rhetoric and Truth." *Economic and Political Weekly*, Vol. LI, Issue No. 37, pp. 36-41.

The World Bank. 2004. "Resuming Punjab's Prosperity: The Opportunities and Challenges Ahead." Poverty Reduction and Economic Management Sector Unit, South Asia Region.

United National Economic and Social Council, Committee of Experts on Public Administration. 2006. "Definition of Basic Concepts and Terminologies in Governance and Public Administration, Fifth Session." Retrieved from https://digitallibrary.un.org/record/566603?ln=en.

United Nations System Task Team on the Post-2015 UN Development Agenda, UNDESA, UNDP and UNESCO. 2012. "Governance and Development." Retrieved from https://www.un.org/millenniumgoals/pdf/Think%20Pieces/7_governance.pdf.

Chapter 3

"Fifth Report of the National Police Commission." 1980. *Government of India.*

Bayley, D.H. 1969. *The Police and Political Development in India.* Princeton: Princeton University Press.

Kumar, P. 2001. "Community Police Interface: Need Assessment Survey." Chandigarh: Institute for Development and Communication.

The World Bank. 2004. "Resuming Punjab's Prosperity: The Opportunities and Challenges Ahead." Poverty Reduction and Economic Management Sector Unit, South Asia Region.

Chapter 4

Arendt, H. 1986. *The Origins of Totalitarianism.* London: André Deutsch.

Allen, V.L. 1975. *Social Analysis: A Marxist Critique and Alternative.* London and New York: Longman.

Bhagat, R.M. 2006. "Census and Caste Enumeration: British legacy and Contemporary Practice in India." *Genus*, Vol. 62, Issue No. 2, pp. 119-134.

Bharti, V. 2019. "The Untold Brutality of Jagmail Singh." *The Sunday Tribune.* November 24.

Census of India. 1931. XVII, Part I.

Chatterjee, P. 2004. *The Politics of the Governed: Reflections on Popular Politics in Most of the World.* Delhi: Permanent Black.

Chowdhry, P. 1997. "Enforcing Cultural Codes: Gender and Violence in Northern India." *Economic and Political Weekly*, Vol. 32, Issue No. 19, pp. 1019-1028.

Dagar, R. 2014. *Gender, Identity and Violence: Female Deselection in India.* New Delhi: Routledge.

Dirks, N.B. 2001. *Castes of Mind: Colonialism and the makings of Modern India..* Delhi: Permanent Black.

Foucault, M. 1991. "Governmentality." In B. Burchell (ed.).*The Foucault Effect Studies in Governmentality.* Chicago: The University of Chicago Press, pp. 87-104.

Fox, R.G. 1987. *Lions of the Punjab. Culture in the Making.* New Delhi: Archives Publishers.

Hans, R.K. 2008. "Dalits and the Emancipatory Sikh Religion in Dalit Challenges to Academic Knowledge: The Great Paradoxes." December 3-5, 2008 Conference, Pennsylvania, University of Pennsylvania.

Ibbetson, D. 1916. *Punjab Castes* (reprint of the chapter on "Races, Castes and Tribes of the People in the Report on the Census of the Punjab 1881"). Superintendent, Government Printing, Punjab.

Jodhka, S.S. (ed.). 2001.*Community & Identities; Contemporary Discourses on Culture and Politics in India*. New Delhi: Sage Publications.

Jodhka, S.S. 2002. "Caste and Untouchability in Rural Punjab." *Economic and Political Weekly*, Vol. 37, Issue No. 19, pp. 1813-1823.

Jodhka, S.S. 2004. "Untouchability in Rural Punjab" in Harish K. Puri (ed.), *Dalits in Regional Context*. Jaipur: Rawat Publications, pp. 62-99.

Judge, P.S. 2002. "Religion, Caste, and Communalism in Punjab." *Sociological Bulletin*. Vol. 51, Issue 2, pp. 175-194.

Judge, P.S. and Bal, G. 2008. "Understanding the Paradox of Changes Among Dalits in Punjab." *Economic and Political Weekly*, Vol. 43, Issue No. 41, pp. 49-55.

Juergensmeyer, M. 1988. *Religious Rebels in Punjab: The Social Vision of Untouchables*. Delhi: Ajanta Publication.

Kalsi, S.S. 1989. *The Sikhs and Caste. A Study of the Sikh Community in Leeds and Bradford* (Doctoral Thesis, Department of Theology and Religious Studies, University of Leeds). Retrieved from https://core.ac.uk/download/pdf/43697.pdf.

Kamal, N. 2012. "Dalit Social Boycott Over Wages, Punjab Village Facing Strains in Social Equilibrium," *Times of India*, July 8.

Korten, D. and Alfonso, F.B. 1983. *Bureaucracy and the Poor: Closing the Gaps.* West Hartford: Kumarian Press.

Kumar, P. 1982. "Communalisation of Hindus in Punjab." *Secular Democracy*, Vol. 15, No. IX, pp. 27-29.

Kumar, P. 2017. "Punjab Politics: Contesting Identities and Forging Coalitions."*Economic and Political Weekly*, Vol. 52, Issue No. 3, pp. 44-49.

Kumar, P. August 28, 2017. "Decoding Politics of 'Messengers of God': Deras in Punjab." *The Times of India*.

Kumar, P. and Dagar, R. 2004. "Gender and Dalit Identity Construction in Punjab." In Harish K. Puri (ed.). *Dalits in Regional Context*, Jaipur: Rawat Publications, pp. 274-296.

Malhotra, A. 2002.*Gender, Caste, and Religious Identities: Restructuring Class in Colonial Punjab*, New Delhi: Oxford University Press.

Manjoo, R. 2012. "Report of the Special Rapporteur on Violence Against Women, its Causes and Consequences." *United Nations. Human Rights Council*. Twentieth session. Agenda Item 3. A/HRC/20/16.

McLeod W.H. 1975. *The Evolution of the Sikh Community: Five Essays*. Delhi: Oxford University Press.

Mendelsohn, O. and Vicziany, M. (1998). *The Untouchables: Subordination, Poverty and the State in Modern India* (Contemporary South Asia). Cambridge University Press.

Mitra, D. 2012. *Punjabi Immigrant Mobility in the United States: Adaptation through Race and Class*. New York: Palgrave Macmillan.

Nandy, A. 1988. "The Politics of Secularism and the Recovery of Religious Tolerance." *Alternatives: Global, Local, Political*, Sage, Vol. 13, Issue No. 2, pp. 177-194.

Punjab Census Report. 1911. Government of India, Registrar General. 1912. Lahore.

Punjab Vidhan Sabha Debates. 1956. Speech by Gurbanta Singh. No. 18, March 23.

Ram, R. 2004. "Limits of Untouchability, Dalit Assertion and Caste Violence in Punjab." In Harish K. Puri (ed.), *Dalits in Regional Context*, Jaipur: Rawat Publications, pp. 132-189.

Ram, R. 2004. "Untouchability in India with a Difference: Ad Dharm, Dalit Assertion, and Caste Conflicts in Punjab". *Asian Survey*, 44(6), pp. 895-912.

Ram, R. 2007. "Social Catastrophe in the Making: Religion, Deras and Dalits in Punjab." Available at http://www.ambedkartimes.com/ronkiram%20page%201.htm#social.

Ram, R. 2013. "Empowering Peripheries from Below. Making Sense of Dalit Identity Formation in Contemporary East Punjab." *Voice of Dalit*, Vol. 6, Issues No. 1, pp. 39-60.

Roy, A.G. 2011. "Celebrating the 'Son of Jats': The Return of Tribes in the Global Village." *South Asian Diaspora*, Vol. 3, Issue No. 1, pp. 89-102.

Seul, J.R. 1999. "Ours is the Way of God: Religion, Identity, and Intergroup Conflict." Harvard Law School. *Journal of Peace Research*. New Delhi: Sage Publications. Vol. 36, Issue No. 5, pp. 553-569.

Shah, G., Mander, H., Thorat, S., Deshpande, S., and Baviskar, A.

2006. *Untouchability in Rural India*. New Delhi: Sage Publications.

Sharma, N. 2012. "Caste in Punjab: Political Marginalization and Cultural Assertion of Scheduled Castes in Punjab." *Journal of Punjab Studies (JPS)*, Vol. 19, Issue No 1, pp. 27-47.

Sikka, S. 2012. "Untouchable Cultures: Memory, Power and the Construction of Dalit Selfhood." *Identities: Global Studies in Culture and Power*, Vol. 19, Issue No. 1, pp. 43-60.

Singh, G. 2012. "Religious Transnationalism and Development Initiatives: The Dera Sachkhand Ballan." *Economic and Political Weekly*, Vol. 47, Issue No. 1, pp. 53-60.

Singh, P. 2012. "Fear and Loathing in Dera Ballan." *Abroo*. Available at (https://pukhraj.me/2012/04/08/fear-and-loathing-in-dera-ballan-abroo/).

Singh, P. 2012. "Punjab's Map of Shame: Caste Atrocities Since 2012." *Abroo*. November 1.

Srinivas, M.N. 1966. *Social Change in Modern India*. Berkeley: University of California Press.

Taylor, S. 2018. "Punjabi Dalit Transnational Mobility: Challenging Caste Inequalities." In Upadhya, C. (ed.), *Provincial Globalisation in India: Transregional Mobilities and Development Politics*, London: Routledge, Taylor & Francis, pp.123-141.

Taylor, S. 2014. "Religious Conversion and Dalit Assertion Among a Punjabi Dalit Diaspora." *Sociological Bulletin*, Vol. 63, Issue No. 2, pp. 224-246.

Thorat, S.K. and Deshpande, R.S. 2001. "Caste System and Economic Inequality: Economic Theory and Evidence." In Ghanshyam Shah (ed.), *Dalit Identity and Politics*. New Delhi/Thousand Oaks/London: Sage Publications, pp. 44-73.

Wallace, P. 1986. "The Sikhs as a "Minority" in a Sikh Majority State in India." *Asian Survey*, Vol. 26, Issue No. 3, pp. 363-377.

World Bank. 2006.*Unequal Citizens: Gender, Caste and Ethnic Exclusion in Nepal: Summary (English)*. Washington, DC: World Bank. Retrieved from http://documents.worldbank.org/curated/en/201971468061735968/pdf/379660Nepal0GSEA0Summary0Report01PUBLIC1.pdf

White, E. 2012. "Religion in England and Wales 2011." Available at https://www.ons.gov.uk/peoplepopulationandcommunity/culturalidentity/religion/articles/religioninenglandandwales2011/2012-12-11.

Index